iii

Contents

WEST PUBLISHING COMPANY
St. Paul • New York • Los Angeles • San Francisco

Public Communication in Business and the Professions

Jerry W. Koehler
Associate Professor
Department of Management

and

John I. Sisco
Professor
Department of Communication
University of South Florida
Tampa, Florida

COPYRIGHT © 1981 By WEST PUBLISHING CO.
50 West Kellogg Boulevard
P.O. Box 3526
St. Paul, Minnesota 55165

Printed in the United States of America

Library of Congress Cataloging in Publication Data

Koehler, Jerry W
    Public communication in business and the professions.

    Includes bibliographies and index.
    1. Communication in management.   2.   Public speaking.
I.   Sisco, John I., joint author.   II.   Title.
HF5718.K63   808.5'024658   80-24646
ISBN 0-8299-0417-4

FIVE **14** EVALUATING PUBLIC COMMUNICATION IN BUSINESS AND THE PROFESSIONS   183

The focus of this book is on the public communication roles most frequently required of the person in business or other professions. In one sense we define public communication broadly enough to include the conference and several types of internal interviews, as well as the public speech. In these instances public communicators may be representing their organization, professional association or themselves, but the purpose for the most part is information dissemination. We have not included in our book attention to small group communication, interpersonal communication, or written communication. Many of the principal concepts examined here are applicable to those communication activities, but the student interested specifically in those forums should examine other sources.

This study is divided into five parts: Communication Essentials, Public Speaking, the Conference, the Interview, and Evaluating Tools. In parts two, three, and four we have distributed some topics broadly applicable to many communication situations but of specific importance to the communication form in focus. We hope this will be particularly useful to the student reading the book in isolation as well as to the teacher adapting the book to a unique syllabus.

At the end of each of these skill-topic chapters we have added a summary of *essential considerations*. We believe that this section, specially tinted for easy reference by the student, will be useful for review. It will also be a useful resource after completion of formal education when one is called upon to apply these skills as part of one's public communication responsibilities.

We wish to express our appreciation to our associates for their assistance, especially Dave Carter, Keith Jensen, Ken Cissna, Lenda Peronto, Sharon Smith, Harold Zelko, Dave Taugher, Chris Mewhinney, Keith Macksey, Noreen Koehler, and Glen Sisco. A special acknowledgment is due to Sharon Eskridge for preparation of the final manuscript.

Preface

First Considerations

In this portion of the text we will consider several first principles, some communication essentials, applicable to all situations which require a sensitivity to communication events. Chapter One provides an introduction to public communication; Chapter Two names principal elements of the process and characterizes fundamental guidelines; and Chapter Three introduces necessary steps to audience analysis and adaptation.

ONE

Peter Franklin is employed as an aerospace engineer. Most of his time is spent in advanced research, work that he finds exciting, challenging and, for the most part, rewarding. He is proud of his personal achievements and of his contributions to his organization.

However, he is now faced with a new and frightening prospect. His company has decided to bid on a major government contract involving advanced technology in his field. Selected as the logical choice to meet with Pentagon officials, Peter must present the case for awarding the contract to his company.

Although Peter was a top student and a product of one of the best American universities, he has never given a formal presentation. He has always avoided anything that resembled "giving a speech." Now, he recognizes that he cannot avoid giving one, and giving it under the most demanding circumstances.

There is Rosemary Edwards, a practicing dentist for 15 years. She has developed a new, effective method of removing stains from teeth, a method which she describes in an article published in a professional magazine. Suddenly, she begins to receive calls to speak at dental association meetings and conferences. She finds herself wishing she had kept the new technique to herself, and she wonders how long she can go on finding excuses not to talk in public. The idea of a public oral presentation terrifies her more than a visit to her office ever terrified a patient.

Everybody either shares the disproportionate resistance to speaking situations experienced by Peter and Rosemary or knows somebody who does. Even many people who become accustomed to the limelight never learn to be comfortable when called upon to make public comment. Jack Nicklaus has won almost every major golfing title and is one of the best-known and respected athletes alive. And yet he confesses that nothing panics him in quite the same way as having to "say a few words" before an audience.

Resistance to public speaking is not quite like any other experience we encounter. It combines irrational fears characteristic of phobias with very specific, objective apprehensions about "going blank," making a fool of one's self, boring the audience, or committing some embarrassing behavior. These are very real apprehensions, even if the individual may exaggerate their threat. Almost everyone has experienced one or more of them, either as

Communication in Business and the Professions

perpetrator or victim. We have induced the apprehension in others or been the victim of the situation.

Robert Mackey, for instance, is not afraid of any audience ever assembled. As chief executive officer of a major corporation, he speaks to groups of people daily. He seeks opportunities to speak and enjoys himself immensely when he is able to do so. Unfortunately, his audiences don't share his enthusiasm. People try to avoid being trapped into listening to him, and those who can't avoid it simply tune him out. Mackey has no idea what a bore he is, and nobody is likely to tell him. He's the boss.

Dan Stanley, on the other hand, is a bank president, a position often supposed to guarantee its occupant a cautious, dry, unstimulating delivery. But Dan is in high demand as a speaker. People love to listen to him because he is informative, witty, relaxed and self-confident when he speaks. He is a constant reminder of an old phrase, "there are no dull subjects, only dull speakers."

The difference between Dan Stanley and the others is not one of information. They are all well-informed on the subjects they are often called upon to discuss. The difference is one of attitude, method and ability. Almost anyone can learn the relatively simple methods required to become an effective speaker. Moreover, the attitude required to apply them effectively is, for the most part, a result of the self-confidence that comes from knowing that one can perform effectively in a speaking situation.

Problems in public communication are not limited to large audience situations. Communication problems faced by platform speakers are basically no different from those involved in briefing a task team, interviewing a prospective employee, explaining a procedure, conducting a performance appraisal, or dictating a letter or memo. In fact, a universal value of "communication" can be stated in an axiom: Your effectiveness in virtually any business or professional situation is improved by communication skill.

Although communication principles are essentially the same in all settings, there are often specific conditions in business and professional situations that affect the communication process in special ways.[1] Organizational structure, climate, management levels as well as styles, assumptions and approaches, etc. affect communication outcomes. One of the most prominent variables affecting communication is the authority structure in organizations. No matter how well it is camouflaged, or how leniently it is exercised, the "boss's" control of the power to reward and punish influences strongly communication processes in organizations.

There is always the threat of being reprimanded or fired for an "inappropriate remark." Sometimes the most important and often most pervasive effects are far more subtle. Advancement, particularly into management, is often dependent on the subordinate's ability to communicate his or her value and accomplishments to superiors.

Let's look again at the aerospace engineering team headed by Peter Franklin. Although Peter is not a skilled communicator, he is group leader because he communicates more effectively than any of the others. The company's hopes for a government contract are pinned on his ability to persuade the Pentagon to accept a technological breakthrough achieved by the team. Everybody on the team knows that the original concept and most of the spadework leading to the breakthrough was the work of Jim Rogers.

Jim is almost a caricature of the boy genius — shy, quiet, socially awkward, more comfortable with ideas and inanimate objects than with people. Hired straight off the campus, he was considered, and proved to be, a major find by the company. It was a discovery that never would have taken place, however, if the company interviewer hadn't been tipped off to Jim's academic record by one of his profs. The interview itself had been anything but impressive. Jim volunteered nothing and replied to all queries in monosyllables. At the time, he had remarked he would rather go through finals again than face the interviewer.

His "negotiation" consisted of accepting the company's offer exactly as presented to him. Since that time, his periodic performance and upgrading reviews have been replays of the employment interview. He accepts them as necessities to be suffered through. If the interviewer doesn't bring up a particular subject, it doesn't get mentioned. At the end, he accepts whatever evaluation, change in status, or raise the interviewer proposes. He recognizes that this passivity permits other people to make all decisions about his status and income, but he accepts this as the price for not having to prolong the uncomfortable interview.

Now, after five years with the company, he is beginning to have second thoughts. Surprisingly, he discovers that he resents the selection of Peter Franklin to present the achievement for which he himself was mostly responsible, even though he would have been terrified at the prospect of having to make the presentation himself. It isn't that he doesn't get credit for his preeminent contribution—he does. But he knows the potential of this new process better than anybody else. Given the required self-confidence and skills, he would approach it in a different and, he believes, more effective manner than Peter does.

Not only that, he is beginning to realize that the same situation exists throughout his professional life—another person, no matter how fair or conscientious, cannot possibly represent one's ideas and interests as well as oneself. He knows that through the years some of the contributions to the company of which he is most proud have gone unnoticed simply because he didn't call attention to them during his performance reviews. How much their recognition might have added to his salary and advancement he cannot guess. But he has a general sense of dissatisfaction with his neglect of the responsibility to himself and to the company to communicate more effectively. He decides to make a systematic effort to improve his communication skills, concentrating on those that will be of greatest benefit to him in the organization.

PURPOSE OF BOOK

The purpose of this book is to provide assistance to people like Peter Franklin, Rosemary Edwards, Robert Mackey, and Jim Rogers. It is not, however, a book intended to bring them sure-fire techniques which will, in three easy lessons, allow them to conquer their communication problems. Rather, the purpose of our book is to prevent such problems, first by anticipating them and, second, by being prepared long before such situations occur. Our book is designed to help people develop a positive, constructive and practical approach to effective oral communication in business and professional settings.

Although the principles of communication we address in our book are applicable to any communication situation, we believe that the most effective way to learn oral communication skills demanded in business and professional environments is to focus on three specific formats. These are:

    A. PUBLIC SPEAKING
    B. CONFERENCE SPEAKING
    C. INTERVIEWING

Prior to discussing these, it is necessary to cover three vital areas: the importance of communication, oral and written messages, and, finally, planned interaction and evaluation.

Importance of Communication

In concentrating on public speaking, conference speaking and interviewing, we will not be examining three distinct sets of communication problems and skills. Each format, rather, presents unique problems in the application of basic communication principles that are essentially universal. Understanding these principles and knowing how to apply them effectively in a variety of situations is very nearly indispensable to career success. This is not to say that one can talk one's way to the top. Nor is it to say that ability and knowledge are of secondary importance. We all can think of successful individuals who possess only the most rudimentary communication skills. The designer who can double the payload of an aircraft without doubling its cost has a very good chance of getting a hearing, even if a translator is needed. But if the designer can explain the concept clearly and persuasively, not only to another individual but also to a small group or a large audience, personal prospects are enlarged many times over.

The ability to express one's thoughts in symbols (words, gestures, etc.) clearly and persuasively in a variety of ways and the ability to detect and interpret the signals of others are two basic communication capabilities. They appear in an infinite number of guises in different communication situations. It is difficult to imagine that an individual could be too skilled in any aspect of communication—even one that is not basic to his or her profession. The three types of communication situations we are emphasizing are interwoven, interacting with and reinforcing each other. Not only that, but the three situations continually emerge in various guises in the business and professional worlds.

The popular image of the attorney focuses on persuasive courtroom oratory—seldom the predominant communication format for even the busiest trial lawyer. But even if the popular image were accurate, the successful attorney is usually involved in many other communication situations. The law-school graduate, for example, is apt to participate in job interviews not very different from those for any other professional.

But many attorneys participate in interview situations on a somewhat continuous basis. Many are called on to represent clients before official bodies. Every meeting with a new client is a type of interview, often requiring a sensitive reading of feedback clues for indications of the client's candor. The same skills are employed in interviewing prospective witnesses, taking depositions, and cross-examining. Perhaps more than many other professionals, lawyers are asked to serve on panels, committees and commissions where small-group participation and leadership are called for. Many lawyers become public speakers by going into politics, either as candidates or as campaigners. Others speak often before service clubs or other groups or on the lecture circuits.

For the physician, skill in interview situations is fundamentally important.

The ability to obtain and impart potentially embarrassing or frightening information with tactful accuracy requires unusual skill in communication and sensitivity to feedback. In addition, doctors, like lawyers, are increasingly called upon to serve on committees and panels or to make public addresses.

Engineers are often noted for their difficulties in communicating. Yet, they often exhibit high precision and accuracy when they communicate among themselves. The latter results from the special engineering symbolism that has evolved in response to their need to express technical complexities and subtle shades of meaning without ambiguity. Whether justified or not, there is also a prevalent impression that many engineers tend to be withdrawn and taciturn in the presence of persons who are not a part of the technical community.

In their organizational and professional life, engineers participate in the same communication situations as those described for other professionals. Communication skills are an especial advantage to the engineer in making presentations and explaining the significance of new work and developments to non-technical career people.

The special language problem, however, is not essentially different for engineers than it is for members of the medical or legal professions. All specialists have to exercise care in translating from the language of their speciality when communicating with the non-specialist world. In our increasingly technological society, it is especially important that communication links be strengthened between the technical/professional areas and other parts of society.

Oral and Written Messages

Some experienced attorneys classify judges whose habits they know as either "readers" or "listeners," according to whether they respond more readily to written or oral arguments. Accordingly, those attorneys try to get their major points before a particular judge in the form with which he or she is most comfortable. With unfamiliar judges, they try to present key material and supporting points both in written motions and in oral argument.

Apart from the preference of an individual receiver, differences between the two modes, oral and written communication, are considerable and require different organization and style. The writer obviously has greater opportunity to shape material—to erase and rewrite, rephrase, reconstruct or even to withdraw the message altogether. The reader also has a better opportunity to analyze and digest the information presented. With a written message, the reader, too, can go back and review earlier sentences in the light of later ones, can proceed at his or her own pace, or can even interrupt the flow of the message to go to a dictionary or other reference. The message itself can be retained for later review or for comparison with subsequent events and statements.

The receiver of an oral message (assuming it is not transcribed) enjoys none of these advantages. There is no assurance of accurate recall for review of the message, and lapses of attention or missed words or phrases cannot always be made up by reference to context. Moreover, a speaker rarely achieves a transmission rate much above 175 to 225 words per minute, while most listeners are capable of comprehending 500 words or more a minute. The busy brain tends to fill the unoccupied time with random thoughts and images to the detriment of message comprehension.

This discrepancy between the sending and receiving rates is perhaps responsible to a large degree for the fact that most of us are poor listeners. At the same time it provides one of the real opportunities to improve listening effectiveness. With practice, one can learn to utilize the unused time and brainpower to make up for the shortcomings of oral communication, fixing the message in memory as it is being received and anticipating the direction and content of the parts of the message yet to be received. The practiced listener learns to foresee and evaluate conclusions foreshadowed in early statements and premises and to take deliberate note of the message transmitted by non-verbal signals, such as gestures, expressions and tone. The residual message—that general conclusion left in the mind of the listener as a result of the communication—is therefore at least partially evaluated and analyzed simultaneously with its receipt.

Even more than the listener, the experienced speaker must be aware of the differences between written and oral communication and adjust for them in the style and structure of the message. For effective reception, the density of data—the number of different facts or images conveyed in a given number of words—is considerably smaller in oral than in written communication. Not only are more words employed orally to convey a given quantity of data, but effective oral presentations commonly make greater use of repetition. The same fact or image, if significant, may well be repeated several times, either in identical form or from different angles.

Planned Interaction and Evaluation

One type of communication situation we are intentionally ignoring is the one where results can be measured only subjectively. These are often mixed social/organizational and social/professional situations. They may come about by accident or coincidence without a planned goal or agenda.

Suppose you are a low or middle echelon employee in an organizational hierarchy. There is not much opportunity to interact directly with your superiors because vertical socialization is not encouraged. You have a table in the crowded snack bar when your boss and his boss come up with their coffee and ask if they can join you. A conversation develops, and you spend the next half hour discussing both social and business topics, all feeling you know each other a little better because of the chance encounter.

No doubt you would have offered a seat to anyone who had asked, but you can't ignore the fact that these two individuals have, or could have, a powerful influence over your progress in the organization. Probably, much of what you contributed to the conversation was affected by your desire to appear in the best possible light. After you have displayed your ignorance or your brilliance, you may have no real clues to whether or not you have advanced your cause. Assuming that the conversation doesn't terminate in an invitation to dinner, you will probably have to rely on subjective evidence and intuition to tell you if the impression you made was favorable.

General communication principles and skills are helpful, of course, in these spontaneous interactions. But the type of situations to be examined in this book are all non-spontaneous. This means that they can be planned and their objectives can be predetermined, making it much easier to decide whether or not the outcomes meet expectations.

In these achievement-oriented situations, we will be concerned first of all with goals. Before any other planning can go forward effectively, it is both practical and necessary to define the precise objectives of the communication and the limits of the effects to be expected. Communication objectives are visually behavioral: the goal is to send messages that will produce a desired effect in the thinking and/or physical behavior of the recipients. The communication process and techniques are tools for achieving the desired effects. The attorney pleading a case, the salesperson making a presentation, the businessperson applying for a bank loan, the physician advising a patient — all are putting their communication skills to use to achieve limited, well-defined objectives. So are the jury foreman, the rescue team leader, and the convention keynoter. Each is faced with the problem of selecting appropriate and effective techniques to achieve the desired objectives within the given or chosen communication format.

Each is equally required to eliminate inappropriate and ineffective practices, as determined by the objective. The objective of a particular interaction is seldom to display the vocabulary and erudition of the speaker. Such displays, when undertaken for their own sake, are almost always counterproductive. Many communicators learn to solve these problems through a combination of intuition and experience. Parts of the solution may depend on the application of simple common sense; other parts may require learned skills derived from experience, practice, study, observation, and the results of communication research.

Approaching Public Speaking, Conference Speaking and Interviewing

Obviously, our approach to achieving successful communication emphasizes planning whether we are speaking to a large group, in a small conference, or in an interview. Our communication begins with the definition of our desired objective. It involves selecting and adapting a message to the format and selection and ordering of the most effective techniques, content, and supporting aids within the competence of the communicator. This does not mean that every communication needs to be written out in advance and read from a manuscript, that every presentation has to be memorized, or that every interview should follow a rigid scenario. It does mean, however, that you should have your objective and materials in mind firmly enough to maintain control of at least your end of the process.

The important point to bear in mind in approaching these three communication situations is that they, like most business and professional activities, are goal-oriented. Unlike informal social communication, which they often resemble, their purpose is seldom merely to pass time, to entertain, or to promote purely personal relations. In business and professional settings, the initiator of the communication and, usually, the other participants as well, have specific, clearly-defined objectives to achieve by means of the communication.

Public Speaking

Public speaking serves as the basic public communication role utilized by business persons and other professionals. Public speaking, whether within the organization or professional sphere or to external and lay audiences brings together a series of complex skills also applicable in the conference and interview situations. The business person who requests special zoning permits, the lawyer making a closing statement to the jury, the clergyman delivering a sermon, the medical practitioner reporting to his colleagues can all utilize the public speech to accomplish desired ends. In addition, the speech provides for the direct personal contact not present in other channels. Each specific audience requires that the public speaker give individual attention to the ways to apply delivery and compositional skills.

Conference Speaking

As the term "conference" implies, this special communication format involves providing direction and coherence in groups, usually numbering up to 30 or 35, whose communication is aimed at achieving defined objectives. In addition to effective communication skills, effective conference management requires a number of specialized skills. The conference leader is usually expected to draw up the agenda, introduce the topic and objective, keep the discussion on track and moving, and summarize the conference results or consensus.

Interviewing

The business or professional interview, for example, usually occurs at critical points in the individual's relationship to an organization—such as hiring, performance review, and separation—and plays a crucial role in the decisions made at those points. It is, in fact, the individual's principal opportunity to participate in those decisions that directly affect his or her career. The interview is perhaps the most common and familiar of the three selected types of communication chosen for this book. It frequently takes place in a deceptively informal atmosphere, making it easy to fall into the trap of treating the interview as though it were merely a version of the social conversation.

Although the interview often resembles a conversation, it is a highly specialized form of conversation with a specific purpose. Generally the interviewee has something significant to gain or lose—a job, a raise or promotion, a recommendation, or the like. The interviewer also has something to gain, of course, but the outcome of an individual interview is seldom so critical for the interviewer as for the interviewee.

It is not only as interviewee, however, that the individual is expected to function in the organization but often also as interviewer. The demands of this role, significantly different from those required for effective communication on the other side of the desk, need to be examined separately. A related communication interaction, among the most common supervisorial responsibilities in most organizations, is the job of task instruction.

NOTES   [1]See J. W. Koehler, K. W. E. Anatol, and R. L. Applbaum, *Organizational Communication: Behavioral Perspectives,* 2nd Edition (New York: Holt, Rinehart & Winston, 1981).

SUGGESTED READINGS

Baskin, O. W. and Craig E. Aronoff. *Interpersonal Communication in Organizations.* Santa Monica, Calif: Goodyear Publishing Co., 1980.

Goldhaber, G. M. *Organizational Communication,* 2nd Edition. Dubuque, Iowa: William C. Brown Co., 1979.

Koehler, J. W., K. W. E. Anatol and R. L. Applbaum. *Organizational Communication: Behavioral Perspectives,* 2nd Edition. New York: Holt, Rinehart & Winston, 1981.

Zelko, H. P. and F. E. X. Dance. *Business and Professional Speech Communication,* 2nd Edition. New York: Holt, Rinehart & Winston, 1978.

The Greeks were the first to make a systematic study of the communication process. Twenty-five centuries ago, the Sophists were teaching logic, persuasion, diction and speaking behavior in terms that would not be much outdated in the twentieth century. The Greeks of the day had more than an academic interest in the subject. Communication—especially persuasive public communication—played an important role in their economic life. Possession of property might be determined by the eloquence of the claimants, arguing their competing claims before a jury that might be made up of as many as 500 citizens. The Sophists were noted for their skill in lofty debate, and their advice and instruction were sought by those with more mundane objectives. Beginning as seers and sages, they wound up teaching litigants the tricks of winning arguments. By their heyday in the second century after Christ "Sophist"—which had been reserved for a person of great wisdom in the time of Protagoras—had come to mean merely "teacher of rhetoric." Today Sophists are chiefly remembered as the first teachers to work for money. *Sic transit gloria!*

Although Plato and his pupil Aristotle were severe critics of the Sophists, both contributed to the systematic study of communication that the Sophists had set in motion. Aristotle in particular provided a descriptive model of the process that was to dominate Western thinking on the subject for the next two thousand years. His three books on rhetoric deal with the three aspects he considered fundamental—the speaker, the message, and the audience. Rhetoric he defined as "discovering in the particular case what are the available means of persuasion.[1]" The speaker's most important attribute, Aristotle held, is credibility; the speaker's most important skill, the ability to shape a message in its most persuasive form for a given audience. Thus, although Aristotle insisted on the highest ethical standards under all circumstances, his concept of the ends and means of rhetoric did not differ essentially from that of the Sophists.

Rhetoric to Aristotle was not a science but a capability that expressed itself in three modes of persuasive power: the influence of the speaker's character, the evocation of the desired emotional response in the audience, and the proof, or apparent proof, of the speaker's claim.

In many respects, modern communication research and theory support Aristotle's insights into the persuasive process. It is apparently more effective to concentrate on the proofs of one's own point of view rather than to attempt to present both sides. For a sophisticated audience, argument by implication is often a more effective approach than argument by explicit

The Communication Process

2

message. The more we learn about the way people think and form opinions, the more impressive Aristotle's analysis appears.

   The purpose of this chapter is to describe the key elements of the communication process. We will discuss each of these elements, concluding with a discussion of communication ethics and of the means of determining what is defensibly sayable in the pursuit of persuasive power.

COMMUNICATION AS A PROCESS

To the telephone company, communication is a simple serial process of sound transmission. If a dog yaps into the instrument at one end of the line and the same yap is faithfully reproduced in the instrument at the line's other end, the communication function has been successfully performed. If you dial a number to report in English that your house has just been torched, and the person on the other end of the line understands only Urdu, you have, nevertheless, communicated according to sound transmission system standards. The standards of such a system deal entirely with form and not content.

   The concern of the human communication specialist is almost exactly the opposite. In human communication terms, the means of transmission are inconsequential except as they contribute to the transfer of message content—meaning—from one consciousness to another. If you're giving notice that your house is burning, it doesn't matter whether you use the telephone or yell, so long as your meaning effectively penetrates the consciousness at which it is aimed.

Figure 2.1
Channel selection must fit objective.

Communication, in this sense, is a complex, interacting process involving shared assumptions and unspoken agreements, feedback and verification, between the sender and the receiver. Its objective is to evoke in the consciousness of the receiver a meaning that is as close as possible to the meaning that originated in the consciousness of the sender. Since meaning cannot be transferred directly from mind to mind (barring ESP), we have learned to attach little bundles of meaning to symbols—usually spoken or written words—that *can* be transmitted. For this clumsy and imprecise procedure to work at all in oral communication, both the sender and the receiver must be making simultaneous contributions to the process. They must be in at least rough agreement on the symbol system or language they are using and the meaning to be assigned to each symbol or group of symbols. There is a

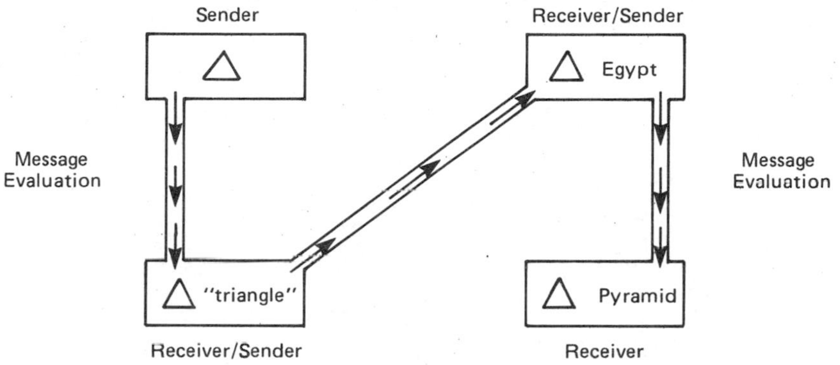

Figure 2.2

Effective communication may necessitate repetition, redrafting, feedback and a simultaneous interaction between sender and receiver.

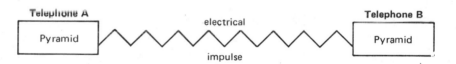

continuous verbal and non-verbal feedback. Often there are repetition and redrafting of the message to bring the intended meaning and the received meaning into alignment.

This is what is meant by an *interacting* process. In contrast, the telephone system represents a linear process.

Figure 2.3

Linear process of the telephone system in which a message is sent as an electrical impulse and is decoded into a reproduction of the original sound (usually).

It translates an input noise into electrical impulses, which are then transmitted to the other end of the connection, where they are decoded and put out as a reproduction of the original noise. Strictly speaking, such a system does not communicate messages; it transports signals. Messages and meanings are beyond its capabilities.

The communication process is most highly and effectively interactive in the face-to-face setting of a conversation, conference or presentation. This may be due in large part to the availability of nonverbal stimuli, as well as to the opportunity for immediate verbal feedback. The process begins virtually simultaneously at both ends of the system when the first word uttered by a speaker is almost instantly received, translated and reacted to by a receiver. Before the first sentence is completed, the speaker is often automatically adjusting the next sentence to a perceived reaction from the listener. In successful interactive communication the message is not the creation of the speaker exclusively. It is a collaborative product, reflecting the influence of listener feedback, both verbal and nonverbal. In an informal setting, this can occur directly, with the receiver asking, "Would you explain that further?" or "Exactly what do you mean by that?" The public speaker usually has to depend on the nonverbal cues many listeners display almost continuously as indications of understanding or confusion, agreement or disagreement.

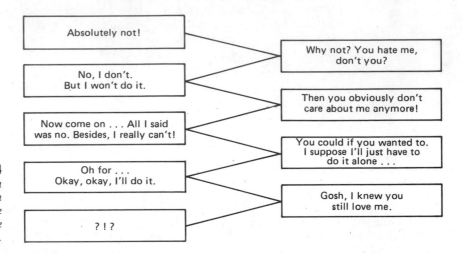

Figure 2.4
*A message, through
the interaction
process, may be
molded into a more
acceptable form.*

THE MANY FUNCTIONS OF COMMUNICATION

Communication is both purposeful and functional. It embodies the objectives of a speaker, and it is also necessary to the accomplishment of numerous tasks requiring agreement and coordination. In addition to a variety of social and entertainment functions, purposeful communication in the business and professional setting can usually be assigned to one or more of four general functions: 1) information, 2) persuasion, 3) understanding, or 4) decision-making.

Such classifications are by nature arbitrary, and these four are designed to describe the main thrust of an interaction that may have the characteristics of more than one function. One part of an effort to promote understanding, clear up a misunderstanding, or create greater sensitivity to a problem, for example, would almost certainly be informational. These are, nevertheless, useful categories for discussion, so long as they aren't treated as limiting definitions.

In addition, these four functions can be thought of as particular forms of a general purpose that has already been described—influence. The objective of purposeful communication is influence over the thinking and behavior of the audience. When the specific function is persuasion, the intention to influence is obvious. But even the purely informational talk can be expected to exert influence on the listeners' thinking about the subject discussed. In general, influence of some sort and to some degree can be assumed to be the objective of all communication.

We can therefore say that communication, as we will regard it, is a systematic process in which a communicator transmits a message intended to influence the receiver in a specific, predetermined way. As mentioned earlier, this is not entirely a one-way process. The receiver also exercises influence on the sender, and the roles of sender and receiver may shift back and forth in the course of the interaction. In the broadest sense communication is the sole instrument through which individuals influence one another.

At the deepest personal level, communication is a tool for breaking out of one's isolation, for establishing contact with others. Once contact has been established, the explanatory or informational role emerges from the desire to have one's needs, feelings, attitudes and beliefs understood and furthered

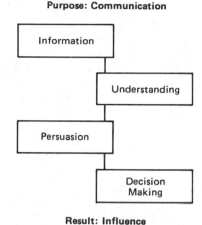

Purpose: Communication

Information

Understanding

Persuasion

Decision
Making

Result: Influence

Figure 2.5
*The objective of any
purposeful commu-
nication is influence,
in some form or
another.*

by others. The persuasive role of communication arises from the resistance encountered in getting a satisfactory response to one's needs and desires.

Persuasion

In contemporary, highly-motivated societies, few communication situations are entirely innocent of direct persuasive intent. It is a rare informational, educational, or entertainment message that does not include some element of persuasion, often artfully concealed or even denied. It is almost axiomatic that the telephone or door-to-door public opinion poll or free gift offer that opens with the reassurance, "We are not selling anything," is, in fact, the introduction to a theoretically irresistible invitation to purchase. One can be comfortably sure that the politician who exhorts the listener to examine the record does not anticipate that the record as presented will lend credence to any opposing point of view. In a world in which there are few completely noncontroversial topics, even the most objective presentation usually betrays a point of view in its selection, order and emphasis.

Persuasion plays a role of unique significance in modern management communication. Charged with responsibility for effective pursuit of organizational goals through the cooperative efforts of many individuals, managers at all levels are required to exercise continuous influence over the thinking and behavior of subordinates, and often, to some extent, over peers and superiors.

Decision-making

Persuasion plays a significant but not exclusive role in the contribution communication makes to the decision-making process in organizations. Sometimes decisions are forged in the clamor of strongly-held opinions in collision. Sometimes they come out of the relatively dispassionate accumulation of information and viewpoints from different sources. Often they reflect nothing more than the will of the strongest, most determined, or most articulate of the participants. But in any case except where decisions are made by a single, isolated autocrat, organizational decision making is a many-faced communication function.

Perhaps nothing places communication closer to the seat of organizational power than its role in internal decision making. Some experts believe that this process is the prime organizational function—that an organization should be defined as a decision-making entity. Others would assign it a slightly less crucial role, but most observers agree that sound internal decision making is basic to organizational health and that effective communication is essential to sound decision-making.

Not all decisions affecting the organization are made inside the organization. Salespeople routinely participate in customer decision making that is vital to the organization. Lobbyists often exert a great deal of influence over the decisions of legislative and regulatory organizations, just as attorneys do over judicial decisions.

An external decision process in which organizational personnel have been called on increasingly to participate in recent years is illustrated by the case of Peter Franklin, our hypothetical aerospace engineer described in Chapter 1. In cases such as his, articulate technical and engineering personnel appear as proposal technicians before government purchasing agencies. They answer a legitimate need in providing information on complicated processes and products, and their role is universally recognized as a key link in their organizations' sales efforts.

In the course of any day's work, this type of technical representative may, in fact, be called on to participate in each of the three communication formats we are examining. The presentation may take the form of an interview, a conference, or a public address. If the technician is a part of a proposal team, it will certainly meet in formal conference sessions to compare notes and map strategy. There may be conventional press interviews to handle, as well as interview-type meetings with key agency personnel and elected representatives. While adapting to each format, the technical representative is expected to maintain an adroit blend of information and sales persuasion in the presentation.

Communication plays many roles in the world at large. In the world of business and the professions, its perennial role is persuasion.

ELEMENTS OF THE COMMUNICATION PROCESS

Objectives, settings and personalities vary from situation to situation, but certain elements remain as constants of the communication process: the sender, the message, the channel, the receiver, and the feedback. In this section, we will examine each of these five functional elements plus a sixth that, a part of the study of rhetoric since the days of Aristotle, has surely earned a place of some sort among the constants: the ethical question.

While it is of a different quality from the other five constants, the ethical question plays a persistent role in selecting the objectives and determining the proper content and tactics of persuasive communication. Every speaker of integrity has wrestled with the problem of establishing ethical standards in the use of persuasive skills. How does one determine the "best interests" of the audience, and how are conflicts between these interests and the objectives of the speaker reconciled? We will examine these and similar problems after a closer look at the five functional constants of the communication process, shown in a typical configuration in Figure 2.6.

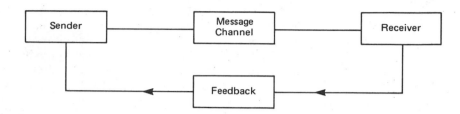

Figure 2.6
*A typical communi-
cation system.*

Sender

As a prime mover in the communication process, the message sender bears
the basic responsibility for its effectiveness. The sender determines the intent
and original encoding of the message and its transmission. The sender also
selects the mode or channel of transmission, verifies receipt of the message,
and interprets the feedback it generates. It is the sender's responsibility to
make the message modifications indicated by the feedback and to correct
any part of the process that fails.

Although we usually visualize the sender as an individual in an interpersonal communication setting, it might be a group of any size or description,
such as a small organization (the faculty committee), a corporation (General
Motors), or an institution (the federal government). The message, rather
than oral, might be a letter or published statement.

Directly or indirectly, the sender is the beneficiary if the objective of the
message is realized. To the extent possible, the sender selects the audience
best qualified to achieve the desired objective.

Among the basic sender responsibilities is the encoding of the message
into appropriate symbols to achieve the desired effect with a given audience.
This means not only selecting the right words but also establishing the tone,
order, and emphasis to convince and motivate the hearers. The crucial principle to remember here is that the words are the means, not the meanings.
Words are merely sounds or squiggles on paper to which we have arbitrarily
attached meanings that exist in our consciousness. The words are the keys
we use to open compartments of meaning in the consciousness of others —
triggers to evoke responses. If we are skilled and lucky, the keys and triggers
we select will evoke the meaning and response we desire.

This principle is embodied in a classic statement that has become almost
a cliche among those who study communication processes: Meanings are
in people, not in words. Unfortunately, it is so easy to quote that its full implications are often disregarded. The sender, therefore, must not develop a "Well,
I said it!" kind of attitude about what has happened.

The first thing that the recognition of where meanings are provides
a guide to selecting symbols. When we undertake to word a message, our
natural impulse is to select those words that convey our meaning most clearly
and forcefully according to our personal interpretations. Our second impulse
is to consult a dictionary, the reference list from which we deduce the meanings commonly associated with a word-symbol by comparison with the
meanings associated with related word-symbols. In the dictionary we may
discover that our personal interpretations do not always agree with those
of the authorities who make up dictionaries. Even the authorities do not
always agree because, to repeat the principle, "meanings are in people, not
in words." Without the meanings people agree to attach to it, a word is an
empty symbol without meaning of its own.

But our message is not directed to ourselves or to a dictionary. It is directed to a person—one of those "people" in whom meanings reside, but not necessarily with the same word-symbols that either you or the dictionary would choose for their expression. In fact, a message expressed purely in your vocabulary, or in the dictionary's, is certain to be interpreted somewhat differently in each new translation. In some cases the differences may be drastic.

The effective meaning of the message, therefore, is not determined by the sender or the dictionary. It is determined in the consciousness of the receiver. This is the reason we communicate most easily with those with whom we share many associations; the reason we communicate best with those we know best; the reason experienced speakers insist on knowing as much as possible about their audiences. This is why the ability to gauge the reactions of another person accurately is possibly the most valuable communication skill one can possess.

Figure 2.7
Messages must be adapted to feedback.

The speaker who has learned to see the world through the eyes of the audience has passed the single most formidable barrier to effective communication.

Since it is the receiver's interpretation that ultimately determines the functional meaning of the message, understanding the receiver's vocabulary and symbol system is of immediate concern to the sender. The problem becomes more complex as the audience grows in size and diversity. Even in the most homogeneous group, no two individuals have identical symbol systems or see the world in identical terms. Thus, the larger the audience, the more the speaker is compelled to use simple, broadly familiar terms that communicate their meanings to a maximum audience with a minimum of ambiguity. This is why the truly great orators usually employ plain, unembellished language, simple illustrations and universal themes.

A second reception factor to be recognized and understood is the listener's state of mind. So far, we have considered the speaker's problem in transmitting messages to cooperative listeners. The problem is enormously more complicated when the listener offers active resistance. When achievement of the message goal depends on the response of the receiver, the receiver is for the moment in absolute control, regardless of the speaker's rhetorical power. The sender's tool is persuasion; if the receiver is sufficiently determined not to understand or respond, there is literally no way to compel cooperation.

We are all familiar with breakdowns in communication that have little or nothing to do with message comprehension but have everything to do with the relationship between sender and receiver. Bias, hostility, the receiver's perception of something offensive in the sender's manner, appearance, tone, or vocabulary, negative experiences with people believed to be similar to the sender in some way—these and a multitude of other subjective factors may cause the listener simply to refuse to receive an otherwise clear message.

Figure 2.8
Any part of the communication process, including events before the verbal message is sent, may contribute noise and, thus, interfere with reception.

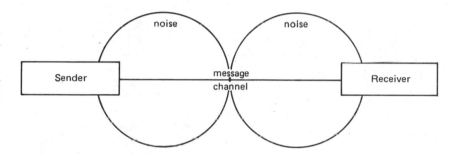

Through extraordinary skill and sensitivity to the receiver's state of mind, the sender can sometimes overcome this stubborn barrier. Sometimes, when the resistance is well entrenched, there appears to be very little that can be done about it.

In addition to creating the message, the sender is also responsible for transmitting it. Far from being a simple matter of standing up and speaking, the available range of possible transmission aids is limited only by the sender's imagination. Even the communicator called upon to deliver a conventional public speech or to chair a conference often has a variety of options— the use of visual aids and graphic materials such as slides, cartoons, illustrations, posters, graphs, summary charts, agendas or other printed material; special formats such as debates, panels, group participation, question-and-answer sessions, music, poetry, skits, role-playing and so on.

This is not intended to suggest that novelty is necessarily and always a virtue for its own sake. Sometimes the simple, direct, conventional approach is the most effective. In that case, it should be used since the most effective approach is, by definition, the best one. But there are situations that clearly call for an imaginative, indirect, unconventional approach.

Message

The sender must understand that the same message can be cast in many forms. The test of any message form is its effectiveness in instilling the desired intent in the mind of a given receiver.

A visit to a doctor's office or to an automobile showroom will provide examples of nonverbal messages and their value in business and the professions. The images of cleanliness, courtesy, and professionalism can be as important as anything the physician actually says to the patient, just as the showroom atmosphere of luxury and comfort probably sells more cars than any particular claim for the piece of machinery on display.

In developing and transmitting a message, the sender selects verbal and nonverbal symbols that are expected to convey the desired meaning most effectively to a particular receiver. In our interactions with others, we send numerous messages that are calculated, consciously or unconsciously, to stimulate desired responses. For maximum effect, our verbal and nonverbal behaviors should reinforce and complement each other. This is why special care has to be devoted to designing and delivering messages, particularly to the meaning that will be attached to the symbols we select.

A blatant example, witnessed by one of the authors, occurred in a sales presentation by a knowledgeable and highly qualified engineer. Entering the office of the prospective customer, the engineer asked permission of his host to smoke and received a barely discernible assent. Reading no clue in the unenthusiastic response, he lit a cigarette. After a few moments, he discovered there was no ashtray in sight. Still oblivious to the implications, he continued to manipulate the cigarette, now with a precariously lengthening ash, until the prospective client, who had begun to exhibit signs of discomfort, rummaged in a drawer and produced a trade-show souvenir ashtray that had obviously never been used. Needless to say, the carefully prepared presentation was shortly in a shambles, along with any hope of success.

The technician having ignored two significant nonverbal messages, the prospective customer became plainly irritated and probably decided that such insensitivity at the outset boded ill for any future relationship. His response was that he really didn't have time to give the presentation serious attention.

Politicians go to extraordinary lengths to establish harmony between their verbal and nonverbal behavior. But sometimes the mask slips. When it happens on national television, the results can be disastrous. At one point in the 1972 Democratic primaries, George McGovern appeared to be seriously challenged by former New York City Mayor John Lindsay. At the press conference at which Lindsay made his announcement, the first opportunity to ask a question fell to a secret McGovern supporter planted in the front row. The reporter asked for Lindsay's evaluation of the crisis in Mexican-American relations. The question caught Lindsay off guard, and for a fatal moment his expression of blank incomprehension and dismay was duly recorded by the cameras.[2]

There was, of course, no crisis in Mexican-American relations. But that dazed instant, so graphically recorded, became the Lindsay image in the critical Florida primary, and there are McGovern strategists who are convinced it was that instant which sealed the fate of the Lindsay candidacy.

Channel

Barring the paranormal, no communication can take place without some identifiable medium of transmission between the sender and the receiver. Even when you are projecting visible or audible signals, no communication occurs unless those signals are brought in some form within range of the receiver's senses. The lecture hall, the conference room, the press, the telephone, the radio, the television and movie screen, billboards, and the postal system are all familiar channels of communication. Selecting an appropriate channel is one of the crucial decisions in the communication process. It is actually a two-part decision: first, whether the channel is appropriate for the target audience; second, whether the form of the message is appropriate for the channel. Richard Nixon had great difficulty in adapting his mastery of radio communication to the new visual medium of television. Similarly, a presentation styled for the public platform is seldom as effective across a conference table or in a one-to-one interaction in an office. Whether or not they recognize it, people are sensitive to the differences in media. Many would select the telephone or the mail over face-to-face interaction when transmitting bad news.

The critical role of channels is attested by the intensity of the competition for access to effective channels by those who need to reach a particular audience. Witness the enormous amount of energy expended by advertisers, promoters, candidates and protest groups to gain the attention and favor of those who serve as gatekeepers for the media and of their office counterparts, agents, secretaries and managers. "Getting past the receptionist" is among the first games sales people learn to play.

An example of using multiple channels was provided by members of a summer speech class taught by one of the authors. Assigned the task of demonstrating multiple avenues for transmitting the same message, three students undertook to use the assignment to solve a practical problem. As they confided to the instructor, the roommate of one of them — also a member of the class — was a sensitive, loveable soul whom no one quite had the heart to tell that his personal hygiene left a good deal to be desired. With characteristic undergraduate ingenuity, they developed a coordinated multi-delivery strategy that would have done credit to Madison Avenue.

The roommate opened the campaign by distributing a Student Health Service leaflet on personal cleanliness. This, he announced, was the inspiration for his own talk, which turned out to be a sometimes hilarious account of the many embarrassments of a personal offense that your best friends won't tell you about. In addition, presumably as a result of his new interest, the same person began making an elaborate ritual of his morning shower and persuaded his offending roommate to act as an independent judge of the effectiveness of his deodorant throughout the day.

Now the second conspirator appeared to catch the enthusiasm. His contribution was an illustrated lecture, complete with slides borrowed from the Department of Health, on the microscopic debris the human body accumulates between baths, with special emphasis on the excretory role of the sweat glands.

Apparently inspired by the first two, the third member of the cabal enlisted the cooperation of the class in a comparative test of various free samples of deodorants obtained from the local drug store. At this point, as an unplanned but delightful development, the student at whom the whole elaborate campaign was directed became genuinely interested. He innocently adopted as his own topic the results of his service as "judge" of his roommate's personal cleanliness campaign.

The project was not only a success with its target; it also had a noticeable bonus effect on the approachability of two other students whose personal hygiene had previously been of marginal social acceptability.

As the deodorant story illustrates, the nonverbal elements may be as significant as — or even more significant than — the verbal message. The students who succeeded in influencing the thinking and behavior of their classmates employed several powerful message techniques that did not depend on articulation for their effect. Drawing the target student's attention to the desirable behavior of his roommate, for example, enlisting his aid in monitoring his roommate's personal cleanliness campaign, and involving him as a participant in the classroom comparison test were shrewd and effective uses of multiple channels.

Receiver

We have already examined important aspects of the receiver's role in clarifying the sender's message. The important point to recall is that the receiver cannot be thought of as a passive receptacle into which meaning can be poured, the way liquid plastic is poured into a mold.

It is true that the objective of communication is to effect some change in the receiver's beliefs, values, attitudes or behavior. And it is true that this is usually accomplished through messages formulated and transmitted by the sender. But messages are also received and translated by the receiver, who is the final judge of what they mean. Unless the receiver is a clone of the sender, the sender who formulates a message purely in terms of his or her private symbol system risks serious misunderstanding when the message is translated in the receiver's symbol system. The sender's job is not to send the message in the form he or she would respond to favorably — but in the form that will motivate the receiver.

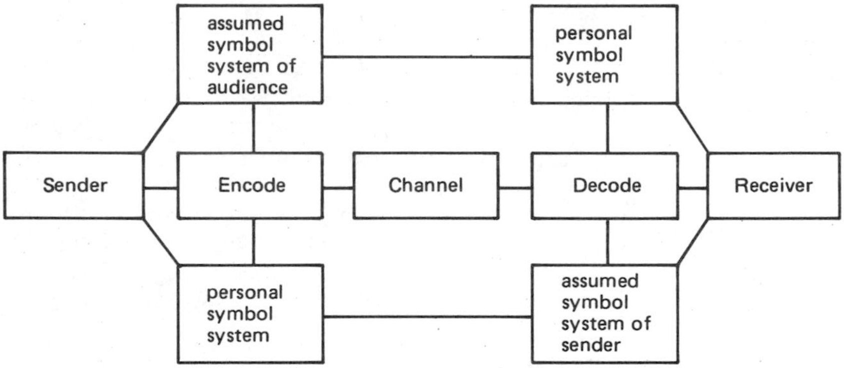

Figure 2.9
Both sender and receiver must be in agreement on symbol system in use in order for communication to be effective.

We need also to keep in mind that the world of communication is not neatly divided into permanent classes of senders and receivers. At one time or another, everybody is a sender and everybody is a receiver, with the roles typically switching from moment to moment in the usual informal interaction. Our common insights into both roles provide a valuable base for more effective communicating if we will only train ourselves to use them. Both the speaker and the listener have an obligation to remember the difficulties of the other role. They should respond, not as they would like to be responded to, since tastes differ, but as if they were the other party.

In a later chapter on listening we will discuss the responsibility the receiver bears for eliminating identifiable distortions in the reception and processing of messages. For the moment, it is important simply to recognize that such distortions range from the innocent to the deliberate, from the banal to the bizarre.

One of the most common sources of message distortion is simple inattention. The inattentive or distracted receiver may receive the message incorrectly and not bother to check it. Or the receiver's perception of the message symbols and the meanings to be attached to them may differ from the sender's. The receiver may not understand some of the words at all but may prefer to guess at their meanings rather than to confess ignorance.

Equally important is the degree to which the receiver, no matter how fair-minded and sophisticated, sees the world through a filter of personal interests, preferences, phobias, biases, prejudices and preconceptions. The listener is responsive not only to the speaker's words but also to the personal images called up by the words.

Communication outcomes are the combined responsibility of speaker and listener, with the primary burden of proof on the speaker. It is the sender's responsibility to take into account as much as possible the receiver's point of view. It is the receiver's obligation to be aware of and resist the influence of his or her own distortion machinery.

Feedback

Although it is perfectly possible to communicate without feedback, for the sender it is a little like dropping stones into a void and never hearing them hit bottom. It is comforting, reassuring, and instructive to have a mechanism that tells you the message has been received, how it has been understood, and what effect it has had. If any of these areas is deficient, feedback can provide the cue to resend or modify and resend the message. It also is a warning system when greater or different means are required in order to achieve the message goal, and it provides valuable information for improving future communication efforts.

Feedback is a process where the sender of a message interprets receiver reaction by listening and observing receiver cues. These cues are called feedback. Both a sender and a receiver share feedback responsibility. For the

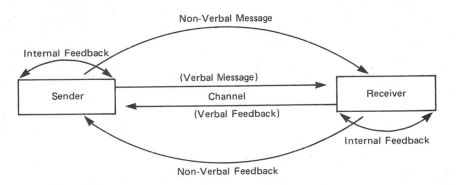

Figure 2.10
Both sender and receiver will be involved in the reception and transmission of verbal as well as nonverbal messages.

sender, it involves conscious attention to all the verbal and nonverbal cues to the receiver's comprehension and reaction—including comments, facial expressions, body language and behavior in response to the message. For the receiver, it involves giving such information consciously, clearly, and in a way that disrupts the flow and distracts the attention of other listeners as little as possible.

For experienced communicators, feedback is a kind of rapport that becomes automatic. For those who are newly alert to feedback, the principal mistake is usually not in misinterpreting the signals but in responding too quickly and too forcefully to superficial indications. A single yawn may be evidence that you have one overly tired listener, not that you are losing the attention of the audience. However, yawning is notoriously contagious, and the first one is certainly a signal to watch for other signs.

If not absolutely essential, feedback is certainly a highly valuable tool for the communicator. Without it, we are almost in the position of those optimistic space explorers who send out messages to unknown intelligences somewhere in the universe without much hope that the messages will ever be received by anyone; or, if received, understood; or, if understood, answered.

Ethics

Robert Jenkins is a member and leading spokesperson for Concerned Citizens Against Pollution (CCAP). A current project is to halt certain kinds of construction activity by Jones Electric, Inc. in his state. Jones Electric is identified as a principal polluter in several areas of the state. The occasion of this speech, however, is to speak to the plans of Jones Electric to build a plant on the Chastity River near a major metropolitan area. CCAP has been convinced that the plant would damage fish life in the river and has financed a study to evaluate the damage. The study reveals conclusively that the new plan will not harm fish life; moreover, it will stimulate fish reproduction and even produce several other positive effects. However, Jenkins believes that in other areas of the state Jones Electric is doing damage to the environment. When asked to speak to the local Kiwanis on the advisability of the Chastity River plant, does he reveal the information from the study?

If you assert that the speaker must not distort nor conceal information, then you must rule Jenkins should tell his audience that in this case Jones Electric, Inc. is doing a good thing. Such an admission will probably weaken his attack on other Jones Electric projects which he believes to be harmful.

In most instances, we would agree that speakers should reveal the sources of their information; speakers should expose their individual biases on controversial issues; speakers should admit lack of information when such is the case. We probably also would agree that speakers should welcome criticism of policies and invite expression of opposing points of view. Speakers should attack arguments and policies but not the spokesperson of opposition.

We share a position first advocated by Aristotle that communication is amoral, that it is a tool used by men who are both good and evil. Therefore, we do not intend to instruct you concerning what kind of morality you should adopt. However, questions related to the ethical choices to be made by every speaker will recur in decisions concerning the use of evidence, modes of delivery, linguistic choices, etc. Of course, the very nature of some of the questions raised suggests a position on the part of the authors; however, the authors do not take exactly the same position on each of the issues raised. We do assert, however, the necessity of an ethical—an honest—communication behavior.

A posture which calls for openness and truthfulness must be endorsed. Public communicators should reveal their biases, welcome the presentation of other points of view, and indicate their sources of information. In our discussions of adaptation to audiences, use of evidence, and selection of delivery methods, we convey ethical judgments necessary to the public communicator.

NOTES   [1]Aristotle *Rhetoric* 1,1355, from Lane Cooper *the Rhetoric of Aristotle*, ny, Appleton-Century-Crofts, 1932, p7.

[2]Mankiewicz, Frank, *Perfectly Clear* (New York: Popular Library, 1974).

SUGGESTED READINGS   Burgoon, M. and M. Ruffner. *Human Communication*. New York: Holt, Rinehart & Winston, 1978.

McCroskey, J. C. and L. R. Wheeless. *Introduction to Human Communication*. Boston: Allyn & Bacon, 1976.

Tubbs, S. L. and S. Moss. *Human Communication*, 3rd Edition. New York: Random House, 1980.

Alice Barry was contacted by the president of the local PTA. As a teacher in a local high school, she was asked to illustrate the various types of audio-visual equipment used by teachers to support classroom instruction. She had several weeks to prepare, and she spent the time familiarizing herself with audio and visual recorders, overhead and opaque projectors, and with filmstrips, slides and films. She also found illustrative materials from colleagues in several academic disciplines and organized an outline of her presentation. She decided to entitle her presentation, "The Tools Teachers Use to Teach Your Children."

When she arrived to make the presentation, she found the five-hundred-seat auditorium to have an audience of about twenty-five people: fifteen teachers who used the equipment regularly and fewer than ten parents. What should she do? Speak from the auditorium stage as planned? Cancel the presentation? Revise and attempt a last-minute adaptation to an audience of teachers who were as familiar with the subject as she?

The purpose of this chapter is to examine the specific requirements of audiences encountered in business and professional situations, such as that experienced by Alice Barry. Alice, for example, will improve her communication effectiveness by anticipating predictable audience reactions to different communication strategies. All decisions we make in communication take into consideration our audience. It is important to understand that effective communication begins with an analysis of who will be receiving our message.

Usually, both parties to a particular exchange are well aware, at least in a general way, of the desired outcome of the communication before it begins. Participants at a production meeting are usually safe in assuming that its objective will somehow involve greater productivity or efficiency. When the sermon topic is "Sin," the congregation will probably not be disappointed if it anticipates that the minister, like the one in the well-worn Calvin Coolidge anecdote, will be "agin it." If the president of Ford Motor Co. discusses the safety features of the Pinto, the listeners can be pretty sure in advance that they will hear evidence for other conclusions than those reached by Ralph Nader.

Thus, in most communication situations there is an advance platform of understanding from which to proceed. This does not, however, give the speaker any right to assume that the audience either understands or agrees

Audiences in Business and Professional Environments

3

with the specific objectives the communication situation is designed to achieve. Many a speaker, many a salesperson, has come to grief by leaping to the conclusion that a listener's willingness, or even eagerness, to listen makes it unnecessary to explain and persuade. The president of a major furniture company entertained his audience with jokes for more than thirty minutes — only to find that everyone enjoyed his speech but no one wanted to buy his company's furniture. Like other foundation structures, a platform of understanding provides a base on which to build, and nothing more that can be taken for granted.

Failure of the speaker to understand and adapt to the processes of the listener is among the most common causes of ineffective communication. Basically, what the speaker is doing is encoding an intellectual/emotional message into symbols. It is vital that the decoder (the listener) attach essentially the same meaning to the symbols that the encoder does. There will always be some loss of meaning — percent agreement between speaker and listener on the exact meaning of symbols is undoubtedly impossible. But below that, there is a range of fairly close agreement on definitions in which reasonably effective communication is possible. Below a certain level of commonly defined symbols, communication becomes virtually impossible. The most effective communication involves both a high degree of agreement on the meaning of the symbols and a high degree of adaptability by both the sender and the receiver. The principal responsibility for adaptation, however, rests with the sender — with regard to not only the definition of terms but also the barriers created by preconceptions and emotional factors as well.

Faulty or superficial analysis of listener processes can be disastrous, as an executive of a major Southern California utility discovered in the early days of the nuclear power debate. He was asked to discuss the subject at the final session of a high-school social studies class, with a social hour to follow and a number of parents attending. Anticipating a relatively unsophisticated audience, he had not made any extensive preparations and spoke informally, inviting questions and discussion.

He tried to keep his illustrations and examples at a level consistent with the knowledge and interests of his audience, and the hour appeared to go very well. At one point he was asked whether there was a chance that a nuclear reactor, such as the one his company proposed to build in the area, might blow up. He responded that any dynamic process, the heating system in the building they occupied or the fuel system in the family automobile, can conceivably blow up but that such systems are designed by people who understand the dangers and provide elaborate safeguards against accidents. This, he added, is especially true in the case of nuclear installations because their designers are acutely aware of the widespread devastation a nuclear accident could cause.

The following day, to his shock, he found himself quoted in the local press as having compared the chances of nuclear disaster to those of an explosion in an automobile fuel system. Apparently a reporter either had been present during the discussion or had obtained a tape from one of the student recorders the speaker had noticed but not given much thought to. It had not crossed his mind that he might be quoted in the press. The accident was particularly embarrassing because the story quoted his thoughtless remark with scrupulous accuracy and the inference drawn, although far from the one he had intended, was not unreasonable. His only recourse was a carefully worded letter to the editor, acknowledging his poor choice of analogies and correcting the false impression he had created.

In retrospect, it is easy to spot several errors he had made in anticipating audience reaction. First, he had failed to recognize that — given the increasing controversy on nuclear installations — anything he said on the subject to any audience was apt to be newsworthy. Second, he never took the time to find out the nature of his audience. Potentially, at least, it was not simply a group of students but the public at large.

It is seldom possible to cover all audience contingencies. As this illustration indicates, it is a mistake not to consider the possibility of an invisible audience, such as the media and their public or the friends and associates of the listener, in addition to the immediate audience. But the key to understanding and anticipating the response of any listener or group of listeners is a grasp of the fundamental characteristics of the decoding process itself — how the individual receiver goes about processing received messages.

DECODING BEHAVIOR

We have already observed that some intended meaning is always lost in the communication process. Even with the best symbol system imaginable, some meaning is lost in the encoding process because the symbols merely stand for the ideas they represent. They are not the ideas themselves. Some additional meaning or clarity is lost to attrition in the transmission process. The words heard are never quite as clear and meaningful as the words spoken, even under the best conditions.

But the greatest hazards to effective communication lurk in the receiving and decoding processes. The other losses in the system are essentially random, resulting in a general, unsystematic erosion of the message. In the listener's receiving processes, however, a dramatic change takes place in the way meaning is lost. Almost as if a malicious saboteur were in charge of the receiving process, clear intended meanings may be ignored, displaced or altered in a bewildering pattern of distortion. Often the unwary communicator is at a complete loss to understand how the message sent out could be so thoroughly transformed — even inverted — in reception.

To the extent that these losses are not caused by deficiencies in hearing or comprehension, they result from a fascinatingly perverse set of screening devices by which the human ego protects itself against the intrusion of disagreeable information. The devices operate in a variety of ways, but the net effect is that when we act as receivers we tend to hear what we want to hear and to ignore everything else.

This general tendency, sometimes referred to as selective attention, can usually be verified by a simple, often dramatic, test. Ask several people to read and describe an objective article dealing with a controversial subject. More often than not, you will find it hard to believe, from the descriptions, that they all read the same material. This is because each of us perceives the world through a highly personal filter of biases, preconceptions, opinions, values and beliefs. Most of us tend to feel threatened when this personal attitude system is subjected to any serious disturbance. Incoming messages that contradict our system are usually ignored, or, if they cannot be ignored, admitted reluctantly and grudgingly.

This phenomenon is observable on a national scale during periods of great public controversy and emotion, such as that surrounding the Watergate scandal. As the charge of corruption moved towards its climax, many of the

President's detractors greeted each new revelation, however trivial, as final proof of his guilt. Meanwhile, his supporters found in the same revelations new proof that the "Nixon-haters" were determined to bring him down. Even when the evidence, much of it from his own mouth, became overwhelming that the President had participated in the "cover-up," defenders continued to favor letters to the editor with pathetic protests against the "injustice" inflicted on the former President. Curiously, their counterparts in the anti-Nixon camp often did not appear to be much better acquainted with the facts of the case.

This selectivity, which runs through all of our perceptions, serves both positive and negative functions in our processes of gathering information and forming attitudes. As a screening device, it does not only hamper the acquisition of new data—it also helps to prevent us from abandoning too quickly the valuable products of our experience and traditions whenever we encounter a new idea. It is also a natural part of the way in which we build concepts out of data acquired bit by bit. Our first perceptions of any phenomenon are usually fragmentary, because we cannot process simultaneously all of the data available. So we select. We absorb an impression and perhaps attach some meaning to it, based on our prior knowledge or experience. As each new bit of information is admitted, it is connected if possible to the data already assimilated, expanding and perhaps subtly altering it. When a piece of information is acquired that will not assimilate, it is usually easier to ignore it than to modify the whole structure to accommodate it. For most people it is more important to maintain the internal consistency of the structure— and perhaps its harmony with their overall value system—than to make room for contradictory information. The process of connecting new perceptions to old perceptions appears to be fundamental to our learning process, and selectivity is both its strength and its weakness. However, our selective processes are capable of operations far more powerful and sophisticated than the simple rejection of undesirable data. They are actually capable of transforming awkward information into a more acceptable form.

Not only are we selective about the messages we choose to accept or send, we are also selective with regard to the senses we elect to heed at a given moment. The only channels through which data from the outside world reach our consciousness are our senses. Whether we realize it or not, all these senses are usually sending a steady stream of signals to our brains to be processed. Fortunately, we are able to select from this avalanche of chaotic stimuli the channels to which we will pay attention. Thus, when you are speaking, your listeners are able to concentrate all but a negligible fraction of their attention on the signals from two channels, sight and hearing.

If, however, a prankster or disrupter releases a stink bomb during the speech, your audience will begin to experience a clamor effect as a neglected channel bids for attention with increasing urgency. At first your audience may be able to disregard the discordant signals by a conscious act of will. But if the level of stimulation continues to rise, it will eventually overwhelm the listeners' selective controls and take over attention from the selected channels. At this point your audience may give up their attempt to concentrate on your speech, leaving the room in order to escape the disagreeable stimulation on their sense-of-smell channel.

A reverse kind of selective attention is taught by defensive driving schools. In this case, the object is to help you avoid becoming fixated on the most attention-getting stimuli in order for you to maintain alertness to other, apparently insignificant, stimuli that could be a warning of impending danger. The good defensive driver has learned to scan a broad range of seemingly chaotic stimuli for possibly significant signals.

At a different level, personal biases and preconceptions play a powerful role in selective perception. We tend to respond positively to people we feel comfortable with and negatively to those who make us uncomfortable. In some cases, the negative reaction is so strong that we avoid seeing, hearing or even discussing the person who makes us uncomfortable. Many people will turn off a television set or leave the room when a personality with whom they deeply disagree appears on the screen.

There is a general tendency to monitor all our senses in this selective manner. To read a publication that confirms and flatters our own point of view is pleasant and bracing; to read material in opposition to our beliefs is not only depressing, but hard work. As listeners, the detection of message elements that offend our beliefs, biases and preconceptions activates all of our devices for deflecting, canceling, jamming or distorting the incoming signal.

Given the obstacles, it is small wonder that communication so often goes awry or that the communicator who understands the obstacles may often feel like an observation pilot attempting to skim his light plane through the massed ack-ack of a heavily defended position. Even in the face of the odds, however, our experience tells us that effective communication is possible when luck, instinct or skill carries us over the mechanical and psychological barriers.

AUDIENCE ANALYSIS When we resolve why we want to communicate to a person or a group of people, we then focus on answering some very basic questions: How can I achieve my purpose? How can I gain their attention, create interest and keep them interested? How do I order my argument? What type of delivery will be most effective? What kind and level of language will be appropriate? Will the audience accept what I say? etc.

To find answers to these questions and many others, we employ a process identified as audience analysis. This process focuses on uncovering the nature and scope of audience interest, values, beliefs, and intent. To uncover this data, two types of analysis are required: demographic and purpose oriented.[1]

Demographic Analysis

The first type of analysis focuses on gathering standard information about the audience, such as occupation, place of residence, income, age, sex, marital status, religion, education, political philosophy, knowledge, reasoning patterns, etc. According to Clevenger, "The demographic characteristics are observed: they are then used as a basis for inferences concerning matters related to the speaker, speech and occasion."[2]

From our demographic analysis we infer how our audience might respond to specific language choices, organizational patterns, lines of argument, content, delivery, etc. This analysis helps the speaker make assumptions about how the audience is likely to decode his or her message.

Purpose-Oriented Analysis

According to Clevenger, this analysis is a continuous process of gathering information needed by the speaker to achieve the desired objective. He states: "Audience analysis which is purpose-oriented is not a stage of speech preparation; it is a dynamic and integral part of every stage of speech preparation."[3]

You begin this process by answering the questions: What is my purpose, what is my objective? Second, what do I need to know to achieve my purpose? What is important about my audience relative to my purpose? Using this process requires a speaker to monitor the audience continuously in light of his or her purpose.

Paul York wants to convince a group of Rotary members that they should support his favorite charity. His purpose is clear: To obtain an endorsement from the club. He begins his preparation by answering the question of how much the members know about his charity. He then may ask what other charities are competing for Rotary funds, what the most effective, persuasive arguments are, etc. He will continue to monitor the audience, even during his speech and after it is completed. If Paul finds he will not have 35 minutes as promised but only 20, he will adjust his speech, taking into account his new time allowance, his purpose and his audience.

ADAPTING, PREDICTING AND ANTICIPATING AUDIENCE BEHAVIOR

Directly or indirectly, all communication aims at creating an effect on the thinking, feelings or behavior of others. In business and professional situations it is uniquely directed to the task of producing a specific effect on the behavior of the receivers. In our earlier example, the power company spokesman made an error in assessing his potential audience and the effect of his remarks on a significant part of it. Assuming that the audience would consist of high school students and a few parents, he thought in terms of long-term behavioral effects. He had supposed that this audience would be primarily interested in the wonders of nuclear technology and the benefits it promised. By explaining these, he hoped to encourage future behavior favorable to his company's plans to install a nuclear generator in the area. He failed to anticipate that his remarks would be projected to a different audience containing a strong contingent actively hostile to his point of view. The immediate result of his communication, therefore, was behavior the opposite of that intended.

The most effective communication is usually well thought out in terms of its purpose, is natural in delivery, and is adapted to the listener or audience to which it is directed. This, as we have suggested, can be a tall order because of the great variety of variables affecting the outcome of any communication interaction.

To further understand audiences in business and professional settings, a speaker may improve effectiveness by knowing organizational variables that could affect communication outcomes. Considering these variables when preparing a message may help a speaker anticipate and predict how one individual or an audience will respond to a message. We will now examine the most important of these factors and their effect on communication in business and professional settings.

Power and Influence

In a relevant article French and Raven describe five different sources of power affecting behavior in organizations: reward, coercive, referent, expert, and legitimate power.[4] Perhaps somewhat more in communication situations than in others, it is more important for power to be *perceived* as existing than for it to exist in reality. The sender may speak with greater deference (and the receiver may listen more intently) to one perceived as holding greater power than to the apparently powerless. This characteristic, in fact, has been the springboard for innumerable comedy scenes in which a natty underling is mistaken for an executive, while a slovenly executive is mistaken for the janitor. Even without the exaggeration of comedy, the contrast in behavior toward the two stereotypes is often striking.

Obviously, the speaker's ability to reward or punish is a significant power to influence behavior. This power has considerable effect upon one's ability to get what one wants. The boss may not have to explain why a particular action is desired, merely that it is desired, whereas the subordinate usually has to make a good argument. As with other forms of power, the effectiveness of reward and punishment power depends largely on the perceptions of those to whom it is directed. Prison inmates can be subjected to enormous pressure not only by the granting or withholding of privileges that would appear trivial to those on the outside but also by more recognizable forms of coercion— shortening or lengthening of sentence, greater or lesser degrees of isolation and restriction, transfer to a more or less desirable institution, and so on.

Depending on the sensitivity of the receiver, the same types of reward and punishment can be observed in all kinds of situations. One in which the value of communication to the individual was emphasized was the British working class tradition of "sending to Coventry"—that is, completely cutting off from communication—an individual who had committed an offense against fellow-workers or union principles. Many people practice an informal kind of "Coventry" by steadfastly refusing to acknowledge the existence of persons who have offended them.

The transfer power of certain types of organizations is also a familiar device of reward and punishment. Former FBI head J. Edgar Hoover was a notorious wielder of this power, often transferring agents to the bureau's "Siberia" posts—areas of disagreeable climate, routine activity, and meager advancement opportunities—for infractions of rules or for personal conduct that he found offensive. In the academic world, the same effect is achieved by assigning the individual to an 8:00 a.m. class.

In addition to the coercive power just described, a third type of power a speaker can use which commands listener attention and affects behavior is called "referent" by French and Raven. Referent power is based on the respect commanded by individuals through their personality, accomplishments, charisma, reputation, status, or office. The Watergate exposures revealed the awesome raw coercive power available to a ruthless administration capable of using the federal bureaucracy to extort personal and party concessions. But in many cases, the favors and contributions do not appear to have resulted from pressure, but from the fact that the donors genuinely liked and admired the President. Obviously, some of those who were persuaded to engage in illegal acts did so because they feared the consequences of refusal. Others, however, seem to have been motivated by their respect for the office of the presidency.

At a less Olympian level, we sometimes see referent power at work on testimonial occasions, when a respected older leader is honored for a lifetime of service and accomplishments. On such occasions, people can sometimes be observed listening in rapt attention to repetitious, meandering reminiscences that they would not endure for five minutes from a speaker who was not loved and revered.

Perceived expertise also creates a form of power in many instances. We listen with greater interest and attention—we are actually more readily convinced—when the speaker, by reputation or manner, wears the mantle of authority in an area in which we are concerned. Our broker may be unimpressive in all other respects, but if we are convinced he or she possesses investment knowledge that can benefit us, we tend to defer to that knowledge as to other forms of power.

"Knowledge is power" is a durable cliché because it is so broadly applicable, even when the knowledge involved is not particularly broad. Many a melodrama plot has been kept alive by the otherwise helpless hero's convenient reminder to the villains: "You can't kill me because I'm the only one who knows where the gold is." For decades about the only quality African villagers possessed that was capable of penetrating the mindless contempt of the white safari members was their superior knowledge of local terrain and the hunt. On the other hand, a simple reputation for breadth of knowledge sometimes confers power. We are all familiar with academics whose pronouncements, even in areas in which they have no especial competence, are accorded oracular stature.

A fifth type of power a speaker may have is called "legitimate" power. It is the power the audience grants to those whose performance, experience, title, status or other attributes testify to effective operation within a value system of which we approve. The founders and effective directors of successful organizations seldom have to wield any power except the perceived legitimate power of their earned position.

The importance of the power variable in business and professional communication situations can hardly be overestimated. From the self-confidence with which the message is encoded and the authority with which it is delivered to the importance and credence with which it is invested by the receiver, the relative perceived power of sender and receiver is the single most effective influence on communication outcome—except in those cases in which the objective itself is so urgent that it overrides all other considerations.

Status

Power and status are related, but they are not identical. Status denotes rank or position in an organizational hierarchy or in the esteem of others. Power usually confers status, and status can be a steppingstone to power. It is possible for persons with high status to have little actual power, but it is quite unusual for a person of low status to achieve and hold significant power.

Status is often associated with the longevity of one's association with a particular profession, organization, project, or locality. Such status is not necessarily accompanied by power. A community's oldest citizen, for example, often acquires status for no apparent virtue beyond durability. The newspaper feature on the town's oldest resident provides a graphic demonstration that people will often read or listen to communications from the very aged that would merit little attention if they came from someone younger.

The term "status symbol" has become attached to those advertisements of standing assumed by individuals and organizations, sometimes unconsciously. The neighborhood one lives in, the size, location and decor of one's home, the clothes one wears, the automobile one drives, and the sports and recreations one adopts can all function as status symbols. In business and professional organizations the symbols are sometimes rigidly dictated—salary, title, the size, location and decor of the office, the type and placement of the desk, the appearance and behavior of the secretary, accessibility—dozens of jealously guarded signals to the status of the individual in the hierarchy. At the other end of the scale, sandals and careless grooming were for a time the badges of status among the antistatus minded.

The effect of status on communication is similar to that of power. In general, persons of perceived high status have greater credibility and are accorded a more respectful and cooperative hearing than those of low status.

Roles

As used in reference to organizational and professional situations, a role is more than an individual's arbitrarily adopted stance and pose—it is a generally recognized and expected mode of behavior. In this sense it is a behavioral norm that fulfills expectations.

While roles are not as rigidly defined as they once were, there are still limits that are rarely violated without diminishing the status of effectiveness of the violator. Today's bank president may not be so easy to identify by his clothes and manner as yesterday's. But it would still be considered highly inappropriate for him to betray a sentimental involvement in the personal problems of his bank's clients.

Roles help to smooth and order business interactions and to eliminate extraneous and confusing elements from transaction. Although every comptroller is a distinct individual, every comptroller's job has certain standard functions and requirements. These can be accomplished with a minimum of friction and confusion if all comptrollers adhere to certain norms of attitude and behavior appropriate to the function.

Either as individuals or as audiences, receivers usually have certain expectations concerning the roles they expect of speakers, interviewers and conference leaders. What they expect is dictated by prior experience, the subject, the occasion, and the speaker's reputation. Entirely different behaviors are expected from a former Big Ten linebacker discussing the upcoming season and a prize-winning poet reading from his latest book although they may, in fact, be the same individual.

Sometimes a speaker who deviates from the expected role can provide a delightful and effective communication experience. This is particularly true if he or she is a skilled communicator and if the unexpected role helps to hold attention or point up a fresh approach to the subject. In such cases it is often helpful if the way can be prepared—if the word that goes ahead of a speaker sets the mood of the audience in the way advance publicity and introductory remarks are intended to do. One of the authors served as director of a university executive program that brought many outside speakers to the campus. He had numerous opportunities to observe audience response to different role situations and advance preparation. In one case he was able to give the class of executives a fairly thorough briefing on what to expect from a speaker whose counter-role style was familiar to him. The response to the speaker was excellent—the more he violated the traditional role, the better they seemed to like it.

In another case, the author did not have any advance information on a speaker who began a talk on effective communication by insulting his listeners' intelligence and then proceeded to erect an apparently insuperable barrier of hostility between himself and them. When they were on the point of walking out, he reversed his tactics and began charming them. He concluded with a striking analysis of the devices he had used in the two halves of his address. He was successful, but the executives never accorded him quite the approval and trust they had given the other unorthodox speaker.

Many factors no doubt contributed to the difference in response to the two men; perhaps one may be that audiences respond better to the unexpected when they are forewarned to expect it. This may occur because role serves a legitimate function in communication. Purposeful communication involves some element of the unfamiliar. Unless one or both parties bring some new data away from the interaction, meaningful communication can hardly be said to have taken place.

In business and professional communication situations, attention is usually focused on a narrow range of data selected to accomplish a specific objective. Any distracting factor tends to reduce the efficiency of the process. Unfortunately, the ability of human beings to adjust to and select among a number of unfamiliar simultaneous stimuli is limited. We tend to become confused and miss the point when too many new things happen at the same time. If, on the other hand, we know ahead of time the general format, pattern, language and attitudes to expect, we don't need to waste any energy or attention on these peripheral matters. We can concentrate on recognizing and adjusting to the new data. Then—unless the new information is highly stimulating—our principal problem may be boredom.

Some communicators refuse to play the role out of a sense that any artificial stance inhibits the communication process, a proposition that may be only partly true. Others adopt alternate roles in order to stimulate interest or to strengthen the theme or point of the address or exchange. In any case, the inexperienced speaker needs to be very sure that a different approach will enhance the process before discarding the role the audience expects and with which it has learned to be comfortable.

THE INFLUENCE PROCESS

In its simplest form a process is an operation in which an intent is converted into an effect. The intent is the input of the process and the effect is the output. In the communication process, the input is the sender's intent to influence the receiver's thinking or behavior in the interests of a selected objective. The output is the receiver's response, which may or may not bear a recognizable resemblance to the intent, depending on the effectiveness of the process.

Sometimes the process is one-way, sometimes two-way. The ship's captain who picks up a microphone and transmits an order over the vessel's communication system intends to produce a specific effect—compliance—in the behavior of the responsible subordinates. He is engaged in an essentially one-way exercise of influence, although it may be that the subordinate is also trying to influence the captain by the smartness or sullenness of the response. It is wrong to view such as an isolated event.

The exchange of influence is more clearly two-way in the typical job-evaluation interview. Here the superior attempts to influence the subordinate to accept the validity of the evaluation and to respond appropriately, continuing the performance that is approved and correcting that which is criticized. At the same time, the subordinate attempts to influence the superior to accept the view that everything is going as well as could be expected or better, under the circumstances.

The effect is the proof and measure of the influence. A quiz is an instructor's tool for measuring the effect of the instructional process—for comparing the produced effect with the intent. Comparative sales figures provide companies with a means of checking the effect of their advertising communication with its intent. Other factors being equal, the greater the correspondence between intent and effect, the more effective the communication process.

Influence: A Four Step Process

The influence process can be looked at as a four-step operation. The first step for the speaker is the planting in the consciousness of the receiver a motivating awareness of the problem, product, or idea with which the communication is concerned. A speaker may cite an interesting statistic or read an alarming quote. Consumer goods manufacturers often move into this phase in a very straightforward manner by giving away free samples of a new product or selling them at a drastically reduced price or tying in the initial purchase with a gift, refund or opportunity to win a prize.

The second stage is the development of interest, usually accomplished by citing a benefit which can be derived from listening to the speaker. If successful, it prompts the listener to evaluate the desired effect in terms of his or her own needs and welfare.

The third step in the influence process is an outcome or evaluation—the adoption of an attitude or a conclusion about the message—and the fourth is the implementation of the conclusion. This fourth step is the action stage of the process and the one that provides evidence of the effect.

A haggling transaction, such as the sale of a used automobile, ordinarily presents the four steps in classic simplicity. Once you have become aware of a particular automobile, by advertisement, noticing it, or being led to it, the salesperson moves directly into step two, extolling the vehicle's virtues, explaining why it is priced so much lower than it should be and encouraging you to sit in it, to start the engine, to drive it around the block. You, in the meantime, are calling attention to its defects, wondering aloud why it's priced so much higher than the same car you saw on another lot an hour ago and protesting that it would be a waste of time to drive it because it isn't what you're looking for.

Assuming there is overtly nothing seriously wrong with the car, your decision to sit in it or test it probably signals that you are well into step two, the serious evaluation in terms of your own needs, resources and desires. It follows that you are prepared for the third, decisive, step—the decision to buy or not to buy. A moderately adroit salesperson can smooth the transition to a positive decision by a well-timed concession to your objections in the form of a price reduction. The fourth step, the sales and payment agreements, becomes little more than a formality.

In this chapter we have examined the role of the audience, or receiver, of messages with particular emphasis on the importance of anticipating audience reactions to specific types of messages, speakers and situations. Among the factors to be considered in preparing for any interaction are the selective attention devices of the audience, the variables of power, status and credibility, role and the dynamics of the influence process itself.

Other Variables

Other factors affect communication outcomes and need to be considered when electing to employ any of the three formats identified in our book. These include the individual, the place, the time and the occasion. Both the public speaking and conference speaking formats also require the speaker to consider the size of the audience, the loudspeaker, and the degree of familiarity among individuals.

In the chapter to follow we will focus on the influence process as it relates to developing a public speech.

AUDIENCES IN BUSINESS AND PROFESSIONAL ENVIRONMENTS: ESSENTIAL CONSIDERATIONS

I.   Consider the Purpose
   A. Intent
   B. Objective
II. Consider the Size
   A. One-to-one
   B. Small group
   C. Mass meeting
III. Consider the Individuals
   A. Educational level
   B. Age
   C. Sex
   D. Informational level
   E. Attitudes and opinions
IV. Consider the Place
   A. Formal-informal
   B. Seating arrangements
   C. Sight lines
   D. Acoustics
V.   Consider the Time
   A. Of day, year, etc.
   B. Earlier speakers
   C. Introductory events
VI. Consider the occasion
   A. Reason for gathering
   B. Degree of familiarity among individuals
   C. Ceremonial, reportorial, or propositional
VII. Consider Organizational Variables
   A. Power
   B. Status
   C. Roles

NOTES   [1]For a full discussion of the two types of analyses identified, see Theodore Clevenger, Jr. *Audience Analysis* (Indianapolis: The Bobbs-Merrill Co., 1966), pp. 43-51.

[2]Clevenger, p. 48.

[3]Clevenger, p. 48.

[4]J. French and B. Raven, "The Bases of Social Power," in *Studies in Social Power*, ed. D. Cartwright (Ann Arbor, Mich: University of Michigan Press, 1959), pp. 128-49.

SUGGESTED READINGS   Brown, C. T. and C. Van Riper. *Communication in Human Relationships*. Skokie, Ill: National Textbook Co., 1973.

Clevenger, Theodore, Jr. *Audience Analysis*. Indianapolis: The Bobbs-Merrill Co., 1966.

Faules, D. F. and D. C. Alexander. *Communication and Social Behavior: A Symbolic Interaction Perspective*. Reading, Mass: Addison-Wesley Publishing Co., 1978.

Rodman, F. *Public Speaking: An Introduction to Message Preparation*. New York: Holt, Rinehart & Winston, 1978.

Sedwick, R. C. *Interaction: Interpersonal Relationships in Organizations*. Englewood Cliffs, N. J: Prentice Hall, 1974.

Public Speaking

The first of three communication situations most frequently required of business persons and other professionals is the public speech. We will discuss several skills which must be developed to make the speech effective: identification of audience demand and speaker purpose, organization, support materials, language choices, and delivery techniques.

The authors believe that the ability to present a public speech is of major importance to career success and basic to the other formats.

"You know, Fred, I would like to have you make this argument before the board of directors. You have expertise about the XL24 which is vital to their decision and important to our plant." With this statement the plant manager looked at his calendar and added:

"Yep! Two weeks from today at ten o'clock be ready with a fifteen to twenty minute speech to the Board. Of course, President Ruggs will be there. You know how insistent he is on good oral presentations. See you there, Fred!"

As Fred left the manager's office he felt anger and apprehension. He knew he had to make the speech, but he had never addressed in any formal sense an audience of more than one or two people. His anger derived from his belief that he was a darn good engineer and that he was informed and correct about the XL24. Now its acceptance by the Board might depend upon his oral presentation rather than on the XL24 itself. "How in the world do I prepare a speech for two weeks from today?" he muttered as he returned to his desk.

Fred has no real choice; he must give the speech and he must do so effectively if he wishes to have his ideas accepted and if he wants to be evaluated positively by his superiors. His concern is not unique. The accountant and the dentist, the salesperson and the physician, the government agency clerk and the nurse, the banker and the teacher—all persons who wish to be successful in their occupational pursuits—will find the inability to complete or an unwillingness to accept public speaking assignments a significant handicap to advancement and personal fulfillment.

A newspaper recently carried a story about a Florida attorney general's reluctant agreement to hire a public speaking coach. His reluctance, according to a quote credited to the officer of the public relations firm who recommended the training, came from a feeling that the time and effort spent on preparing the speeches is "significantly less important than performing his duties as attorney general."[1]

The story also carried an admission by this politician that he had never had a speech course in college. He, or his advisors, have discovered only now how important attention to public communication is to professional success. They are not alone. Every year associations of professionals and organizations from business and industry spend thousands of dollars to purchase special public-speaking training for their members or employees. In listing areas of

Basic Considerations for Public Speaking 4

study which they wish they had included in their formal educational experience, business people regularly rank training in public speaking most prominently.[2] When a representative sample of the U. S. adult population was asked to identify what things produced for them the most fear or tension, public speaking appeared at the top of the list.[3]

Unfortunately, the Florida attorney general still believes, apparently, that the public speaking activity is not related to his duties as attorney general. What he should realize is that public speaking is a vital part of his role as politician and attorney general. Through efficient public speaking he does his job, accomplishes his objectives, and wins acceptance for himself and his ideas.

Among specific experiences of communication consultants is that of a public utilities company preparing to announce a request for a rate increase from its consumers. When the executives and middle management personnel of the company were being asked to give speeches on the reasons for the rate increase, the company realized the need for training them in public speaking.

In another instance, a dental surgeon had developed a series of surgical techniques which resulted in requests for his presence at conferences around the country. When the doctor sought help in preparation of these speeches, he thought his major difficulty was delivery and management of his voice and body. In truth, he discovered his speeches were disorganized, lacking in any attempt to adapt to specific audiences, and filled with the most technical language. His delivery was only a minor dimension of his correct assessment of his failure as a public speaker. As a result of some study, he has not become one of the country's great orators; however, he does continue to be widely known as a brilliant practitioner of dental surgery. Furthermore, he is an articulate and coherent speaker who can efficiently communicate new procedures to fellow professionals or to layperson.   •

In addition to such direct applications of public speaking as these, the general public-relations value of employees and associates who can speak intelligently and effectively on a variety of topics is also an important asset. Speeches on the individual's personal interests or concerns, when done well, reflect positively on one's company and colleagues. Thus, a group of citizens may decide to patronize a particular bank because one of its cashiers spoke effectively on some economic question; or they may select the bank because that cashier spoke in an articulate and interesting manner on some topic totally unrelated to banking. Some might decide to avoid a particular medical doctor because of a poor speech he made in support of a favorite project unrelated to health concerns. In another instance, we might choose to do business with a particular concern because one of its sales force gave an effective speech on a local community question.

One of the authors received the latest of several mailings from J. J. Graham, manager of public affairs for Exxon Company, U.S.A., a copy of a speech made by the president of that company. It was important to the company that its president was asked to give a speech as part of a university lecture series, that the presentation put forth a point of view important to the industry, and that the approach to the topic was important to building goodwill toward big business.

All of this leads to the conclusion that public speaking 1) is an important dimension in the lives of business men and women and other professionals; 2) is a skill which frequently distinguishes outstanding individuals from their fellows; 3) is of major value to businesses, industry and government agencies who regularly purchase such training for their employees; and 4) is a significant element in the public relations dimension of any organization.

If you have come to accept the importance of public speaking for business people and other professionals, let us now consider a few additional generalizations about public speaking which you should have in mind.

1. *Public Speaking is a one-to-many form of communication.* The form usually would suggest an event in which one person (the speaker) directs his thoughts and ideas in an oral message to a group of persons (audience) in a face-to-face situation. The size of the audience for the public speech would usually be more than one or two and is limited in size only by the ability of the speaker's voice to reach each person. We have deliberately refused to characterize public speaking as one-way communication because the effective speaker receives communication from an audience throughout a speech. We will discuss this further in another section of this book.

As a one-to-many form of communication, public speaking imposes significant responsibility on the speaker whose voice will be given full claim to the floor for a period of time. The audience has a right to demand a speaker prepared for the speaking assignment with a message aimed at this particular assemblage. The audience also has a right to expect an ethical speaker who avoids deliberate falsehoods and misleading information.

2. *Public speaking ability is learned.* Few persons within our experience were born with ability as public speakers. Public speaking is a learned behavior, as are writing, singing, or jumping. True, some of us are born with different kinds of voices, but it is a mistake to believe that the principal ingredient of public speaking is a beautiful voice. Many fine speakers were born with weak voices and minimized this handicap through study and practice in other major aspects of public speaking.

3. *Public speaking requires broad reading habits.* In addition to the expertise from your occupational activity and training, you will also have to be prepared to function as an informed citizen. Although it is probably the case that you most often will speak on questions related to your business or profession, this may not always be so. In either type of situation, you will be most effective if you also have an awareness of and interest in a wide range of subjects. This means that you must regularly read newspapers, news magazines, opinion magazines, books and book reviews. Keep in touch with events in the arts and new developments in science. The public speaker who has this kind of broad preparation is in a much better position to hold audience attention and secure understanding with appropriate examples and illustrations.

In addition, being broadly prepared through regular reading habits will better equip you to speak to audiences outside your own professional groups. One author who has worked with professional groups finds one of their major liabilities to be the inability to adapt to audiences outside the professional circle. The public speaker needs to have a language, illustration, and definition within the experiences of his audience. Even when speaking on his specialization, an accountant will need to explain a procedure for income tax credits to his PTA audience in their terms, not his. A medical doctor will need to describe a dietary plan for business people in terms of the Chamber of Commerce audience, not in his professional jargon. To have this ability, these professionals will need broad resources for examples and vocabulary.

4. *Public speaking requires specific training and experience.* When you deliver your speech, you will have spent a significant amount of time preparing

it. In addition to having selected a thesis and identified your purpose, you will have gathered a rich supply of substantive material. You will have considered the possible structures available for this audience, the kinds of language choices to be made, and methods of enhancing delivery of the speech. The chapters which follow will provide you with assistance in developing your skills for making this specific preparation.

5.   *Public speaking is the delivery of a message.* Some persons believe that public speech exists to fulfill a formality or pronounce the obvious. Business men and women and other professionals do not have time to waste; therefore, the public speaking we discuss in this book is that which contains a message. The speaker has made specific preparation of his thoughts and ideas and communicates them to an audience. It is true that many political speakers and others have become skillful at filling air space by pronouncing the obvious. This type of speech is outside the purposes of this book.

6.   *Public speaking is directed toward a speaker-selected purpose.* For every speech which you give we will ask you to respond to this question: What do *I want* to do *in this speech* with *this audience*? You will want first to decide why you are giving the speech and what your objectives are. Second, you will need to decide what ingredients are necessary for the substance of the speech. Finally, you will need to determine what audience reaction you want to secure.

It is common practice to think of general speech purposes as to inform, to persuade, or to entertain. We will try to avoid use of these broad concepts of purpose in our discussions of public speaking. Every speech should be informative, persuasive and entertaining. Although some may have an essentially expository purpose, they must be persuasive as well. To inform us about an important and new invention, you must also persuade us that the information is related to us or of value to us in order to cause us to listen. Conversely, it will be difficult for you to persuade us that we should visit Redhood Island unless you also inform us about some of its features.

Some public speakers believe that their principal purpose is to entertain. For most of us this is unrealistic. Yes, speakers can be entertaining, but business people and other professionals ought not attempt to compete with entertainers. The era of the public speaker who might tell one joke after another as his total speech content is over. The audiences for our speeches have heard comedians far more sophisticated in delivery and timing than we will ever be. Of course we are not ruling out humor which derives naturally from the topic and the situation. It can be an important device for gaining and maintaining attention and in accomplishing our specific purposes.

Our concern, however, in this book is to direct the speaker toward methods of achieving desired results. The speaker identifies a specific goal, sets forth a message to a particular audience, and evaluates the outcome.

Note the simple drawing on the following page. Consider the line A-C as a continuum descriptive of different phases of audience attitude. Allow point A to be that point of audience attitude represented as hostile to the message of the speech or ignorant of the subject matter of the speech. Let point C indicate an audience which is either accepting of the speaker's message or now has understanding of it. In other words we can characterize speeches as being in the business of moving audiences from point A to point C— that is, from hostile toward accepting or from ignorant toward informed. The objectives we set for our speeches might describe the degree by which

Acceptance = Understanding Scale

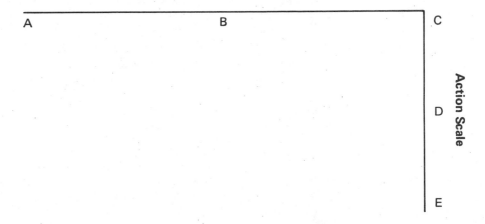

we move audiences from A toward C. Let us call A-C, the acceptance-understanding scale.

Note also line C-E. Consider line C-E as a continuum also descriptive of different phases of audience attitude. Allow point C to represent audience attitude characterized as informed or accepting. Let point E represent an audience ready to act on the topic of the speech. Let us call C-D-E the action scale.

Some speech situations in which we might concentrate our efforts on the understanding-acceptance or action scale might be the following:

A.   The speech to honor or award. One kind of speech we may frequently have to make will be to explain an award (a retiring employee, an award-winning suggestion, an athletic accomplishment). Although these speeches may be short, the speaker has the responsibility of moving the audience from ignorance — or from a state of being uninformed — to understanding why the praise is merited.

B.   The speech to explain a procedure or process. Here is another illustration where the speaker's purpose is to move the audience from whatever point they occupy on the A-B-C scale to as near C as possible. An accountant may need to explain a new bookkeeping procedure to a board of directors. A sales manager may need to deliver a speech explaining a new billing and distribution procedure to the company sales force. A police officer may be speaking to the PTA about how school riot-control measures will be implemented. These speeches will be successful when the majority of the audience understands the process.

C.   A speech requesting support. In this example an audience might already be informed about the necessity of collecting and distributing money through the United Fund (point C on the action scale). The speaker who wished to obtain volunteer workers in the collection campaign then would have to move them to a position of action, toward point E on the scale.

In these three brief illustrations the task of the speaker can be realistically charted. The speaker's purpose can be defined in terms of the position or attitude of the audience toward the subject of the speech. No speaker should expect to be able to move an audience from point A to point E on the scale (from hostility to action in support of some cause). Speakers can, however, set objectives designed to move an audience *toward* a desired attitude or position.

7.   *Public speaking serves as a basis for judgments about speakers.* The public speech is a situation in which the speaker exposes himself for appraisal. Members of the audience will make evaluations based, we hope, on the merits of the information and/or arguments set forth in the speech. However, judgments will also be made about the adequacy of our educational background, the amount of personal confidence we seem to have, our capabilities in the use of language, our seriousness and sense of humor, our credibility, grooming habits, and an entire list of things which have little connection with the purposes of our speeches. And, of course, some members of our audiences will develop notions about us directly opposite to the reactions of another portion of our audience.

THE MOMENTS OF THE PUBLIC SPEECH

Now we will deal with three different types of public speaking situations. They are the ceremonial, the reportorial, and the propositional. We believe these labels most effectively describe the *moments* for public speaking by persons in business and other professions.

We have decided upon these labels as most appropriate because we believe they describe the kind of *demand* the audience for a particular occasion puts upon a speaker. This is not to say that the speaker's role, thesis and purpose remain outside his or her control. However, the audience and the occasion in every instance place demands upon the speaker which may not be ignored. These prescribe much about how to approach the speech and how to relate the speaker's specific purpose to the demands imposed. These expectations—these demands—must receive a primary consideration.

The Ceremonial Demand

Aristotle, one of the earliest and most influential persons to label different kinds of public speeches or places for oratory, referred to a certain type of speech as ceremonial. While his description of the purposes and places of ceremonial oratory was ancient Greece, his label and some of his ideas are incorporated in our characterization of this as one form of public speaking frequently used in present-day America.

Imagine that you are requested to give a speech at an association banquet honoring this year's outgoing officers; or that you wish to inspire members of your company sales force to redouble their efforts; or that you must give an award. In each of these instances, the members of your audience demand that you express *their* feelings of appreciation; that you articulate *their* goodwill; that you embody in your speech the kinds of significance which *they* neither have the opportunity nor the ability to express. The ceremonial speaker must represent the audience members and speak for them.

The Reportorial Demand

There are also instances in which the audience and situation demand the expertise of the speaker, an expertise derived from particular training or specific experiences. In many cases that expertise will have been gained for the instance of the speech situation exclusively. In any case, the audience needs information and sometimes conclusions from a person who knows or is expected to know. The engineer's evaluative report on several proposed alternatives in compliance with governmental environmental pollution control standards meets the board of directors' demand for expert information. The explanation of a new accounting procedure is needed by the organization's membership before a proposed budget can be implemented. In professional associations you may be called upon to explain or evaluate a new technique, method, or process for laypersons or colleagues. In each of these situations your audience demands that you be well prepared and that you give the information needed for understanding.

The Propositional Demand

In a third type of speaking situation, the audience demand may be characterized as propositional. The audience realizes that a controversial issue is pending or that the speaker is identified with a cause, with a point of view, or with a person. In this instance the audience expects you to attempt to move a gathering of voters to active support for a candidate or issue in which they already believe.

On the issue of expending organizational effort and/or funds for a project, an audience also makes a propositional demand. Speakers on this issue are expected to take a position. Clearly, to simply report on the issue would not meet these expectations.

Whether audiences are sympathetic or hostile to the position of the speaker, the speaker must support a proposition. The audience does not demand that the speaker be persuasive; they only demand that he/she take a position. For personal purposes the speaker will want to be persuasive, but the audience is less concerned about personal success or failure than that the speaker use the time to advocate a proposition.

Of course, none of these moments for public speech for business people and other professionals is mutually exclusive of overlapping demands from the audience. To some extent the demand for expression of the emotions, feelings and attitudes of the audience which are primary in the ceremonial speech must also be a part of both the reportorial and propositional speeches. The demand of the reportorial speech for expertise continues to be an element for the propositional speech. It is not our purpose to suggest that the propositional speech is of greater importance or necessarily more complex. In every speech situation the principal demands of the audience and the occasion are of major consequence.

Others who characterize speeches in terms of the speaker's purpose use the label of speeches to entertain, speeches to inform and speeches to persuade. This strongly implies that speeches to persuade are the most significant, most complex and most useful. We, however, find that classification misleading and inaccurate. To some degree all effective public speaking is persuasive, informative and entertaining. In business and the professions for one to assume any ranking of importance among the different kinds of speech is a serious mistake. The speaker's purpose must be very closely derived from the audience and situation. As you will see in the next chapters, the speaker's identification of purpose and statement of thesis are vital to effective speech, yet secondary to audience and situation demands. As you prepare to structure a speech, ask first what the principal audience demand is. Is it ceremonial, reportorial, or propositional? When this question is answered, you can frame your own thesis and purpose with greater potential for success.

Audience Demand	Speech Type	Desired Outcome
"Say it for us."	Ceremonial	Praise/Inspiration
"Give me expertise."	Reportorial	Understanding
"Take a position."	Propositional	Acceptance/Rejection Decision

The following chapters discuss these three types of speeches as most significant for the person in business and the professions. We examine organization and structure, support material and gathering of evidence, language choices, and delivery of the speech. The ceremonial, reportorial, and propositional demands placed by the audience have implications for each of these skills.

ESSENTIAL CONSIDERATIONS PRIOR TO THE DEVELOPMENT OF THE PUBLIC SPEECH

I. Is a speech the best route to accomplishing my communicative goal? Are there other communication options available?

II. What is the assumed audience demand?
  A. Ceremonial?
  B. Reportorial?
  C. Propositional?

III. What is the outcome which I desire for the audience?
  A. Reduction of hostility?
  B. Acceptance?
  C. Action?
  D. Understanding?

IV. What about the topic for the speech?
  A. What information is available?
  B. To what additional resources have I access?
  C. How much time will be needed for preparation?
  D. How long shall the presentation be?

V. What will be the presentational mode?
  A. Face-to-face?
  B. Recorded?
  C. Radio?
  D. Television?

VI. What delivery format will be most appropriate?
  A. Manuscript?
  B. Memorized?
  C. Extemporaneous?

NOTES   [1]"Attorney General Agrees to Polish Speaking Style," *Tampa Tribune*, October 30, 1979.

[2]Becker, S. L. and Ekdom, L. R. V. "That Forgotton Basic Skill: Oral Communication. *The Association for Communication Administration,* (Aug. 1980), pp. 12-15.

[3]"The Bruskin Report" (New Brunswick, N.J: R. H. Bruskin Associates, July, 1973).

SUGGESTED READINGS   Bradley, Patricia Hayes and John E. Baird, Jr. *Communication for Business and the Professions*. William C. Brown Co., 1980, pp. 213-33.

Howell, William S. and Ernest G. Borman. *Presentational Speaking for Business and the Professions*. New York: Harper & Row, 1971, pp. 3-21.

Treece, Malra. *Communication for Business and the Professions*. Allyn & Bacon, 1978, pp. 17-36.

Zimmerman, Gordon, James L. Owen, and David R. Seibert. *Speech Communication: A Contemporary Approach*, 2nd Edition. West Publishing Co., 1980, pp. 176-187.

Martin Gomez was to be the featured speaker for his company awards banquet. He was to speak on the topic "The Giant Transit Company Is a Valuable Resident of the Space City Community." "Don't worry about it, Martin," said the old veteran speaker to whom Martin had gone for advice. "Just tell some good jokes and in the middle of them say how great it is to work for Giant Transit. Finish up with a little poem or prayer of some kind about the American way."

Martin protested a bit, "Shouldn't I have some kind of organizational plan for getting my point across? I certainly don't know many jokes either."

The veteran speaker seemed to lose some patience. "Look," he said, "get yourself a couple of joke books and pick out some good ones. By the way, have you heard the one about the . . . ."

Let's hope Martin will follow his instincts and ignore the veteran speaker's advice. Unfortunately, many persons will think the man's directions are adequate. They are not and will result in no real presentation related to the topic. You recognize that Martin is now prepared to identify his purpose and characterize the demand which this particular audience makes upon him. What should he do now? How should he organize the speech? What kind of structure would be appropriate?

The place to begin is with your general objective for the speech. Write a note to yourself specifically answering the question, "What do *I* want to do in *this speech* with *this audience*?" Complying with the ceremonial demand, the answering note might say "I want to highlight accomplishments of retiring supervisor Fred Jones for an audience of fellow workers." Responding to a reportorial demand, you might express the purpose as "I want the Board of County Commissioners to know the implications of the plan to reroute County Road 19 around Meadows Subdivision." Or if the audience demand is in the propositional mode, the purpose might be expressed as "I want to cause this group of college students to work in Frank Green's campaign for governor."

You may want to characterize the preceding activity as mere busy work. Be assured it is more than that. Speakers who decide on a topic or who select a title before they have stated their purposes to themselves invite disaster. To be sure, many actually deliver so-called speeches when all they have developed is to name the subject or devise a catchy title. Until, however, you can clearly tell yourself what you are up to in this particular speech,

Structuring the Speech 5

you will not be able to accomplish a meaningful objective or meet specific audience demands.

After you have made this effort to state your purpose to yourself, you need to live with that purpose for a few days—or a few weeks, if you have the time—before the speech must be delivered. During this time you will regularly be reminded of the topic, audience and purpose as you go about your normal routine.

If your topic is to deal with a better route for the new county road, you will probably find others with whom you work discussing the question. Your local newspaper will very likely be carrying information about progress on the project. If you drive through the proposed route site on your way to work, you will note certain developments and characteristics. To write down some of these items of information may be a good idea, but if you don't, at least make a *mental* note of them.

During this period of gestation, you will enlarge also your sensitivity to the particular audience. Since the topic of your upcoming speech will be in your mind, it will find its way into many of your casual conversations. Responses to your ideas about the project will suggest many of the different attitudes and levels of information about the topic which will be present in the actual audience for your speech. Some of these discussions may even point to directions of investigation as well as necessary preparation for explanation and argument. Additional insights and materials will occur to you which will become substance for the speech itself.

We are now ready to begin to develop the speech. Notice we say "develop" rather than "write" the speech. In Chapter 8 we have more to say about written speeches, but be informed at this point that the authors share an aversion to the notion of "writing" a speech. The speaker should develop an outline of the speech from which to speak extemporaneously. The outline is a device to remind the speaker of things to be said, the order for saying them, and the specifics to illustrate major points.

THE OUTLINE Begin the outline by writing at the top of the page what is usually called a thesis statement. This statement is similar to the topic sentence that your English teacher used to ask you to identify when writing paragraphs. In this instance the thesis sentence identifies the central idea of the speech in a simple declarative sentence. Below are listed three theses which illustrate each of the different audience demands discussed in the previous chapter.

Thesis: Fred Jones has made major contributions to our lives.
> or

Thesis: The plan to reroute County Road 19 around Meadows Subdivision has complex implications.
> or

Thesis: Young voters should begin active political participation at the state level.

Each of these illustrations is a simple declarative sentence and each parallels the examples of purpose statement listed earlier. The speaker is well advised to avoid using only phrases, such as "County Road 19 Improvements" or "Fred Jones" or "The Gubernatorial Contest." Always make sure that the *verb* is present in your thesis statement.

Be sure to take seriously this first step, writing the thesis statement. Many times people working on speeches report to teachers that they have a great title and will be eager to describe a clever introduction. "But what is the thesis?" the teacher asks. "Oh! I haven't figured that out yet, but isn't this a good introduction?"

Introductions and conclusions are important parts of the speech. When compared to the thesis development, the selection of the main points and the collection of support material and evidence to enlarge those main points, however, introductions and conclusions are only frills. Later in this chapter we will discuss them in detail, but for now let us concentrate on development of the body of the speech.

Through the use of the thesis statement, the speaker states in a concrete way the principal message of the speech. The thesis should set the limits of the topic and should also be narrow enough to fit the time constraints.

A thesis expressed as "Capital Punishment" in no way limits the aspects of capital punishment with which the speaker will deal. "The History of Capital Punishment" is somewhat more limiting, but "The Application of the Death Penalty in Florida is a Twentieth Century Phenomenon" gives direction to the speaker for organizational and research activity. The speaker should experiment with several different ways of wording the thesis statement. Keep the form simple and limited to one single idea. Frequently we settle on the first wording of a thesis that comes to mind. While this decision is certainly better than to begin preparing the speech with no thesis statement in mind, a little experimentation with alternative wording will yield profit.

PATTERNS OF ARRANGEMENT

Once the thesis is determined, the speaker should consider alternative organizational arrangements for the main areas of the speech. The organizational plan selected is known as *the pattern of arrangement*, the rationale which explains the relationship among the main points. Of many possible arrangement patterns available we recommend attention to four:

1. Time pattern
2. Topical pattern
3. Problem-solution pattern
4. Reflective pattern

Some patterns of arrangement will be readily applicable to one kind of purpose and audience demand, but very inappropriate in a different demand situation. The speaker is encouraged to consider several possible patterns of arrangement for every thesis being considered. The specific topic, the nature of the occasion, the make-up of the audience, and/or the data available might determine that one organizational scheme would be more effective than the first pattern of arrangement which came to mind.

PATTERNS OF ARRANGEMENT AND THE CEREMONIAL DEMAND

When the thesis is clearly expressed in a simple declarative sentence, the speaker can readily identify major points or divisions which might be developed in support of the thesis. These main points or divisions will usually be developed according to some pattern or sequence or order. If we go back to the speech honoring Fred Jones, the main points to be developed might appear as follows:

Thesis: Fred Jones has made major contributions to our lives.

1st Main Point:	A.	Fred served as an introduction for most of us to the company.
2nd Main Point:	B.	Fred advised and supported us during our years with the company.
3rd Main Point:	C.	Fred will leave his mark on us after his departure.

Note that the main points developed under this thesis have been organized on a *time* pattern of arrangement. The main points result in a chronology derived from the audience members' years with the company. We have chosen to use three main points in this instance, but a speaker could elect to use as many as five or as few as two. Decision about the number of main points should be determined by the thesis statement, but three major points for a speech of about twenty minutes seem appropriate. Of course we could have opted for an alternative time pattern which used moments in Fred's period of employment, such as his first years, his first promotion, and his latest contribution.

Now let us consider another possible arrangement pattern for this same speech.

Thesis: Fred Jones has made major contributions to our lives.

1st Main Point:	A.	Fred taught us our professional responsibilities.
2nd Main Point:	B.	Fred taught us our civic sensitivities.
3rd Main Point:	C.	Fred taught us our familial obligations.

In this organizational division of the thesis we have used what we might call a *topical* pattern of arrangement. That is, rather than the time sequence described in the first example, we selected topic areas which indicate how Jones has made contributions which influence our lives. Of course we could have used any of several divisions for this same speech. We might have selected a set of topics based on his contributions to the company by areas such as sales abilities, customer-relations abilities, and employee-evaluation capabilities.

In these illustrations of the time pattern and the topical pattern you can see that many more possibilities exist even within a single thesis. Some change in the thesis is also possible in this example, where your purpose was to "highlight the accomplishments of retiring supervisor Fred Jones for an audience of fellow employees." When the obligation to the audience requires compliance with the ceremonial demand, the speaker will most often wish to use a time pattern or a topical pattern of arrangement.

PATTERNS OF ARRANGE-MENT AND THE REPORTORIAL DEMAND
These same two patterns of arrangement—time and topical—will also be frequently used to develop main heads for theses when the purpose is to comply with the reportorial demand. An earlier example described the speaker who wanted to have the Board of County Commissioners know the implications of the plan to reroute County Road 19 around Meadows Subdivision. Note some possible organizational schemes for the theses and main heads, using time and topical patterns.

Time Patterns

Thesis: The plan to reroute County Road 19 around Meadows Subdivision has complex implications.
1st Main Point: A. Initial citizen requests for rerouting.
2nd Main Point: B. Development of the plan.
3rd Main Point: C. Present citizen opposition to the plan.

Thesis: The plan to reroute County Road 19 around Meadows Subdivision has complex implications.
1st Main Point: A. The county traffic program adopted in 1968.
2nd Main Point: B. Development of Meadows Subdivision 1972-76.
3rd Main Point: C. Changed traffic patterns of County Road 19 today.

Topical Patterns

Thesis: The plan to reroute County Road 19 around Meadows Subdivision has complex implications.
1st Main Point: A. The plan for rerouting County Road 19.
2nd Main Point: B. The disadvantages of the plan.
3rd Main Point: C. The advantages of the plan.

Thesis: The plan to reroute County Road 19 around Meadows Subdivision has complex implications.
1st Main Point: A. The period of traffic confusion during construction.
2nd Main Point: B. Rerouting plan and county master plan.
3rd Main Point: C. Cost of construction.
4th Main Point: D. Improved service benefits.

The speaker should be aware that in the topical pattern of arrangement the decision about which topic should be introduced first, which last, etc. is arbitrary. If you look at the above examples of topical patterns, you can see that the order of these main points might very well be modified. It may be important, however, in meeting the reportorial demand, to order a series of topics in certain ways to best insure understanding of an idea or plan or procedure.

PATTERNS OF ARRANGE-MENT AND THE PROPO-SITIONAL DEMAND

The propositional demand may use the time or topical patterns of arrangement. You will recall that we spoke of a propositional demand purpose to cause the audience of college students to work in the campaign of gubernatorial candidate Green. We illustrate below some ways in which the time or topical patterns might fit a thesis designed to accomplish such a purpose.

Time Pattern

Thesis: Young voters should begin active political participation in this major state contest.

1st Main Point:	A.	Young activists in the party primaries in June.
2nd Main Point:	B.	Young activists in the July party convention.
3rd Main Point:	C.	Young activists' participation during October.
4th Main Point:	D.	Post-election rewards.

Topical Pattern

Thesis: Young voters should begin active political participation in this state-level contest.

1st Main Point:	A.	State-level contests provide opportunities to work in several different constituencies.
2nd Main Point:	B.	Young voters have the opportunity to evaluate various interests and inform candidate Green.
3rd Main Point:	C.	Young activists will find positions in a Green administration.

In addition to these patterns of arrangement, the speaker attempting to make his purpose meet the propositional demand of an audience might make use of two other patterns for arrangement. These are the *problem-solution* and the *reflective patterns*.

The Problem-Solution Pattern

This arrangement suggests that frequently in the propositional speech the speaker will need to have two major parts. Part one would require the statement and illustration of a problem, and part two would require a stated solution to the problem and an illustration of that solution. To characterize a problem, the speaker must cause the audience to realize that the problem is serious; that it will continue to exist or grow worse; and that it is harmful to members of the audience. To demonstrate the solution, the speaker will need to show that the solution will eliminate or minimize the problem; that the solution is practical; that it is the best solution; and that it can be implemented. If we use our young voters example, we might have a skeletal outline such as this:

Thesis: Young voters should begin their active political participation in this state campaign.

1st Main Point:	A.	Young voters are frequently excluded from political campaigns.
1st Sub Point:	1.	Young voters have not been active in gubernatorial campaigns.
2nd Sub Point:	2.	Young voters are excluded from local campaigns and remote from national campaigns.
3rd Sub Point:	3.	Most state candidates are ignoring young voters.
4th Sub Point:	4.	Interests and needs of young voters are not represented in state government.
2nd Main Point:	B.	Young voters can be involved and active in this state-wide campaign of Mr. Green.
1st Sub Point:	1.	Young voters are the big element in Green's campaign philosophy.
2nd Sub Point:	2.	Young voters have fresh insights and energy to make a campaign successful.
3rd Sub Point:	3.	Green activist groups exist on each of the major campuses in the state.

You will notice that the subpoints under each main point are arranged according to a topical pattern of arrangement.

The Reflective Pattern

This arrangement derived from John Dewey's[1] ideas, identifies a pattern of reflective thinking used by the individual in problem-solving. The concept has long been used to prescribe ways for small groups to solve problems systematically. The speaker confronted with an audience making propositional demands but hostile to the speaker's specific proposition might want to select the pattern of arrangement which we describe here as reflective.

The speaker attempting to recruit student workers for Mr. Green may discover that the audience consists of persons not supportive of Green but supportive of some other candidate. Consequently the speaker might develop a five-step organizational plan including (a) defining the problem; (b) analyzing the problem; (c) suggesting possible solutions; (d) evaluating possible solutions; (e) selecting best solution. A skeletal outline might be similar to the following:

Thesis: Young voters should begin their active political participation in this state campaign.

1st Main Point:	A.	How can young voters participate and be influential in state politics?
2nd Main Point:	B.	What problems of young people have been addressed neither by state government nor candidates?
3rd Main Point:	C.	Which candidates might use and be influenced by young political activists?
4th Main Point:	D.	How does each candidate appear in the light of a young person's interests?
5th Main Point:	E.	Mr. Green is the only choice.

Each of these patterns of arrangement gives only the broad structural plan for the speech. The substance—the support material and evidence—will need to be gathered and organized to uphold each of the main points. This support material will be discussed in the next chapter. For now, let us attend to one more organizational detail—the introduction and conclusion.

ADDITIONAL ORGANIZA- TIONAL ELEMENTS After the outline of the body of the speech is completed, including the development of support material (to be discussed in the next chapter), the speaker can attend to the development of an introduction and a conclusion. Readers will remember that we said earlier that while introductions and conclusions are important elements of the total speech, they are certainly secondary to the body of the speech.

Introductions

In the introduction you should attempt to do three things which will aid in the accomplishment of your purpose. The first of these is to *indicate the thesis* of the speech. Notice that we say "indicate" rather than "state" the thesis. In some instances it will suit the purpose of the speaker to state directly to the audience the thesis as it appeared at the top of the outline. In the examples of theses stated earlier in the ceremonial and reportorial mode, the speaker might choose to assert the thesis very specifically in the opening of the speech. In the example of the reflective pattern illustrated earlier, the speaker might wish the audience to arrive at the precise thesis statement at the end of the speech. In any case, the audience must have some idea, from the very beginning, of the speaker's purpose. Even though the type of demand imposed on the speaker comes from the audience, the speaker should remind the audience of that demand.

Another aspect of indicating the thesis requires that the audience have an idea of how the speech will be developed. Sometimes the speaker may want to name the main points to be discussed; in other situations the speaker may wish to be more subtle in outlining the direction the speech will take. It is true, however, that listeners who can see the structure for a yet-to-be-received message tend to follow and retain more of that message. Thus, a speaker who says, "In order to show the influence that Fred Jones has had on our lives, I intend to point to his professional, his social, and his familial influences," has given the audience a frame of expectations to assist them in following the speech.

The second important ingredient for introductions is to *develop a positive feeling toward the speaker*. The positive reaction occurs as a result of the context of the introduction, the mannerisms of the speaker, and the relationship a speaker implies toward the audience. Audiences like speakers who are confident rather than hesitant; who are prepared; who are interested, rather than nonreactive. We are favorably disposed toward speakers who are excited about their topics. The speaker who appears witty and responsive to audience needs and concerns secures early support from that audience.

The third requirement of the introduction is to *gain audience attention*. Of course, attention must not only be gained initially but must also be maintained throughout the speech. The speaker might think of attention-gaining devices in three classifications and should plan to incorporate all of them during the speech.

The first of these is that attention device which gives the audience no options but to attend. A loud noise, large movements, the presence of a horse at the lectern are of this type. Only limited use of this kind of attention device is recommended, but occasionally it can be very effective.

Attention gained because the information provided is so vital to the interest of the audience is a second and most important device. When the audience becomes aware that the topic of the speech has possible impact on their pocketbooks, grades, or family interests, attention is automatic. When the information to be provided will answer specific questions, will give needed directions, or will have implications for our status, we attend.

A third attention device is more subtle and not so easily defined. This category includes that attention got from an audience simply because the device arouses curiosity, whets interests, or otherwise entices. When a speaker begins with an illustration, we may be intrigued by the characters in the story, by the humor, or by the suspense. We give our attention, not because we couldn't do otherwise nor because we need the information, but because the subject matter of the introduction captures us.

Introductions, then, are required to indicate the thesis, secure a positive audience response to the speaker, and gain audience attention. The authors of this text discourage brief introductions which begin with muttered asides to other speakers. We do not believe it is necessary to go through long lists of people to be recognized nor to assert trite expressions of how "happy I am to be here," etc. We do believe that the speaker should get to the prepared introduction immediately. The speaker loses effectiveness who mutters about being inexperienced as a speaker, runs through a series of recognition statements to other dignitaries or speakers, or tells an unrelated "joke" before the speech. One would be better advised to make the first thing something like "I am here to talk about utility bills" or "Fred Jones has influenced your life," etc.

More specifically, one might begin with an illustration. Since the introduction should not be written out and read to the audience, the examples which follow are only meant to characterize the nature of introduction content:

Introduction 1: "Last evening as I looked through the mail which arrived at my house yesterday, I found the monthly notice from Smithville Power and Light Company. The size of this bill gave me pause. I discover I am using less power, paying twice as much for it, and receiving poorer service than just one year ago. It is for this reason that I am here today to discuss utility bills, the use of power, and the service provided."

Introduction 2: "When I heard that Fred Jones was retiring, I spent a few minutes reviewing my years of working with Fred. I discovered that there were many times when he played a key role in my life. And this is true for many of us in this company. In the areas of professional responsibility, civic responsibilities, and familial obligations, Fred Jones has influenced your life."

Conclusions

Conclusions should accomplish two major tasks: The audience 1) should be reminded of the major points which have been developed and 2) should be given some direction for the future in the application of the subject matter discussed. Conclusions, like introductions, should be brief. Conclusions should provide for a pointed end to your speech. Can you recall a speaker who couldn't seem to find the end to his speech? Someone who just continued to search for one more superlative after another to attach to the topic before finishing the speech?

To remind the audience of major points may require no more than to assert each main point. The speaker might say, "Therefore, your active participation in this campaign will give you new insights into state politics; will allow you to work close to a candidate who will listen to you; and will provide you with important career opportunities later in life."

Direction for the future might simply be a statement of some action to be taken by audience members such as "sign up immediately after the meeting" or "evaluate other candidates against this set of criteria." This objective might also be accomplished in a less direct way by an appropriate quotation or with another illustration.

This chapter has dealt in a very deliberate way with the process of developing the skeletal outline for several different kinds of speeches. We believe from our experience in aiding speakers and evaluating speeches that this plan of organization is a vital first step. The process of selecting an appropriate structure from many possible alternatives makes for coherent speeches and gives additional guidance to the speaker in selecting his support material.

Many of us have had unpleasant experiences with outlines in other contexts. You may have done an outline because someone required it. Perhaps you did the outline after the report or the essay or the book was completed. Avoid making this kind of association with the outline for a public speech. Public speech outlines are the tool in developing and delivering the speech. Without an outline a speaker limits his potential and risks negative outcomes. Plan carefully through the outline preparation from thesis statement to the conclusion. You will know where you are going and the audience will know where they have been.

STRUCTUR- ING THE SPEECH: ESSENTIAL CONSIDERA- TIONS

Successful Speeches Result From Careful Organization of Main Points and Subordinate Materials Into Outline Form for Use in Rehearsal and Delivery!
These steps seem to be very simple and little more than busy-work, but they are *vital to a reasoned, successful communication.*

1. Write in a simple declarative sentence the point you want to make. For instance: "Giant Transit Company of the Southwest is a valuable resident of this city.

2. Determine what main points you must establish in order to gain understanding or win acceptance of your central idea as stated above. Write them out in uninvolved declarative sentences. For instance:

   A. As a valuable resident, GTCSW contributes to the economic well-being of our city.
   B. As a valuable resident, GTCSW contributes to the educational advancement of our community.
   C. As a valuable resident, GTCSW contributes aesthetic values to the appearance of our city.

3. Consider all the material from your personal experience, conversations, reading, etc. which can be used to illustrate and support the accuracy of each of the *main points above.* For instance:

   —In support of main point A above, you might use the statistics identifying the amount of taxes paid by the company which was available to the local community.
   —For additional support of this first main point you might also cite the statistics which indicate the size of the local payroll.
   —For additional support of this first main point you might use the testimony of the president of the Chamber of Commerce, who said, "The GTCSW has made it possible for our city to live; without the company this city would have blown away."

4. When you have completed the first three steps, you will have completed the body of your speech. This is the most important part!! Now you are ready to add one of the fringes—the introduction. The introduction is not unimportant, but it will take you nowhere if the body has not been well planned. In your introduction, attempt to accomplish these three things:

   A. Get their attention!
   B. Indicate the subject of your talk.
   C. Favorably dispose them toward you.

5. Now add the second fringe—the conclusion. Attempt to accomplish these things in your conclusion:

   A. Restate your main points and your central idea.
   B. Suggest direction for your audience.

6. Rehearse by reading through your outline several times; talk it through, referring to the outline only when necessary. Repeat until the ideas, *not the wording,* are fixed in your mind.

A completed outline of the speech discussed on the preceding pages might be similar to the following. Note that it uses a topical pattern of arrangement.

Purpose: In this speech I wish to cause this audience of Rotary Club members to recognize the significance of GTCSW to this community in order to reduce the negative response to our proposed plans for expansion in the park area.

Thesis: The Giant Transit Company of the Southwest is a valuable resident of this city.

I. Introduction

Opening
    A. "Good citizens produce prosperous and beautiful cities.

Statement
    B. Initial summary

II. Development
    A. As a valuable resident GTCSW contributes to the economic well-being of this city.

Statistics
        1. $000,000 in local taxes

Statistics
        2. $000,000 paid in wages in fiscal 1965

Testimony
        3. President Martin of the Chamber of Commerce

Analogy
        4. Tax rate for personal property compared to nearby towns

    B. As a valuable resident GTCSW contributes to the educational advancement of our community.

Example
        1. Audiovisual equipment is made available to schools.

Example
        2. Company employees serve on the school board and bring wide range of abilities.

Example
        3. The Wire-stringers Union caused the development of adult education program.

    C. As a valuable resident GTCSW contributes aesthetic values to the appearance of the city.

Example
        1. Landscaping around central office.

Testimony
        2. Lady Bird's estimate.

Example
        3. Company equipment during clean-up week.

III. Conclusion
    A. Summary

Closing
    B. GTCSW is one of our city's good citizens; it has

Statement
        accepted the burdens of citizenship.

NOTES   [1]John Dewey, *How We Think,* Boston: Heath, 1902.

SUGGESTED READINGS   Berko, Ray M., Andrew D. Wolvin, and Ray Curtis. *This Business of Communicating.* William C. Brown Co., 1980, pp. 190-216.

Mudd, Charles S. and Malcolm O. Sillars. *Speech: Content and Communication,* 4th Edition. New York: Harper & Row, 1979, pp. 204-20.

Vasile, Albert J. and Harold K. Mintz. *Speak With Confidence: A Practical Guide,* 2nd Edition. Winthrop Publishers, 1980, pp. 93-117.

Marie and Sam were seated in the company cafeteria enjoying their coffee break. "You know," said Sam, "Phil Downs is the best supervisor in this organization."

"Why do you say that?" asked Marie.

"Well, he simply has a way of manipulating interpersonal situations with efficiency and concern," replied Sam. "He is a master of such events."

"What do you mean by interpersonal situations?" persisted Marie.

"I mean he has the ability to treat individuals in confrontations in such a way that each feels that his or her interests are being considered. Phil is sensitive to individual needs."

"Can you give me an example of how and when this happens? Can you give me a specific instance of his ability to function in such a way?" asked Marie.

In this situation Marie is functioning in precisely the way that all of us do when we hear people make assertions. We want to know how the speaker knows; we want to know more specifically what he means; we want illustrations and definitions to be sure we understand the speaker. In normal conversation most of us would recognize the need to clarify or prove our statements. We would elaborate to make sure the listener understood. If we failed to provide this elaboration, the listener would probably ask questions, just as Marie did in the scene above. Similarly, in public communication we must provide this elaboration; we must anticipate the kinds of requests for proof or clarification the audience would request if given the opportunity.

In one of the earliest treatises on public speaking, Aristotle indicated that the task of the speaker was to state his case and prove it. Our last chapter dealt with developing a clear statement of your case; we now turn to the matter of proof or support for the speech.

Once the thesis and main points have been asserted, each must be developed and demonstrated. When your friend asserts that IBM is a good company for which to work, you, functioning in the role of audience, will very likely ask why. If he responds by an additional assertion that the company provides fine fringe benefits (his first main point), your normal demand as audience would request that he explain. His explanation would be the development or the demonstration of support. He might state that the company also provides a pleasant working environment (a second main head). Again, you would ask for explanation and clarification.

Support Material and Data Collection 6

Audiences, whether composed of one or many persons, can be expected to say to speakers who assert things, "How do you know?" "What do you mean?" "In what way?" "Explain that." "Give me an example." "For instance?" "Prove it!" The effective speaker anticipates these reactions and locates materials to provide answers to these demands for additional information. Support material is required for the ceremonial, reportorial, and propositional demand speeches. The nature and application of support material will vary somewhat to meet the different demands but must be developed for each.

It is customary to discuss support material as that developmental or substantial part of the speech which *proves, clarifies,* or *reinforces* the statements of the speaker. A speaker could claim that consumer use of electricity has declined during recent years. Then the speaker could *prove* the statement by presenting a summary of the numbers of kilowatt hours of electricity used in the last two years as contrasted to the number used in the five previous years. The same speaker could also probably *prove* that decline in usage by quoting statements from several governmental officials or company executives whom you believe.

Sometimes the speaker will simply need to *clarify* a point, not necessarily prove it. To clarify the point that there are more government regulations for a particular industry than one person could know, the speaker might explain that if the paper on which the regulations are written were stacked, it would total eight stacks six feet high. Sometimes clarification will require only additional definition or synonyms.

In other instances, the speaker will use some additional support material to reinforce what he has said. He may refer to the illustration from the previous paragraph by quoting an administrator of a company who says, "We are being drowned in a sea of paper which threatens to engulf all of us." Of course, single pieces of support material may serve each of these purposes. To the extent that we have a wealth of proof, clarification, and reinforcement, we will have a forceful speech.

Support material must be selected in terms of the audience's interests and knowledge. Support which proves must prove for the specific audience. Proof is what the audience *accepts* as proof; clarification is that which makes clear an assertion for a particular audience; reinforcement is that material which reinforces for the audience of the speech. Specific items may prove, clarify, or reinforce for the speaker, or for the speaker's associates; but, unless these ends are accomplished for the majority of audience members, the speaker fails. If you will review some of the material from Chapter 3 on audience analysis and adaptation, you will recognize the implications of this point.

FORMS OF SUPPORT

While they may be given various labels, there are essentially five forms of support. We will characterize them as 1) *example,* 2) *statistics,* 3) *testimony,* 4) *analogy,* and 5) *definition.* Although we primarily focus here on support forms for oral communication, the reader should consider the application to written discourse as well.

Example

"Give me an example" is heard frequently in our day-to-day communicative activities. The individual requests clarification through an illustration to help understand and/or accept some previous assertion of the speaker. Sometimes you will need only a brief naming of a specific instance to accomplish understanding. Occasionally, you will have to provide several such instances. At other times you will have to or elect to give much more information rather than just naming the specific instance. A speaker may assert in one of the main points that the recall of American automobiles has been significant, choosing to provide a series of detailed and undetailed examples:

series of undetailed examples	The recall of American automobiles has been significant. Ford recalled the Pinto; General Motors, the Corvair; Chrysler, the Horizon and Omni; AMC, several recalls. Thus the recall required has resulted in much expense in time and energy.
detailed example	The recall of American automobiles has been significant. In 1978 the Ford Motor Company made the decision to recall all Pinto and Bobcat automobiles for the years 1971 through 1976.
	The decision was made after Ford experienced several law suits involving serious fires resulting from construction defects and from location of the gas tanks on those models. Charges and counter charges flew back and forth concerning the extent to which Ford knew about the potential hazard engineered into these automobiles. This is only one instance where the recall of American automobiles has involved much expense of time and energy.
undetailed examples	The telephone consumer now has more than the basic black instrument. He can now have a telephone on the wall or on a stand; she can have a phone in green, red, white, or several other colors; he can get one in a box. Some phones are equipped to handle multi-lines, conference calls, etc. A customer of the local company has many services available.
detailed example	The telephone consumer now has more than the basic black instrument. From many options the consumer might select an instrument which can be carried in a briefcase. It requires only the simplest of connections in most locations and, of course, can incorporate the radio-telephone systems present in automobiles and boats. A customer of the local company has many services available.

The speaker in the previous illustrations used what we refer to as *real examples* or factual illustrations. Sometimes a speaker may wish to combine elements from several different instances into one detailed, but *hypothetical*, example. The speaker is not saying that the example is real but that it could be real. This implies that the instance is certainly possible or that it contains characteristics important to note. The audience certainly understands these characteristics. One might develop a hypothetical example such as this:

detailed hypothetical example	A signal light needs to be installed at the dangerous intersection of Morgan Street and Oak Avenue. You may one day see a loved one or a neighbor off to the shopping center. Your friend may be an excellent driver and comply with all the rules of the road. As your friend approaches the intersection, traffic will be mov-

ing along smoothly. But because there are no lights or even stop signs on the corner, your friend could become the latest in a series of persons killed on that corner in the last year.

The example is probably the most important and most often used support material selected by effective speakers. Teachers of public communication find themselves saying over and over again to business people or professionals who seek to improve their public speaking, "Use more examples!" Examples bring life to all speeches by populating them with illustrations of real people and real events. They catch and hold attention in a way that much descriptive discourse does not. Use examples freely and extensively; use them in the introduction and conclusion as well as throughout the speech.

Statistics

Frequently support material in the form of numbers, percentages, averages, etc., would be most useful and important for proving or clarifying an issue. Statistics are really an accumulation of similar examples or instances expressed in numerical form. If you state that the intersection named above is dangerous, an example might help to illustrate and clarify. However, if you can also state that 14 persons were killed in the last 10 years, that 37 persons have been injured in the same time period, and that the cost in property loss has totaled $93,753 in that period, you will have gone a long way toward proving that the corner is dangerous and costly.

Statistics should be used carefully because, of course, none of us wishes to listen to continuous recitations of numbers. When used, numbers should usually be rounded off, especially when a series is presented. Statistics should also be used in ways that emphasize the significance of the number. We frequently hear numbers in the millions and billions and have no way of knowing the significance of those when the reference is to dollars or people. These numbers can be made real when they are contrasted with numbers from other periods or instances.

Sometimes such numbers can be made more meaningful when dollars are described as "equal to the combined budgets of Georgia, Florida, and Alabama." A large number of people may be expressed as "the equivalent to the combined populations of Memphis, Montgomery, Atlanta, and Miami."

Often speakers, especially when meeting the reportorial demand, will wish to illustrate statistics with visual aids. A large amount of necessary statistical support can be presented quickly and clearly with visuals in the form of graphs or scales. A more extensive discussion of visual aids can be found in Chapter 10.

Testimony

Frequently we prove, clarify, or reinforce our assertions by reporting the statements of other persons. These statements we use to support our own we call testimony. When we quote someone in a position to know or someone whose opinions are respected, our own credibility is enhanced. Three variations of testimony follow:

Expert testimony is that type of statement which comes from one whose training, experience, or previous judgments have demonstrated knowledge on the subject. When the comptroller of the company predicts a profit level;

when the professor of chemistry declares the composition of a compound; or when the major pollster of public opinion tells us that a certain number of U.S. citizens support a particular foreign policy, we tend to accept the expert's statements as true.

Audiences are also very often willing to accept our statements when some person of high or respected status agrees with the statements. If that person happens to qualify as an expert, such *prestige* testimony may also have persuasive impact. When Arnold Palmer or Jack Nicklaus says that longer drives and more accurate putts result from the use of Federal Golf Clubs, the testimony is convincing. The speaker who quotes the university president as saying that enrollments have declined over the last four years has located the statement of one who can be regarded as an expert. That is, the speaker supports his assertions with those of persons who are in a position to know. Such testimony has both expert and prestige characteristics. However, persuasive value may also be realized even if the person quoted is not an expert. Some members of audiences may simply accept the words of any famous person as support. You need only look at television to be confronted with the extensive use of prestige testimony in advertising: the football player who supports the assertions of a beer company that its brand has "less calories." The dog-food company who uses a well-known actor to support the company's assertion that its product makes for long healthy dog lives is using the prestige of the actor to secure acceptance of the claim. When an actor supports the claims that an engine additive makes for more efficient automobile operation, the support comes from the person making the claim rather than from the assertions of the manufacturer

A third kind of testimony we recommend for use as support material can be referred to as *lay* testimony. This testimony is most useful when expressed in statistical form. When we state that 35 persons out of 50 persons said they were apprehensive about the future, we are using lay testimony. Sometimes we will select the testimony of one layperson as a representative example of how a group of people feel or believe.

In a speech where a main point asserts that "Persons in business and the professions are poorly trained in public communication," the support content of the speech might be similar to the following:

> My second main argument is that persons who enter business and the professions are poorly trained in public communication. In his book on organizational communication, Professor Fred Smith states, "Most breakdown in communication within large companies is directly attributable to the fact that employees had no training in public communication."
>
> But even more significant is the testimony of the Personnel Director for Devron Corporation who said in a speech last winter, "When I interview job applicants, I always discover that the area of study most obviously absent from their credentials is coursework in public communication, especially public speaking."
>
> In an interview with top executives of six corporations in a southern city, the most frequently named skill desired was that of public speaking. It is easy to conclude therefore, that training in public communication is inadequate for persons entering business or the professions.

The above illustration shows three different pieces of testimony to support a single assertion. Naturally, the speaker could, and probably would, include some other forms of support. The assertion would be made clear and strongly supported with the addition of some example and statistical support.

Analogy

A fourth form of support is the analogy. The comparison of items of similar substance is referred to usually as the literal analogy. If we argue that the experiences of one person in budget planning parallel the experiences of another with similar activities, we might attempt to make the argument of an assumed similar result.

Most analogy support serves the principal objective of clarification. This is especially true of the figurative analogy. If we attempt to explain the process of executive maturation by comparing it to the metamorphosis of a butterfly, we have compared two things not really alike in substance. However, a comparison of stages of development or the idea that there were different phases to the creation of a mature executive is clarified by the analogy.

The comparison of something known to something unknown provides insights not easily accomplished with other support forms. The discoverer of the circulation of the blood made his explanation in terms of what was known about waterway systems of arteries and pumps, a figurative analogy. As a result, we still refer to the heart as a pump and to arteries and the blood circulation processes with that terminology. The analogy gives us an orientation by comparing the unknown to the known. To explain a grammatical characteristic of a foreign language, the teacher must almost always do so by comparing that language with a known characteristic of the English language. In this instance literal analogy becomes the route to understanding an unknown concept.

Definition

The last type of support we discuss is definition. Definition is probably the most important method of initiating idea development. Limits are imposed by using definitions. The concept or term is restricted to mean for the audience what it means for the speaker in this speech. Definitions frequently describe processes. The following illustration of definition is from a speech by Stewart Udall, the former Secretary of Interior, on a college campus a few years ago in which he defined "environmental crisis" thusly:

> "That in the last 25 years while our per capita income or production of our industrial system — the amount of energy we are generating in our energy system — our GNP has been going up constantly. That our living standard, the livability of our cities, the cleanliness of our rivers and our land and air and water has been on a draft going down like that at the very same time. That's — the "Environmental Crisis — the paradox."

Defining does not have to be lengthy or involved to be effective. Stewart Udall demonstrates this point:

> "We are getting quite radical as we go along. Radical, a good word you know, a very good word; it means get to the root of things."[1]

GATHERING DATA The support material forms which we have been discussing will require the speaker to engage in some research. Much of the material will already be available through the speaker's experience and expertise. Most often our speech topics result from our professional roles or our specific employment assignment. Our professional and trade journals will give much of the resource material such as statistics, example, and testimony. Often definitions for technical processes will derive from the publications of our field. Yet, for other topics and for sources for analogy, we need to investigate other potential resource materials.

In an earlier chapter we made the point that effective speakers must read a wide selection of materials. The support material necessary to prove, clarify, and reinforce our statements accrues from this reading. Many regular public speakers keep a file of materials, clipped from a variety of sources, on different and potential speech topics. This is a good policy, and we encourage you to follow it.

Sources

In addition to the material resulting from *personal experience* in our professional contexts, we should use other resource material. If you were asked to speak on the contributions of your company to the community and/or the country, you would probably begin by examining the company public relations or *promotional materials* as well as financial records. This would provide information on salaries paid to employees, contributions made to civic improvement, and taxes paid in various areas.

By consulting the reference materials at a local *library* you might also locate a feature story in *Time* a few years ago on one of the principal executives. You might locate an article from *Business Week* describing the company's activities in Community Chest or United Fund drives. These kinds of items from periodical literature, especially from news magazines, can be a major source.

Additional support can be obtained from *interviews and incidental conversations*. To develop the topic about your company's value to the general welfare, you might get some expert testimony as well as additional examples and statistics from an interview with a city official. You might collect some useful lay testimony by discussing the topic with your neighbor over the back fence or a beer. In the process of living with the topic for a period of time, you will find pieces of information as a result of informal conversation.

On-the-spot observation will provide some information for certain topics. You might examine the new antipollution devices at a particular plant. You might discuss the plant with neighboring residents and note their reactions. You can check on the ways in which the environment has been improved, has worsened, or is not considered at all. You could speak to employees in the newly remodeled office building, examining their work areas and recreational facilities.

We have chosen not to discuss with you a specific procedure for making notes on your findings. Each of us probably has developed procedures which are habits of long standing. In any case you will want to develop note-taking and clipping-saving habits to preserve the materials for when you need them.

One final direction relating to your data-gathering activity: Be sure to identify the sources of your information! If you use an example from someone's speech or writing, identify your debt to that person who did the original work. You wish not only to give credit to your sources but also to increase your own credibility. Crediting sources shows the breadth of your own research and makes you recognizable as a person who has prepared for this specific speech.

We have now discussed the complete development of structure and substantive materials necessary to a speech. The outline which follows is similar to the way we think your outline for your speech should appear. You will see that in this example we include several items which will probably not appear on your own outline. Note that a purpose statement is provided and that we have attempted to label some different kinds of support material. If one were familiar with the substance of the examples, testimony, statistics, and analogy which appear under each main point, one could easily deliver the speech. Often pieces of testimony, statistics or sources of information will have to be written out very specifically and read to the audience. However, in most instances words or phrases such as those which appear in this outline will be adequate to remind the speaker of what to say as well as the order in which to say it.

A completed outline of a speech might be similar to the following. Note that it uses a topical pattern of arrangement.

Purpose: In this speech I wish to cause this audience of parents and taxpayers to examine the arguments in support of merit ratings for public school teachers.

Thesis: A workable merit-rating system for public school teachers will improve school efficiency.

I.   Introduction

opening statement . . . . .   A. "An eminent Chinese philosopher, Sin Yu, complained to the Imperial Rater as long ago as 200 A.D. He said, 'He seldom rates men according to their merit, but always according to his likes and dislikes'."

initial summary . . . .   B. Define 'merit rating' in public school education.

statistics . . . .   1. Utah study (Gallup).

example . . . .   2. Florida law (30%).

II.   Development

main head . . . .   A. A workable merit rating system would have distinct values toward efficient school operation.

example . . . .   1. It provides for rewarding "good" teachers.

example . . . .   2. It provides for punishing "poor" teachers.

hypothetical example . .   3. It creates faculty harmony.

example . . . .   4. It insures uniformity.

testimony . . . .   5. It decreases the number of teacher-referred disciplinary problems.

main head	B. A workable merit-rating system would make use of qualified "raters" already associated with schools.
subhead	1. Members of the school boards.
example	a. They know community needs.
hypothetical ex.	b. They may have association with industry.
subhead	2. The school administrators.
testimony	a. Their useful background *(New Republic)*.
example	b. Their closeness to teachers.
main head	C. A workable merit-rating system would make use of criteria to insure the best teachers.
subhead	1. "Good" teachers would meet these criteria for personal characteristics.
example	a. Barr study.
example	b. Supplemental lists.
subhead	2. "Good" teachers have demonstrated these additional characteristics of habit.
example	a. The New England School Development Council.
example	b. The Pomona, California, criteria.
subhead	3. "Good" teachers should probably be rated in their knowledge of their subject area.
hypothetical ex.	a. Industry measures a person's worth by production.
hypothetical ex.	b. A point system based on student success.

   III. Conclusion
      A. Summary by restatement of main points.

closing statement	B. You have positions which allow you to exert some influence on educational procedures; make yourselves heard on this policy of merit rating. This discussion was prepared to help you develop strong convictions on the topic.

The speaker who prepares an outline of short phrases or single words as reminders of the support material items will be able to direct attention to the audience rather than to reading from a manuscript. Once familiar with the outline of main heads and the word or phrase reminders, the speaker can present the material in a fresh and spontaneous way. The extemporaneous way in which the support material is stated will help the speaker react to what is said and observe audience response.

    Support material is vital to strong and stimulating public communication.

SUPPORT MATERIAL AND DATA COLLECTION: ESSENTIAL CONSIDERATIONS

I.   Determining Topic and Potential Resources

The following are not meant to be possible topics for you. They simply illustrate the vast resource areas which are available to you. Do a similar analysis to determine whether you have overlooked some resources for your own speech topics and for potential support material.

A.   How about some personal experience?
   1.   Have you *seen* anything to talk about?
      a.   A slum area in your community
      b.   The accident potential of some corner in your city
      c.   The progress being made on public camping facilities in Florida
      d.   The uniforms of the local high school band
      e.   The confusion in preparations for the annual city celebration
      f.   The conditions of our county highway system
      g.   The enthusiasm of out-of-state tourists during holidays
   2.   Have you *done* anything worth speaking about?
      a.   Worked in the last political campaign
      b.   Moved from one community to another
      c.   Taken some course
      d.   Investigated the local philosophy in teaching first graders to read
      e.   Bought a new car
      f.   Sold an old car
      g.   Eaten at an unusual restaurant
      h.   Taken up a new hobby
      i.   Installed some new procedures in your business operation
   3.   Have you *thought* anything worth speaking about?
      a.   The Panama Canal Treaty was a mistake
      b.   Public school teachers ought to have a minimum of five years of higher education
      c.   There could be better ways to finance the purchase of a new home
      d.   If I were president of this company, I'd . . .
      e.   What supervisors really need is a course in conference methods
      f.   The public would certainly appreciate a new form of billing
      g.   How can our city find qualified police officers
B.   How about some conversations you have had recently?
   1.   Discussions with your fellow workers
   2.   Discussions at social gatherings
   3.   Discussions with the next door neighbor
C.   How about something you have read recently?
   1.   That editorial in this morning's paper
   2.   That article on the institutional problems for the mentally retarded
   3.   A feature story in a weekly news magazine
      a.   *Time,* the industrial developments in Western Canada

     b. *Newsweek,* women in politics
     c. *U. S. News and World Report,* incomes in various professions
    4. Magazines of opinion
     a. *Nation,* the LSD problem
     b. *The National Review,* the Panama Canal
     c. *The New Republic's* appraisal of Senator _____
     d. *The Saturday Review* article on the legal profession
  II. Support Material
    A. Testimony—Source? Expert? Prestige? Known by audience?
    B. Analogy—Literal comparison? Figurative comparison?
    C. Statistics—Brief—Simple—Clear
    D. Example—Detailed? Hypothetical? Undetailed? Real?
    E. Definition

NOTES [1]Stewart Udall, *Speech Delivered in fall of 1970, University of South Florida,* Tampa, Fla.

SUGGESTED READINGS Gorden, William I. and John R. Miller. *Speak Up for Business: Career Communication Development.* Kendal Hunt Publishing Co., 1977, pp. 110-17.

Mudd, Charles S. and Malcolm O. Sillars. *Speech: Content and Communication,* 4th Edition. Harper & Row, Publishers, 1977, pp. 120-50.

Samovar, Larry and Jack Mills. *Oral Communication: Message and Response,* 4th Edition. William C. Brown Co., 1980, pp. 79-100.

Walter, Otis M. and Robert L. Scott. *Thinking and Speaking: A Guide to Intelligent Oral Communication,* 4th Edition. Macmillan Co., 1979, pp. 33-60.

Beth and Arnold Pearson were eager to hear the presentation by the principal of their son's school as they sat in the audience of PTA members to hear his plans for the gifted-child project of the school. Principal Barnes greeted the assembly and launched immediately into his speech, a description of the project.

"We are delighted to be gettin' the grant to start the project," he said. "The representative of the granting agency don't have any doubts that we have the necessary faculty to staff the program. He tells me that the data shows that our staff will be as qualified as those of any gifted center in the country. Furthermore, . . ."

When the speech ended and the Pearsons were on their way home, Beth said, "You know, I have some real doubts about that project and Mr. Barnes' ability to get it started."

"He seemed to know what the program needed, but you're right. I, too, have the feeling that Barnes isn't the most competent person to head it. I'm not sure what it was, but he didn't give me confidence."

Of course, we do not know all the things involved in the Pearsons' negative reaction to Principal Barnes, but some explanation might be found in the short excerpt presented above. Perhaps without being consciously aware of it, the Pearsons were reacting to the way in which Barnes used, or misused, language. The lack of careful articulation and the grammatical errors are only two instances of language usage which distract from our message and cause audiences to make judgments about us or our ideas. "Unfair!" you say. Maybe, but the truth of the matter is that audiences frequently react to the way we say things rather than to what we say.

Before we discuss delivery of the speech, we must commit this section of the book to a consideration of language and the language choices which a speaker must make. During rehearsal of the speech, the speaker will need to select certain phrases, words and sentences for particular emphasis and order. In addition, certain word choices and usages appropriate to one audience might be quite inappropriate for another. Even though the purpose might be the same when speaking in support of the university athletic program, the principal of the school might make significantly different language choices in speaking to the faculty on one hand or the coaching staff on the other. And just as the choice of support material and evidence may be different for speaking to the Downtown Quarterbacks Club, so will the language choices.

The Speaker's Language 7

We have not yet stated the obvious fact that the vehicle for public communication is language. Novice—and many veteran—speakers frequently are very much concerned about the use of voice and body but give little thought to language. Perhaps you also think that since you have been using language since the age of three you can take this skill for granted. Skill in the use of language, or the characteristic of public speaking which we will call *style,* should be given some attention by all of us. We hope you will make some effort to evaluate your style and weigh the items discussed in this chapter.

The speaker's language and the writer's language have a good deal in common, of course. However, there are significant differences between the two which have been noted from the time of Aristotle to the present. If you listen to a recording of an extemporaneously delivered speech and attempt to transcribe it, you will have dramatic evidence of some major differences from written discourse. You will discover in oral communication a greater use of contractions and interjections; a larger number of simple sentences and sentence fragments; more personal pronouns and familiar or common words; and an amount of repetition and a use of direct quotation not usual in written messages. A speech is not written to be read; a speech is prepared to be heard. This suggests, then, that the speaker must make language choices for the ears similar to the way a writer makes choices for the eyes. In addition, the social context of the public speech is different from the scene where the writer's creation is received.

When considering language choices, the speaker must remember that oral style is significant in two important ways. The first consideration is the responsibility for carrying the content of the speech. What the audience understands the speaker to mean can be altered by the substitution of a word or phrase. The word or words which flesh out an example or the way in which a source is cited may significantly change the meanings for different audiences. The selection of jargon or slang appropriate to the content in one situation may be entirely inconsistent with the speech content in another. The second consideration relates to the way in which the speaker's language style reveals things about the speaker. Judgments are made based on vocabulary, grammar, and pronunciation.

CHARAC-TERISTICS OF STYLE

For our purposes in this chapter, let us attend to three frequently named characteristics of oral style: *clarity, correctness*, and *appropriateness*. Each of these items is going to be heavily influenced not only by your experience, training and fluency but also by the communicative purpose you have in mind with a specific audience.

Clarity

In oral communication one must remember that there is no opportunity for the listener to go back and rehear in the way the audience for written messages can reread. The listener must comprehend each phrase and sentence as it is uttered, or it is gone forever. Statements of the speaker must arouse meanings in the auditor through a careful selection of words, deliberate and clear articulation and enunciation, and repetition and emphasis. Clarity in the use of language must be a first ingredient in oral style.

One aspect of clarity to which additional attention may be given is the selection of nouns, verbs and adjectives which are currently in general use. If you are asked to speak to a lay audience on your area of expertise, avoid using the jargon or in-words of the professional field. You would have to select a different set of words in explaining zero-based budgeting to the PTA than you would in describing the process to the Accountants' Club.

Frequently professionals assert that they must use the technical terms because they are precise and correct. Perhaps this may be true in some instances; if so, the speaker has the responsibility of making those terms meaningful to the audience. Sometimes technical or in-group terms are used only with the notion of impressing an audience with the complexity of the speaker's field. This not only is poor communication; it also raises an ethical question about responsibilities of speakers and the rights of audiences.

A second point is that attaining clarity requires the use of concrete words and phrases rather than abstract ones. The more details in a given amount of discourse, the more solid, concrete and effective is the speech. "An animal" is significantly more abstract than "my neighbor's dog." "My neighbor's red cocker spaniel" is more concrete than either. Often speakers find themselves discussing terms for which the concrete referent is difficult to determine. As a speaker, you should make more concrete what you mean by such terms as *censorship, government intervention, welfare, love, success,* and *honesty.* Just as a more concrete reference to "Fido, my neighbor's red cocker spaniel" adds meaning to "animal;" so also the "federally required anti-pollution devices" is more concrete than "government intervention."

Choose words which express your thoughts, but make use only sparingly of highly abstract words. Avoid the use of vague words such as good and nice as single descriptors since no specific characteristic is conveyed. If you tell me that "Fred gave a good speech," I understand that you mean to identify some favorable attitude about the speech or some aspect of it. However, I do not know whether you mean that it was persuasive, articulate, literary, direct, appreciated by the audience as an effective statement of position, long or short.

Because concrete wording is essential, meaning may often be more accurately transmitted to an audience through the use of metaphoric language. The metaphor and simile are useful in making an audience, unfamiliar with your meaning or concept, understand a relationship or intent. The speaker who describes the New York Yankees as "the A.T. & T. of baseball" conveys an entire idea about the wealth and power of one club and its owner. The speaker who says that "finding persons who will say they like to give speeches is like finding persons who will say they voted for Nixon" conveys the entire notion that, although many persons do enjoy the public speaking experience, it is not fashionable to admit it.

Correctness

A second concept for your consideration is correctness or accuracy. We list it second to clarity because we believe that one might very well be accurate or correct and not be clear. Ideally, a speaker will be both; but we would opt for understanding as of major significance. By correctness, we refer to the speaker's ability to choose words which best reflect his/her thoughts to the audience.

One reason for attention to correctness is so that one may develop the ability to select the specific label or term most appropriate to a variety of audiences. To do this, effective speakers and writers make regular efforts to enlarge their vocabularies. When necessary, these speakers can provide synonyms and/or antonyms in response to any momentary, bewildered feedback transmitted to them by the audience. An immediate adjustment to indications that the audience does not understand is made possible by selecting other words. Vocabularies are enlarged by extensive reading and by the regular use of a dictionary and a thesaurus.

Another aspect of correctness is the necessary elimination of grammatical errors and mispronunciations. It is true that the speech requires less attention to punctuation and complete sentences. Nevertheless, subject-verb disagreement, substitution of plural for singular (data/datum, media/medium), inappropriate pronoun case, and other grammatical errors have negative impact upon speaker success. The audience member not only will be distracted, perhaps to thoughts irrelevant to the subject, but will make negative judgments of the speaker's credibility. While you may feel that it is irrational for an audience member to make judgments about the speaker and the subject based on misuse of some conventions of language, be assured that such evaluations will be made. We cannot change that habit of the audience; our only alternative is to eliminate the errors from our oral language.

Mispronunciation can have a similar negative impact. One of the authors remembers clearly his mispronunciation of the word "awry" many years ago. Each of us can recall experiences of our own or others when a mispronounced or misused word called attention to itself rather than to the intended message.

Effective speakers take pride in their ability to use language correctly. This is a pride resulting from the confidence in one's ability to accurately pronounce most words needed and to place them accurately within a grammatical context. It is not some notion of social status or class separateness. You have heard of politicians who can switch from a good-ole-boy dialect to their best Harvard accent, depending on whether they are in their rural constituency or in Washington. Although one might see this ability to adapt to audiences as desirable, it also raises some ethical questions.

Appropriateness

One more dimension of style worth our attention we will call *appropriateness*. The language choices which the speaker makes are for that one particular situation; other situations will require other choices. The style must be appropriate to the occasion, the audience, the speech subject, and the speaker. What is appropriate might also influence what will be clear and what is correct.

Appropriateness to the occasion requires those adjustments necessary to the event which calls for the speech and the location for delivery of the speech. A commencement address requires stylistic choices different from a speech to the board of county commissioners; a speech in the Astrodome requires langugage adjustments not appropriate to the same topic when presented in the staff conference room.

Appropriateness to the audience is probably the major area for concern. Certainly the adjustments of style to be made when speaking even on the same topic to your child's third-grade class or the directors of your corporation are not difficult to discover. But adjustments must also be made from one adult audience to another on the basis of the relative expertise and familiarity with the subject. All our previous discussion of style has emphasized the necessity of appropriateness to audiences.

Appropriateness to the subject of the speech suggests that one not treat commonplace events with an especially literary style. Wilson and Arnold suggest this type of inappropriateness in the following passage:

> To depict a sunset in plain vernacular is to rob the subject of meaning and inherent emotional quality. To say "the sky was kind of red, sort of like a tomato or a radish," would be as inappropriate as to say of a tire, "the shiny black vulcanized rubber besmirched with dust and grime ought to be carefully loosened from the band which girdles the wheel."[1]

Appropriateness to the speaker need only remind us of the necessity of a style natural to us. To pretend to be someone we are not is not only dishonest and therefore inappropriate, it is also dangerous to our communicative objective. The encyclopedia salesperson who comes to your house and attempts to use arguments and a style suggesting expertness in child psychology will probably not get inside the door. One who is considering adopting a style unnatural to himself should remember that many professional comedians have entertained us by illustrating a person making similar attempts.

The various aspects of style considered here are only named for initial consideration. The speaker should take on the task of developing an effective language style. In her book, *A Sense of Style*, Jane Blankenship compares the style of "The Gettysburg Address" as delivered by Lincoln with a second version of the speech as it might have been delivered by another person. Professor Blankenship effectively demonstrates that although the content of each speech is essentially the same, the differences in style make for two very different speeches. "Their different ways of using that language reveal not merely a different set of techniques, but a different mode of vision."[2]

SOME ADDITIONAL NOTIONS ABOUT LANGUAGE

After considering the stylistic aspects of your speech, you should also attend to some realities of language which help you understand what will happen when you use it. The general semanticists remind us of several such realities:

1. *Remember that words are only the names of things and not the thing itself.* Of course, you say! However, we have many misunderstandings occurring every day because we forget this truth. When you tell me that Fred is a mechanic, I frequently react as though I have the precise information. I may be correct if I understand you to mean that he is an overall-wearing auto engine expert, who works at a gas station and has dirt under his fingernails. However, Fred may also be a student of literature, a soccer fan, a guitar player, etc. To name a thing is not to describe it — at least, not to describe it completely. The naming only calls up certain kinds of experiences we have had with other persons called "mechanics."

Words only refer, then, to a part of reality. There is no thing or person "mechanic;" there are only "mechanics." There is no such thing as "accountant," there are only "accountants." Perhaps by the naming you can be sure of the occupation of the person referred to, but you must not infer much more than that. You must wait for additional information.

2. Keep in mind that *meanings are in people, not in words*. Frequently we hear speakers who say, "Well, I told them at the beginning of my speech."

Another says, "I said it." The suggestion is that if they pronounced certain words, the meaning was conveyed. This must not be assumed. Our secretary tells us that each faculty member was told that "registration begins on September 20th." The assumption was that naming the time of registration meant that every faculty member would understand that the chairperson wanted each available during that time.

3.   The reminder that meanings are in people and not in words suggests the extended realization that *we must be careful not to project our meanings to members of our audience*. One of our faculty colleagues has just been named to an *ad hoc* committee on faculty parking. He is the only faculty member on the committee. All other members are deans and vice-presidents. All deans and vice-presidents have reserved parking spots with their names on them. Faculty members have to hunt for any open space in faculty-designated lots. During their first meeting, our colleague tells us, he was the only committee member, not surprisingly, who perceived a real problem.

We can easily discover when others project their meanings to us. Do we recognize the danger of doing this ourselves? Your new boss tells you that your project report is satisfactory. Your past experience suggests that "satisfactory" means "adequate" or the "minimum quality acceptable." Your boss's experience gives meanings to "satisfactory" such as "well-done," "meets the objective," "a good work." This misunderstanding of the limitations of language and our tendencies to project our meanings could very well result in tragic communication breakdown.

4.   *Words refer to a changing world*, and successful speakers should remember to reject categorical attachment of meaning. The semanticists suggest that we should subconsciously attach the words "to me — today" to all assertions. The boss described above who described your work as satisfactory might have been viewed by you as an unappreciative, pompous, feelingless lout. However, when you receive the next day a copy of a letter to the board of directors in which the boss praises the quality of your work, your skill and your sensitivity to the project, you might have wished that you had added the words "to me — today" to your earlier characterization.

Although much misunderstanding about the nature of language results in significant distortion in communication objectives, the public speaker who attends to the concerns cited above can offset its impact. Language choices which are made with attention to clarity, correctness and appropriateness must include consideration of these potential distortions. Recognize communication as imperfect at best and design messages and make word choices with the receivers' perceptions as clearly ascertained as possible.

THE SPEAKER'S LANGUAGE: ESSENTIAL CONSIDERATIONS

I. Selecting Appropriate Language
   A. Is the occasion formal or informal?
   B. What is the relationship of the speaker to the audience?
   C. Does the nature of the topic suggest specific language choices?
   D. Location?
   E. Expectation?
II. Correctness
   A. Adequate vocabulary for technical or lay audience?
   B. Grammatically accurate?
   C. Pronunciation? Sure of each name or technical term?
III. Clarity
   A. Is Repetition and Restatement required?
   B. Is the presentation free of jargon?
   C. Are the images concrete rather than abstract?
   D. Is the speaker's articulation in need of special attention?

NOTES

[1]John F. Wilson and Carroll Arnold, *Public Speaking as a Liberal Art*, 2nd Edition (Boston: Allyn and Bacon, 1968), p. 283.

[2]Jane Blankenship, *A Sense of Style: An Introduction to Style for the Public Speaker* (Belmont, Cal: Dickenson Publishing Co., 1968), p. 10.

SUGGESTED READINGS

Bradley, Patricia Hayes and John E. Baird, Jr. *Communication for Business and the Professions*. William C. Brown Co., 1980, pp. 310-14.

Ehninger, Douglas; Alan H. Monroe; and Bruce E. Gronbeck. *Principles and Types of Speech Communication*, 8th Edition. Scott, Foresman and Co., 1978, pp. 206-23.

Millar, Dan P. and Frank E. Millar. *Messages and Myths: Understanding Interpersonal Communication*. Alfred Publishing Co., 1976, pp. 126-39.

Samovar, Larry A. and Jack Mills. *Oral Communication: Message and Response*, 4th Edition. William C. Brown and Co., 1980, pp. 127-42.

As they left the banquet after listening to the featured speaker, one member of the audience said to an associate, "I wonder what he was talking about? I don't think he cared whether anyone could hear him or not. He never once looked up from his manuscript."

"Yeah, I know, but he is the leading expert in his field," replied the associate. "He doesn't have to be concerned about entertaining us. If we want to follow his speech, we need to work at it."

"Not me, Baby! Anybody who speaks in such a mumbling, inarticulate manner is wasting my time. If I am going to listen, the speaker better seem eager about the topic and appear eager to talk to me as a member of the audience. I figure I deserve that."

The discussion above represents a frequent dialogue among many persons who debate the importance of subject matter quality versus efficiency of presentation. We believe that the two elements are essentially inseparable and that a speech (the content and arrangement) is not a speech until it is delivered to an audience. The presentation *is* the speech. We agree in part with the views of the first speaker above. There are some persons who will even argue that the content of the speech is secondary to the delivery. Indeed, one of the authors had a first sergeant in the army who used to say he could present a fifteen-minute lecture to the troops on any subject. To be sure, he could hurl an uninterrupted flow of vocal noise at an assembly of men. The content of the message varied little from his discussion of the M-1 rifle, to military courtesy, to soldier hygiene. Mostly, the sergeant made noise in several different ways. His greatest problem was that he thought making a speech meant using the voice and body effectively. Making a speech, as we have already emphasized, means using one's *head* effectively. Only after we have analyzed the purpose of our speech and the demands of the particular audience, then organized our principal points and support material, does the use of voice and body become important.

One left the sergeant's lecture impressed with the way he could use his voice and body to hold audience attention. Unfortunately, one also left without very much information about the M-1 rifle, military courtesy, or soldier hygiene. The best delivery is that which does not call attention to itself. When one's manner of delivery distracts from the content of the message, the principal objective is being subverted. Thus, our first and major recommendation to our students is to regard delivery as important, but certainly secondary to content and preparation.

Delivery 8

MODES OF DELIVERY Frequently, the situation for your public speech will demand that you use a particular mode of delivery. In most instances you will find yourself standing before an audience. However, you might find yourself seated before a committee, seated or standing behind a microphone, seated alone in a studio, standing with part of your audience in front of you and part behind you (spokesperson for a citizen's group before the county commission). The mode of delivery you use will be selected in terms of these situations as well as in terms of your purpose and the audience demand.

Extemporaneous Mode of Delivery

The extemporaneous mode of delivery is the type we have been suggesting throughout the book. In this mode the speaker makes careful preparation by gathering materials and developing a word or phrase outline of the type illustrated in Chapter V. He or she rehearses the speech and gets the order of the main points and the forms of support clearly set. The speaker probably varies the word choices each time through but has the principal points well in mind. The extemporaneous speaker has almost everything except the specific word choices planned. As a result, the extemporaneous speaker gives the audience the impression of thorough preparation and organization and

Photo 8.1
Extemporaneous speaking allows for direct audience contact.

also transmits a freshness and spontaneity which adds interest. Of course, this does not mean that there are no portions of the speech where certain phrases or statements are fixed or planned. In some instances a specific planned statement is included because of the impact of saying it just that way. During rehearsal you will decide on a number of such instances.

The value of this form of delivery is that it is the most direct. It provides the best opportunity for the speaker to be in constant touch with the audience. Eye contact can be developed with all portions of one's audience, interrupted only occasionally by brief reference to one's outlined notes. The speaker and the audience can both develop the feeling that the speaker is speaking *to* the audience, not *at* it.

The speaker who has rehearsed for an extemporaneous presentation will also be much more flexible and will be able to adapt to the unexpected. When the size of the audience turns out to be considerably smaller than originally anticipated; when the age of the audience is different from that expected; or when the room arrangements are unusual, the extemporaneous speech can be adapted with greater ease and effectiveness. Probably the most important value of this flexibility is that the speaker, monitoring feedback from her audience, will be able to restate items which seem unclear. The speaker can recognize from the audience response the need for another example. Communication is more complete, more natural and more conversational in this type of delivery.

Manuscript Mode of Delivery

The manuscript delivery mode also requires the speaker to prepare carefully the collection of data and the organizational plan. But, in addition, the speaker must make specific word choices and write out the speech word for word. We have said earlier that we are not enthusiastic about the speech read to an audience. There are, however, some situations which require one to prepare a manuscript of the speech to be read by the speaker. Spokespersons for governmental bodies, large corporations and certain special interest groups sometimes must select every word very carefully. The impact of a bad word choice or a hastily-selected example by an executive might cause a corporation's stock to drop, might offend some friendly nation, might provide the basis for a lawsuit. We have a number of examples from recent history in which people in important positions made extemporaneous statements which had significant negative impact on their careers. Some readers may remember presidential candidate George Romney's statement that he had been "brainwashed," presidential candidate Jimmy Carter's statements about ethnic selective neighborhoods or U. N. representative Andrew Young's statement about political prisoners in the U. S. In these instances the phrases returned regularly in the press to haunt the speakers.

The speaker who is on a very strict time schedule will also probably want to use the manuscript mode of delivery. Radio and television usually impose such schedules. When speaking to the Rotary Club or similar groups, a twenty-five minute speech might actually take somewhere between twenty and thirty minutes. But when scheduled to be twenty-five minutes on radio or T.V., the speaker will have to fit more precisely the time requirements.

The manuscript speech may have an additional value which should be noted. The speaker who wishes to spend a good deal of time on her or his language choices has the opportunity in rehearsal to concentrate much more specifically on this dimension. Although it is our opinion that what is lost in spontaneity and flexibility is more important than the demonstration of linguistic dexterity, certain situations and audiences may demand this feature.

When the manuscript mode is used, the speaker must not approach the preparation as if writing an essay. We have earlier discussed the differences between written and oral discourse. A manuscript speech is written to be heard, not read. Therefore, the manuscript speech should be prepared in just the same way as the extemporaneous speech, including an extemporaneous delivery. The speaker should prepare an outline and talk through the entire speech. In this way, when the speaker now begins to write the manuscript, it will have that oral flavor; it will sound like a speech and not like an essay.

Photo 8.2
Speaking from a manuscript requires special preparation.

While continuing to rehearse with the manuscript, the speaker will want to make revisions in word choices, phrasing, etc. But rehearsal should also include plans for handling the manuscript and preparing its final form. Remember that one of the principal problems with the manuscript speech is that the manipulation of that manuscript is distracting. The final copy should probably be triple-spaced, have words marked for emphasis, and pauses indicated. The speaker should not memorize the manuscript but should be so familiar with the wording that he or she can read entire sentences at a glance and return to eye contact with the audience.

Novice speakers frequently see the manuscript speech as a way out of, or at least around, the speech necessity. Such persons think that if they can get it written down they can stand up there and read it. Wrong! The manuscript speech makes it much more difficult for the speaker to be an effective communicator. Effective manuscript speakers are those who are first of all effective extemporaneous speakers. Have you been in an audience and experienced the dissatisfaction when a speaker goes from a direct and extemporaneous opening to the reading of a manuscript? Have you heard the groan when an audience sees the sheaf of papers from which the speaker is going to read? Do you remember the enthusiasm in many a movie when the hero tears up the prepared speech and speaks from the gut, or heart, or mind, or something? Although the manuscript mode of delivery is an important skill for the public communicator, the speaker must remember that it is more difficult and requires a special kind of preparation.

The Memorized Mode of Delivery

The memorized mode is named here because it is an option that also frequently has some appeal to the novice speaker. *We are categorical in our rejection of this mode of delivery.* Do you remember the old saying that in a college lecture the words go from the notes of the professor to the notebook of the student without going through the head of either? The memorized speech is much the same. The speaker must spend so much energy trying to remember what words come next that there is no chance to think about the content, to react to it, nor to reinforce it with voice and body.

For most of us, the memorized speech has another major liability. There is the great fear that memory will fail. The extemporaneous speaker can make on-the-spot transitions to the next major point or item of support, but the memorizing speaker cannot proceed until the recall of another sequence of words. One of the authors remembers a terrible experience where a speaker who obviously had memorized his speech was blocked by memory failure during the introduction of this speech. In desperation he turned to the master of ceremonies and said, "May I start over?" Of course he could start over in one sense; but, in terms of the audience, he could not. The experience had happened; we couldn't erase it as we might a tape recording. As you can imagine, the balance of that speech was an uncomfortable experience for both the speaker and the audience, and neither gave much attention to the content.

We have tried to avoid an unusually large number of categorical do's and don'ts in this book. But here is one: DON'T MEMORIZE! Yes, in the extemporaneous speech you will need to memorize a sequence of main points; and in the manuscript speech you will need to be very familiar with most words and phrases; but do not attempt to deliver a speech memorized word by word.

Impromptu Mode of Delivery

The last of these modes to be discussed is the impromptu delivery. As the dictionary definition suggests, it is that speech for which you have had no chance to make *specific* preparation. The person in business or other professionals will frequently be called upon to make speeches of this type. When you are called upon to explain how your company's new computer will change consumer billing procedures or when you are asked to summarize how the county immunization program will be conducted, you might have no opportunity for *specific* preparation. But if you follow the procedures for the extemporaneous speech, you will have a basic *general* preparation to equip you for the task. Since you are called upon because you have experience with or knowledge about the subject, all you need to do is bring to bear your general information about available patterns of arrangement and the main points to be used. You may even have the opportunity to write them on a note card or napkin. Give some attention to an opening and closing statement. With this plan you will be able to provide the information sought by this audience in a coherent and convincing presentation. The speaker will usually have *some time* for preparation and only on rare occasions will be called upon without some prior notification, even if only a few minutes.

The speaker who has prepared and delivered extemporaneous speeches in the form and manner which we have discussed here and in earlier chapters will never be completely comfortable with impromptu speaking requirements. However, he or she will be equipped to handle the responsibility in a satisfactory manner.

In many cases the speaker can anticipate being called upon to speak at meetings. In such instances there is time to make specific preparation and deliver an extemporaneous speech. A responsible program chairperson or master of ceremonies who plans to call upon people to speak should, of course, give prior notice to the speakers.

Let us conclude this discussion of these four modes of delivery by recognizing that they are not precisely parallel alternatives. Some get their identity from the situation while others from the way the speaker has prepared. We will continue our discussion of public speaking with the assumption that our students in business and the professions have agreed that the extemporaneous mode of delivery is the most useful preparation for all situations. In rehearsal, the extemporaneous speaker will be able to reduce an outline to a few note cards, each containing items to jog the memory or quotations to be read precisely. We will have a few more words on this topic when we discuss nonverbal dimensions of delivery.

REDUCING TENSION

We suppose that almost any book which discusses public speaking needs to acknowledge the popular topic of stage fright. This is about all we will do. We recognize that each of us experiences tension when called upon to speak before an audience. The tension ought not to be related so exclusively to the speech event. We experience tension whenever we find ourselves in an unknown situation in which we must take some kind of risk. In the speech situation we must reveal ourselves, our thinking patterns, and our ideas to an audience not completely known. This is true for every speaker, singer, golfer, tennis player, etc. Therefore, the best way to approach this question of stage fright is to acknowledge it in the same way we acknowledge that grading is a part of testing, that bookkeeping is a part of doing business, that billing is a part of providing professional services. We deal with those things by planning for them.

Tension can be managed by being well prepared to deliver the speech. When we have confidence that our subject is significant, that we have learned about and adapted to the audience, that we have researched the topic and organized the speech appropriately, tension will still be there. However, with this preparation the tension will not be disruptive. In fact, most authorities and the authors' experiences support the notion that the tension is necessary to effective, spontaneous and energetic presentations.

Instead of wasting time and energy characterizing butterflies in the stomach or shaking knees, let us simply accept the fact that tension is a normal reaction. It results from certain physiological events which occur in the organism faced with an anxiety-filled situation. Among other things, the rate of respiration probably increases as well as blood pressure. More energy is produced by an increase in the burning of blood sugar by the body. The speaker can actually feel this energy and use it as the source of extra strength for his presentation.

We are inclined to respond to the novice speaker who claims nervousness or stage fright by saying, "Swell; it will be a big help to you."

As a summary of these considerations on tension and its management, we outline here some steps that speakers might take to reduce fear of the speaking situation. These activities will allow speakers to prevent the tension from causing communication breakdown.

1. Make thorough preparation. Develop confidence in your own knowledge of the subject and with the thoroughness of your research. Allow time to prepare and refine your outline.
2. Become as familiar as you can with the speaking situation. Plan for the unexpected.
3. Make use of movement during the presentation. Using arms, hands and purposeful movement from one position to another before the audience will engage the larger muscles and help reduce tension.
4. Recognize that the tension you experience is probably not communicated to the audience. Research on the subject suggests that speakers regularly report having experienced more stage fright than audiences report having observed.
5. Omit expressions of how "inexperienced I am at public speaking" or of how "nervous I am about this speech." These kinds of statements only call attention to your tension and do nothing toward its reduction.
6. Speak often. As you gain more experience you will come to appreciate that a certain tension level is, indeed, normal for you. As you gain experience you will recognize that you can control this tension through careful preparation for each speech situation.

MAJOR ELEMENTS OF DELIVERY Of course the elements of delivery are the use of the voice and the use of the body. We will talk first about vocal aspects of delivery and then the nonverbal elements. Although we have maintained that use of voice and body are not the primary elements of public speaking, they are obviously very important adjuncts to effective public communication. Do not excuse yourself from the necessary role of public speaking with some notion that since your voice is not like Walter Cronkite's or John Chancellor's or Jane Pauley's or Barbara Jordan's, you will never be an effective speaker. Each of us has unique characteristics of voice and mannerisms of body which, with preparation, can make our communication efforts more effective.

Vocal Aspects of Delivery

We assume you have some understanding of the physiology and physics involved in sound production by the human organism. Fundamentally, the voice must allow the speaker to *be heard* and to *be understood*. There are two areas of consideration we wish you to heed. The first is articulation and the second is vocal variety.

Articulation

Articulation refers to the use of speech articulators, such as lips, tongue, teeth, etc., to produce distinct sounds. You could recognize most of these individual sounds and the necessary manipulation of certain articulators in order to produce them. The ability we have to combine these sounds in the production of syllables, words, sentences, etc. is remarkable; but that we can decipher meanings when bombarded by a group of sounds rapidly presented is even more astounding. Therefore, as speakers who wish to be heard and understood, it is important that we articulate these sounds in such a way that the listener can discern them without significant effort. One of the authors once heard a teacher say that the speaker must be articulate so that the audience could work with its mind on the content of the message rather than work with the ear trying to identify sounds. We are not talking about an exaggerated articulation which calls attention to itself and distracts from the message. An effective speaker does not call attention in any way to articulation. Perhaps the most desirable response from an audience member to a question about a speaker's articulation would be "I didn't notice it."

Unfortunately, many speakers do cause us to notice it. When we hear endings of words dropped, such as "quittin'"and "runnin';" when we hear sounds omitted, such as "singlar" for "singular;" when we hear substitutions, such as "ek cetra" for "et cetera" or "excaped" for "escaped," we may easily become distracted from the speaker's message. Flagrant shortcomings in articulation may very well result in adverse judgments about the speaker's general credibility, competence, and education. We have spoken of the importance of selecting that evidence and support material which will enhance our credibility with an audience. We must not destroy those efforts by allowing a lazy voice to work to the contrary.

The speaker must also be willing to open his or her mouth and make articulation possible. Many a good idea or carefully researched speech fails to be communicated because a lazy lip or lazy jaw blocked delivery. Open your mouth! What may seem exaggerated articulation on first try might come to be quite appropriate and effective.

The speaker should record his or her speech during rehearsal and listen during playback for evidence of distracting articulation behaviors. In fact, until we hear ourselves making these distractive sounds, correction is doubtful.

Vocal Variety

By this concept we mean to identify those aspects of voice which can be controlled by the speaker and can significantly contribute to being heard and to being understood. Through careful articulation the speaker can attempt to convey literal or denotative meanings. Through variations in rate, pitch, and volume, the speaker can suggest more subtle and/or connotative meanings as well. Remember that old high school cheer, "We like our team"? Our cheerleaders directed us to place the emphasis on "we" the first time we said it, then on "like" the second time, then "our," and finally on "team" the last time through. The change in emphasis caused us to change the meaning each time we yelled the sentence. If you let the underline indicate the word to be emphasized, you would have the cheer written as follows:

<u>We</u> like our team
We <u>like</u> our team
We like <u>our</u> team
We like our <u>team</u>
<u>We</u> <u>like</u> <u>our</u> <u>team</u>

Although you may feel self-conscious asserting that simple example, read it through, placing emphasis as directed. Do you hear the meaning change? Could others hear this shift in meaning produced by your shift of emphasis?

Consider what different emphases would do for a sentence such as "This year the Franklyn Corporation will produce four hundred units of Box M." Experiment with vocal variety by applying alternative methods of emphasis. For instance, the emphasis can be created in several different ways by using vocal variation. A selected word or words can be emphasized by simply using greater volume or loudness. Emphasis can come by using a different pitch level; it can come by inserting a pause after the underlined word or by other variations in rate. It is to the potential for these variations that we next give some attention.

Rate

Variations in speed are important to effective public speech. Frequently the rate will be determined by the content of the message. Parenthetical information might very well be delivered at a faster rate than the substantive parts of a statement. Effective pausing and phrasing are characteristic of a well-managed rate. Words grouped into meaningful units and pauses placed strategically provide variation and emphasis vital to maintaining audience attention. Although variation in rate is important to convey attitude, meaning, and importance, change for change's sake is a minimum necessity. No speech is more deadly than that which is delivered at one steady pace from beginning to end.

We are sure that each person interested in variety in rate could make up some personal illustrations, but the following exercises may help get you started:

1.   Read the following sentences by pronouncing each word and syllable at approximately the same speed all the way through.
"For the county to construct a bridge, <u>one that will last for at least twenty years</u>, many federal/guidelines must be met. <u>When these guidelines are complied with</u>, the project has only reached/phase one."
2.   Now reread the paragraph at the same rate, but speak faster when reading the underlined portion. Many other shades of meaning are possible by variations in rate.
3.   Now reread the paragraph once more. Where the diagonal appears, pause for a longer interval before pronouncing the word which follows. Experiment with the pause. Note you can emphasize what precedes as well as what follows.

Pitch

Monotone in pitch is perhaps even more deadly than the unchanging rate. Even though each of us has a normal pitch range, some speakers adopt unnatural pitch levels. The normal pitch level is where one's voice is most easily produced with the least strain and effort. It is the level to which the speaker will return after variations for emphasis.

The novice might find a passage of prose and attempt to read with specific change in pitch. Some changes are perhaps natural. The rising inflection in questions and the pitch levels appropriate to different moods can be checked through playback of tapes during rehearsal.

In the following illustrations note some emphases and meaning changes which result from rising or falling pitch:

1.   Say the following statement with a falling pitch at the end.
"You have seen the X company's annual report"
2.   Now say the same statement with a rising pitch at the end. If we had given the end cue punctuation of a period for the first reading and a question mark for the second, you would have probably given the appropriate falling or rising pitch.
3.   Note how the meaning of the sentence changes if you use either a higher or lower pitch when you reach the word "seen."

Volume

Sometimes referred to as intensity, this feature suggests that the variation is not only in the direction of greater loudness. Sometimes a much greater emphasis can be achieved by a sharp decrease in volume.

Volume should be adjusted to the speech situation, and the speaker has the responsibility to be sure that everyone can hear. When possible one should avoid the use of a microphone and other amplifying devices. When such items must be used, the speaker should attempt to try them out before the audience is present. Determine the capability of the microphone. Is it sensitive enough so that you can move some distance from it without losing its support? Is some type of lapel mike available so that your extemporaneous movement and general delivery mode is unhampered? Be sure also to check the volume level in different parts of the audience so that no portion is irritated by too much while others are losing the sound. Do not use the microphone as a crutch or because it seems the thing for speakers to use. Use it only if it is needed for audiences to be able to hear you.

Our lack of enthusiasm for microphones results from observing and hearing many speakers who adopt weird postures to guarantee that they are being picked up. The microphone also tends to restrict one's movement and decrease audience contact.

In addition, appropriate volume means more than just being loud enough. Emphasis can be created by a decrease in volume as well as in increase. An audience may listen very attentively if some portions are delivered with a sharp decrease in volume for a brief period.

Nonverbal Aspects of Delivery

The use of the body in public communication events is, of course, well known to most of us. Let us spend some time reviewing three major categories of *nonverbal behavior associated with public speaking:* movement, posture, and gesture.

Movement

One's speech actually begins the moment one is identified as the speaker. The way we respond with our body and face to the introduction and the way we approach the lectern or speaking area are a part of our speech. Then, our words and voice are saying that we are excited about our topic and the opportunity to speak to the audience, our nonverbal behavior should also reinforce, not contradict, those messages.

When called upon to speak, the speaker should do so with energy and enthusiasm. Too frequently the mutterings of speakers about how they are unused to speaking and unskilled in the practice are also supported by a hesitant step and timid voice which make those of us in the audience wish we were elsewhere. The general rule about movement is to do so with purpose and conviction. When at the lectern, the speaker prepared for an extemporaneous delivery is free to move about to confront different parts of the audience with a directness that is effective. The novice probably has some fear of becoming trapped at some distance from notes left on the lectern, but one soon learns to return to the lectern without awkwardness. Note that we said to move with purpose and conviction. Of course movement must be for purposes of emphasis and directness. Movement for movement's sake is not to be encouraged.

In addition, the speaker need have no hesitation about holding the notes in hand while moving about. Although one can be freer without them, there should be no effort to hide them from the audience. These notes should, however, be on small cards to eliminate the distraction of gesturing with and manipulating large sheets of paper.

Posture

There was a time when teachers of public speaking advised specific postures, but today we suggest a posture supportive of your message and conducive to good communication. It does make sense to recognize that if weight is evenly balanced on the feet, you can avoid the distraction of shifting from one foot to the other. And, of course, a posture which has the speaker draped over the lectern is also not one which suggests great enthusiasm for the subject. An upright, not stiff, posture does maximize one's ability to use the voice and body in the many ways we have been discussing in this chapter.

Gestures

One cannot avoid the use of gestures when really involved with one's message, and with a little additional attention the speaker can learn to punctuate with hand and arm gestures.

The best gestures and facial expressions are those which are a natural part of our communication behavior. However, in the public speaking situation, we should consider giving them an additional emphasis. One way is to exaggerate them during rehearsal of the speech. This will help us to make appropriate gestures and facial expression during the speech.

Some Additional Generalizations Concerning Delivery

The speaker should approach these matters of delivery with what we have regularly called *a keen sense of communication.* Avoid some of the common notions which have been around for some time, such as "Look just over the heads of your audience." This is nonsense and not good communication behavior. Make every effort to be direct. The speaker who seemed to be speaking directly to me is one who had my attention. To the extent that the speaker can establish eye contact with many persons in the audience, he/she will hold their attention. A well-known teacher of speech communication used to say that the speaker should look the audience in the eye and the speech should look the audience in the mind. At any rate, the speaker who seems to be looking at the floor, ceiling, or just over the heads of the audience is distracting them from the message.

The speaker should react to himself/herself and to the audience. When audience members respond to an idea or a statement in a way clearly apparent to all members of that audience, the speaker should respond with them. A speaker should be listening to his or her own speech so that facial and gestic responses consistent with the message will be observed by the audience.

The speaker should not leave or start to leave until the speech is finished. Frequently we hear a speaker who has developed an effective conclusion destroy its effect by delivering it while he is picking up speech notes and other materials. Finish crisply, allow a moment for this final statement to be considered, collect your materials and return with confidence to your seat. Gestures and sighs of relief do little to reinforce the impact of the speech.

Finally, as we have been implying throughout this chapter, *the speaker must plan to rehearse the speech aloud* as often as possible before delivery. If you have a sympathetic family, ask someone to listen. If not, use a tape recorder and playback. Make efforts to practice the entire speech all the way through. Rehearse all aspects of the talk—introduction, pattern of arrangement, support for each point, language choice, and delivery—just as you plan to present it to the specific audience. Have only the notes you will actually use. Practice until you are comfortable and familiar with your material.

DELIVERY: ESSENTIAL CONSIDERA- TIONS

For this speech situation what particular attention do I need to give to the following:

I. Vocal Delivery
   A. Articulation
   B. Pitch
   C. Rate
   D. Volume
II. Nonverbal Delivery
   A. Posture
   B. Dress
   C. Movement
   D. Gestic Emphasis
   E. Line of Sight
III. Attention and Audience Contact
   A. Energy Level
   B. Proximity
   C. Reacting to Self and Audience
   D. Mode of Delivery
      1. Extemporaneous
      2. Manuscript
IV. Tension Reduction
   A. Subject Matter Prepared
   B. Prepared for Specific Audience
   C. Prepared for Different Settings
   D. Rehearsed

SUGGESTED READINGS

Mudd, Charles S. and Malcolm O. Sillars. *Speech: Content and Communication,* 4th Edition. Harper & Row, 1980, pp. 246-64.

Tacey, William S. *Business and Professional Speaking,* 3rd Edition. William C. Brown Co., 1980, pp. 121-39.

Zimmerman, Gordon I.; James L. Owen; and David R. Seibert. *Speech Communication: A Contemporary Introduction,* 2nd Edition. West Publishing Co., 1980, pp. 47-75.

A second moment of importance in the communication roles for the person in business and other professions is conference speaking and participation. Of course all the skills we have discussed earlier as related to the public speech and to audience analysis and adaptation are specifically applicable to conference speaking. In addition, we have chosen to focus special attention on the use of visual aids and listening as skills significantly related to the conference. These skills, too, are supportive of communication in all instances.

THREE

After the production meeting, George Mackey felt vaguely frustrated and dissatisfied. It was a familiar feeling. These conferences, held on an irregular basis every few months, when he couldn't put them off any longer, were to remind the responsible department heads that plant productivity left a lot to be desired. But they never seemed to accomplish anything. This one had been no exception.

To begin with, a couple of people who were supposed to be there had somehow failed to be notified and had to be summoned from something else they were working on. As a result, the meeting started late and in something less than the best possible atmosphere. Whoever had used the conference room last had left it in a mess, and the first fifteen minutes were spent emptying ashtrays, moving dirty coffee cups aside, erasing the blackboard, and starting a fresh pot of coffee.

He'd opened the meeting more or less as usual, with a reminder that there hadn't been much improvement following the last meeting. To get the ball rolling, he'd reviewed the suggestions he had made at that meeting and at several meetings before it. Then he'd asked for comments. There were none.

He went back over some of the ground he had just covered and repeated his request. This time, surprisingly, a new department head, about whom George knew practically nothing, offered what sounded like the germ of a pretty good idea. Even more surprising, Bob, who never had anything to contribute, picked up on the idea and seemed to be about to expand on it. Then Al, who'd been in the same job for years and who'd never been known to let a good story suffer for lack of exaggeration, interrupted to describe the monumental confusion he said had resulted when a similar suggestion had been tried once before. It was a long, rather funny recital, followed by an unrelated incident called to mind by a detail in the first story.

By the time the two stories were finished, the mood was more relaxed, but it was difficult to get back to the subject. There was some general discussion, but the new man made no further contribution, Bob had gone back into his shell, and there were no more original suggestions. George had a couple more points he had meant to bring up, but it was now almost lunchtime and he noticed some people checking their watches. He asked for

Conference Speaking

9

*final comments and closed the session. Now he wondered what
he had done wrong.*

Almost everything, actually. In this chapter we will discuss group processes
and the particular responsibilities of the conference leader as they apply in
the planning and preparation stage and in the actual conduct of the meeting.
We will examine the root causes of the frustration, wasted motion and lack
of focus that so often characterize conferences and small group meetings in
general. Then we will describe the measures the group leader can take to
convert them into effective communication events.

The group, in a face-to-face setting, working cooperatively toward a desired
end, is an integral part of our modern organizations. It is made increasingly
necessary by the growing size and complexity of the organizations. Regardless of the type of organization, the higher you rise in it, the more time you
will probably spend in conference. Thus the better your perspective should
be on the types of problems and responses arising at various organizational
levels.

The limitation of lower-echelon viewpoints and suggestions is that they
are too often narrowly focused on details of a particular job or department.
There is little grasp either of the overall picture or of the effect of an action
in one part of the organization on its other parts. Higher-echelon perspective,
on the other hand, frequently suffers from the opposite problem. Higher
management tends to concentrate on the overview while neglecting the effect
of general policies on specific operations. In the modern organization it is
necessary, either through an effective middle-management level or through
vertical conference in which all echelons are represented, to provide the perspective missing at both ends of the hierarchy. However, it is not just the
greater size of modern organizations that has made the small-group meeting
a vital part of corporate life. It is the whole trend of contemporary management. It is true that fewer formal meetings were required when the typical
owner-manager was a part of the work force and knew each employee by
name. But it was not the management style of that era to do much consulting
with employees under any circumstances. Today, organizations of all size
reflect the impact of the "democratic management" revolution. They grant
at least token recognition to employee participation in making decisions that
affect all personnel. They listen to the voice of the employee in matters once
jealously reserved for top management consideration and encourage an informal give-and-take interaction to a degree unthinkable only a few decades ago.

Nor is it management thinking alone that has changed. Employee attitudes have evolved in step with the development of the democratic style in
management. By and large, today's employees have adapted to the informal,
nonauthoritarian, consultative organizational atmosphere and would resent
or reject a more rigid climate. In addition, today's employees have learned
to expect greater organizational emphasis on human relationships as well
as on training, development and on-the-job technical education to keep abreast
of change. Increasing group communication is thus promoted by both the
democratic management style and the needs and expectations of employees.

All of these factors—the growing size and complexity of organizations,
human-centered management philosophies, and new employee outlooks and
requirements—work together to make the conference process an increasingly
important part of the modern organization scene. Understanding the process
is, therefore, vital to effective participation in organizational activities. More-

over, skill in conference leadership is a valuable instrument of success in the organizational structure, regardless of your profession or place in the hierarchy.

WHAT IS A CONFER-ENCE? A conference is an intensified communication process in which the ideas, information and skills of two or more people are pooled to achieve a common objective. A conference may last anywhere from a few minutes to several days, usually with an effort made to eliminate or reduce interruptions. It is essentially a small-group discussion process—the actual work of large conferences is usually done in small groups who bring the results of their work back to the general body for final discussion or action.

Conferences serve as a tool for *information, instruction,* and *training;* they are ideally suited for group *problem solving* and *decision making* and for *pooling ideas and skills;* they are useful for *building team spirit,* for providing an opportunity for *individual contribution,* and for *giving a sense of participation.* They can offer new channels for communication in all directions in the organization; upward, downward, and horizontally.

For all of these reasons, the conference has become an important part of organizational activity, often consuming 60% to 70% of the time of top executives—an estimate one of the present writers was able to verify while serving as special assistant to the chief executive officer of a major corporation. An incident from this experience also tends to confirm the value of conference participation in promoting a sense of individual security and belonging, even among those who are seemingly most critical. The names of several persons who had complained that meetings were boring, useless and time-consuming were eliminated from the list for a meeting at which their presence was not essential, although they normally would have been asked to attend. Before the day was over, all of them had lodged a complaint that they had been passed over!

The charge that conferences are great time-wasters can also be misleading. There is no denying that a conference such as the production meeting described in the opening paragraphs of this chapter can be an expensive waste. But even a moderately well-planned conference is among the most efficient communication tools for such tasks as disseminating information, obtaining a cross-section of opinion, and making generally supported and understood decisions.

All in all, most serious observers would probably agree that the advantages of small group communication outweigh the disadvantages. Groups generally come up with better, or at least more thoroughly examined, solutions to problems than individuals do; motivation is usually better for group-planned projects; group processes help individuals to better understand how their own activities fit into the larger picture; and they often help to improve understanding and communication all around.

Goals and Objectives

The difference between a conference and a bull session is that a conference is designed to achieve one or more specific objectives: to disseminate or elicit certain information, to provide training, development or instructions, to mobilize for a particular task or goal, to solve a problem or reach a decision. The goal of a long-range planning conference is to develop goals and objectives. A regular weekly or monthly meeting may have a continuous objective (such as coordinating production activities) and an agenda that may vary from meeting to meeting.

Participants

Considered as inputs to the conference process, the participants play a role whose value can hardly be overemphasized. Where the conference will serve what some observers call its integrative function—reinforcing an individual sense of participation and identification with the group—some participants will no doubt be included for no other reason, as suggested by the anecdote related earlier in this chapter.

Obviously, those participants are most valuable to a conference who have the knowledge and skills required to achieve its purposes. But attitude and specific small-group communication skills are almost as important in determining the contribution they actually make. The participant willing to do some advance preparation may contribute more in the final analysis than one who is an expert on the conference topic, particularly if the well-prepared nonexpert is more eager to see the conference succeed than the expert is. The participant who assumes responsibility for a share of discussion and debate but doesn't hog the floor, who is a listener as well as a speaker, and who cooperates without competing with the conference leader often makes the difference between success and failure.

Agenda

An agenda is not just a meeting convenience; it is a necessary tool. It should, therefore, be treated with the thought and attention it deserves. If it is well planned and organized for a logical or psychological building effect, it can contribute greatly to the interest and success of the conference. Distributed ahead of time, it is an invaluable aid in advance preparation.

Group Size

A successful small working group can consist of anywhere from two to about twenty people. Above that number it becomes difficult to maintain the visibility and communication distance that enables each participant to interact with any other member of the group. Except in unusual circumstances, the actual work of larger meetings is best done in small subgroups or buzz sessions. By definition, the conference atmosphere is one that encourages the widest possible participation and interaction within a controlled framework. The larger the group, the more important it becomes to have a strong, skillful leader to maintain diversified interaction and, at the same time, to hold the proceedings to the established agenda, schedule, and objectives.

Physical Setting

Conference-room size, decor, lighting, acoustics, temperature, ventilation, seating comfort, and the adequacy of personal and tabletop space have a significant bearing on the success of the conference. No matter how dedicated the participants are, their performance is affected by overcrowding, depressing surroundings, physical discomfort or inconvenience, and inability to hear or see what is going on. It is particularly important that the conference leader and any blackboard, chart easel, or projection screen be clearly visible to all participants.

The longer the meeting lasts, the greater the toll taken by a bad physical setting. People who do not actually walk out can still be converted into non-participants by physical discomfort or negative reaction to their surroundings.

Conference Aids

In addition to visual aids, discussed at length in Chapter 10, it is usually important to provide conference participants with scratch pads, pencils and an adequate surface space to use them conveniently. It is a good idea to provide fresh copies of the agenda and any prepared notes, background or supporting material, even though they may have been supplied to prospective participants in advance.

CONFER-ENCE LEADERSHIP

As the preceding section indicates, the conference leader is responsible for advance arrangements which may have a significant impact on the conference well before it begins. With the actual opening of the meeting, two leadership factors become crucial to its ultimate success. These are the attitudes with which the leader approaches the task and the actual conduct of the conference.

The role of the conference leader is to initiate structure and show consideration for participants. The leader's role is seen as having two dimensions, one directed to the task at hand and the other to the human factor. In one half of the role, the leader structures the communication in such a way that the objective is achieved and, in the other, helps the people involved to make their maximum contribution and enjoy a sense of accomplishment in doing so. The requirements differ from group to group and situation to situation, and few individual leaders are equally proficient in all skills. Some outstanding leaders seem able to maintain balanced, high-level performance in both dimensions. Most people, however, appear to have a natural tendency to emphasize one role or the other. They need to make a conscious effort to develop and utilize skills in their weaker area. If you tend to concentrate on the task aspect of leadership, you should make a conscious effort to relate to the individual participants on a warm, human level, and vice versa, until you can be sure you are not unduly neglecting either of these key responsibilities.

There is more at stake than the development of an aesthetically pleasing leadership style. Studies indicate that success in achieving small-group communication objectives is directly tied to the ability of the leader to function adequately in both areas. The leader who emphasizes human interaction and neglects task considerations is apt to wind up with a lot of friendly conversation and no accomplishments. Excessive attention to task, on the other hand, can be equally unproductive, if in a less immediately obvious way.

It is said that a major typewriter company lost its one-time preeminence in the market largely because of the cold, autocratic task-oriented leadership of its senior executive. His staff meetings were one-man shows, without warmth or spontaneity. Suggestions and contributions were treated with contempt and rejected out of hand. One such suggestion, turned down without discussion, was that the company might look into the possibilities, then being explored by competitors, of an electrically powered carriage return.

By the time the executive got around to considering the idea on his own, one of his competitors had utilized the idea to capture a lion's share of the market.

So it is not merely the leader's professional excellence that is involved in the development of both task and socialization skills; it is also the quality of the conference output itself. So close is the correlation, in fact, that one observer, Fiedler, suggests that, just as athletic coaches are often judged by the performance of their teams, the best way to evaluate a conference leader is to look not at his or her activity but rather at the group's effectiveness in achieving its objectives.[1]

This does not mean that the effective leader is one who imposes his or her will on the group. The leader enjoys a certain status and authority by virtue of being leader, but this leverage is properly used only to preserve orderly discussion, maintain fair play and offer direction. For the leader to impose a conclusion is to defeat the purpose of the group effort. The leader may, and should, enter into discussion, debating, questioning, responding, playing devil's advocate. The success of the conference, however, does not hinge on whether the leader's point of view prevails but on whether the group processes the conference inputs in a thorough and healthy way, achieving the best outputs that particular group is capable of. The leader's role is to stimulate and influence the process in such a way that the best possible results are achieved.

Influencing the Process

As we have seen, the leader's influence begins long before the conference opens, selecting objectives and participants, arranging the details of the physical setting, and drawing up the agenda. Once the conference is under way, the leader is expected to influence the group process, without dominating it, in order to get the best results with the least waste of time and energy. How is the leader's influence exercised? What specifically does the leader do to prompt the group to produce its best work?

A variety of answers has been suggested. About thirty years ago some people suggested that leaders exert their influence through the exhibition of certain traits in which they characteristically excel when compared to the typical member of the groups they lead, including such traits as intelligence, scholarship, dependability, economic status, and social status. Many organizations still employ a traits matrix in their search for leadership material. Many others have abandoned the practice after spending a large amount of money and time on research that seems to indicate that real traits are not that easy to define and identify and, in any case, do not seem to produce the anticipated results.

A crucial leadership quality is the kind of personal magnetism Max Weber credited for a large part of the answer to his question, "Why do people obey as they do?"[2] He called this quality charisma. Although it is not easy to define or validate experimentally, charisma is fairly universally recognized as the extraordinary personal quality that causes large numbers of people to gravitate to and respond to certain individuals.

Not everybody has charisma of the kind described by Weber and by others later. But everybody has a personal magnetism, if it is only allowed to be expressed. The leader who can overcome personal reticence, shyness, and the fear of exposure of personal foibles and weaknesses has taken the first great step toward developing his or her own charisma. Naturally, one's ideas about the subject of the conference are of great importance; but, in communicating them, how one reveals oneself as a unique human being, with personal qualities and a special way of regarding and relating to others, may be even more important in the long run.

Either as a participant or as a leader, you will usually find you have far more to gain than to lose in allowing your real self to emerge in the conference process—and it may even strengthen your leadership with your own brand of charisma.

Task

Among all the complex details of conference organization and management, the one fact that shoud be kept constantly in view is the reason for it all— the job to be done. How well this crucial responsibility is discharged is almost invariably related to the quality of the conference leadership. Consistently firm, flexible leadership can make the difference between moderate and maximum success or between moderate performance and none at all.

Even the best group can founder for lack of adequate leadership. A recent conference attended by the writer offers a typical example. It was well attended by informed and concerned people, but the leader, either through incompetence or misunderstanding of his responsibilities, refused to give it guidance and direction. Inevitably, a topic having little to do with the conference task was injected into the discussion; furthermore, the leader permitted the extraneous matter to dominate through a long, meandering and pointless argument. When both the subject and the participants were exhausted, it was all but impossible to get back to the job at hand. It was only after several irritable demands to know why we were assembled that the meeting finally found its way back to its agenda, dispirited and with far too little time left to do its work. Needless to say, the conference was not a success.

The leader's most important single responsibility is to keep the group on track and progressing toward its goal. It should be done with tact and grace if possible, but done, no matter how. There are many tools at the leader's disposal for accomplishing this purpose. A well-thought-out agenda is one, particularly if it has a realistic time schedule. Allocating each point a specific, limited period for discussion serves two purposes. It keeps the participants constantly aware of the number of items to be considered and the need to budget time, and it helps to prevent neglect of items near the end of the agenda. It also helps put the responsibility for wasting time on the time-wasters. It is less important that the time schedule be adhered to down to the second than that the group, if it changes the schedule, does so knowing that time added to one item has to come from the time allotted to another.

The leader also keeps the group's attention directed to the task before it by the liberal use of suggestions and questions when there is a tendency to bog down or stray from the point. It is far less effective for the leader to say simply, "Let's get back to the point" or "Let's get on with it" than to say something like "We need to consider the effect of this approach on R & D" or "Jim, can't we come up with a more flexible funding plan? How did your organization handle it when. . . ?" This usually calls for the leader to have a list of questions prepared in advance for each agenda item. Some of them will be answered in the course of the discussion, but when a need arises for a fresh stimulus, a question not yet answered often provides it. In drawing

up such a list, the leader may be helped by keeping in mind that most discussions deal with matters of fact, practicality, and policy. The order of possible questions to ask, therefore, moves from those that ask "What are the
facts in this case?" through "Is this the best approach?" to "Is this what we
should be doing?"

Consideration

As emphasized earlier, the leader bears a large responsibility for developing
a conference climate that demonstrates consideration for the comfort and
needs of the participants. This is, first of all, a human consideration, but
it is also one of great practicality, as experience has shown repeatedly. The
employer whose only thought is for the task at hand, with none for the fact
that it must be accomplished by human beings, almost invariably complains
about the low motivation, the poor production or the sloppy work with which
the employees respond. The same psychology applies in conference situations.
A leader's lack of consideration for the human requirements of the participants will almost certainly be reflected in disapppointing results.

   At the same time, the leader is only one person, who is expected to interact
on a personal level with each member of the group. Since this is difficult
to do, even with only two or three, and manifestly impossible with a larger
assembly, the effect of personal interaction must be created in some other
way. The leader must, first, project a genuine attitude of friendly, personal
interest in all members of the group. Then the leader must employ communication techniques that help to sustain the illusion that this attitude is in
continuous effect between the leader and each participant. Almost all
speakers utilize the device of speaking as though to one individual member
of the audience—as though, in a group of ten, carrying on a conversation
with one recipient and nine listeners. The important part of the illusion in
small groups, however, is to convey to *each* listener the impression that he
or she is the one to whom the remarks are directly addressed and that the
others are the eavesdroppers. It is not, of course, supposed that the listeners
are intellectually deceived—it is the general feeling and atmosphere that are
important. The impression is usually achieved by frequent direct address
to individuals, by making sure you do not habitually favor or neglect one
part of the room over another, and by impartially speaking directly to each
listener in turn. Since the attention of even the most rapt listener is necessarily discontinuous at best, each can be encouraged to carry away the feeling
that a large proportion of the discussion took place in direct interaction with
the leader.

Intrapersonal Communication Systems

Over 2,300 years ago, Aristotle provided us with an invention system which
he called "topoi," a rote list of general topics that one could utilize in the
effort to think of "sayables," things to talk about. In keeping a conversation
alive, for example, one might thumb through an imaginary compilation of
topics—music, literature, art, theater, politics, sports, health—testing each
for interest and appropriateness in the interaction.

   This valuable concept for the conference leader is one we have already
touched on in advising ways to use prepared suggestions and questions to
keep the discussion moving on track. Many leaders find it helpful to have

in mind a more general list of considerations for reference throughout the conference, such as these: (1) goals: What are they and how does the discussion under way or just completed relate to them? (2) participation: Are some people dominating the discussion while others are being left out? (3) sensitivity: What are the individual participants thinking and feeling? What might be the effect of an insensitive or offensive remark on a particular individual? How does the leader handle the situation if offense appears to have been given? (4) style: What has been the response to the leader's style? What alternatives are available if the one in operation isn't effective? (5) language: Is there general mutual understanding and stimulating cross-interaction? (6) recognition: Are the participants getting enough recognition for their contribution?

Each leader develops his or her own style of topoi; the important thing is to have in advance an idea of all of the processes that should be going on simultaneously. Then thinking on your feet is less a matter of inspiration than of preparation.

The challenge to the conference leader is ultimately one of personal development to the limit in all directions. In urging the task-oriented leader to learn socialization skills, and vice versa, the object is not to reach for phony tricks and devices but to give effective expression to the natural human qualities that lie, often deeply buried, in each individual and to encourage development of the self-confidence to utilize them.

Perhaps there is no universally applicable list of traits that mark a good leader, as it was once supposed. Fortunately, it is far more likely that skillful leadership can be learned by anyone who will spend the time and energy to learn how to set goals and describe them clearly, how to plan with attention to detail and possible problems, and how to guide the communication process with respect and consideration for others.

**CONFER-
ENCE
PROCESS
AND LEADER-
SHIP: ESSEN-
TIAL CON-
SIDERATIONS**

I. Participants
    A. By virtue of position
    B. Invited
    C. Peers
II. Purpose
    A. Information
    B. New research data
    C. New ways of doing this
    D. Team building
    E. Creative problem-solving
III. Facility
    A. Rooms
    B. AV equipment
    C. Furniture arrangement
    D. Eating and sleeping
    E. Relaxation opportunities
    F. Pads, pencils, etc.
IV. Agenda and organization
    A. Topics
    B. Section leaders
    C. Schedule
    D. Registration
V. Promotion
    A. Invitations and announcements
    B. Press releases
    C. Directions, maps, etc.
    D. Program description
VI. Leading the conference
    A. Maintaining control
    B. Showing consideration for each participant
    C. Enforcing agenda
    D. Recording proceedings

NOTES

[1]Fiedler, F. and M. Chemers, *Leaders and Effective Management*, New York, Scott Foresman, 1974.

[2]M. Weber, *The Theory of Social and Economic Organization*, translated by A. M. Anderson and T. Parsons (New York: The Free Press, 1947).

SUGGESTED READINGS

Applbaum, R. L.; E. M. Bodaken; K. K. Sereno; and K. W. E. Anatol. *The Process of Group Communication*, 2nd Edition. Palo Alto, Cal: Science Research Associates, 1979.

Gulley, H. E. *Discussion, Conference and Group Process*, 2nd Edition. New York: Holt, Rinehart and Winston, 1968.

Shaw, M. E. *Group Dynamics: The Psychology of Small Group Behavior*, 2nd Edition. New York: McGraw-Hill Book Co., 1976.

Zelko, H. P. *The Business Conference: Leadership and Participation*. New York: McGraw-Hill Book Co., 1969.

Although Phryne was the most celebrated beauty of fourth-century B.C. Athens (she was the model for the Aphrodites of the sculptor Praxiteles, one of her countless lovers), the famous courtesan always went veiled in public except during certain religious festivals, when she ritually disrobed and bathed in the sea. Hailed into court on a charge of impiety, she was defended by the equally famous orator Hypereides, also one of the industrious lady's admirers. Not only did Hypereides plead eloquently that one so fair could not possibly be guilty of such a charge, but he underscored his peroration by dramatically opening her tunic, exposing her to the judges. She was acquitted, and "The Defense of Phryne" became an imperishable milestone not only in legal strategy, but in the use of visual aids.[1]

Not all graphic aids, unfortunately, are so directly related to the point the speaker wants to make although they may be impressive from a design or aesthetic standpoint. This lesson was learned the hard way by an engineer hired to sell the merits of a small but excellent firm in competition with some of the largest builders in the South. He was given a free hand and a virtually unrestricted budget to attract contracts from government agencies and private industry. He made a careful study of audio-visual equipment and selected the best. His slides and other graphic materials were prepared by experts.

For several months, he made presentations throughout the South, always to the same enthusiastic and appreciative response. He was repeatedly complimented on the excellence of his materials, and one important prospect commented that they were perhaps the best he had ever seen. His company congratulated itself and waited for the orders to start pouring in.

Six months later, still waiting, it called in one of the authors for consultation on what it was doing wrong. Despite the universal applause, despite the lavish promotion budget, despite the enthusiasm and knowledge of their representative, not a dollar's worth of new business could be attributed to the vigorous and expensive campaign.

A quick review of the presentation confirmed the general consensus — it was a stunning piece of work. If the company had been selling photography or audio-visual equipment, it probably would have been fantastically successful. But in the final analysis, what it said was that construction projects can be beautifully photographed. It said it so well that it overwhelmed any other point the presentation might have been trying to make verbally. Nowhere did it say graphically that this company could do an outstanding

Visual Communication 10

construction job or that there was any particular reason why it would be a better company to deal with than its competitors. The presentation was a smashing artistic success and a dismal business flop because it broke the cardinal rule of results-oriented communication. It did not harness its materials to the single task of achieving its goal: acquiring new construction contracts.

Fortunately, however, it had served one important purpose. It had created a positive feeling toward the representative and his company with regard to their ability to put on a good show. Thus it provided an excellent entree for a second presentation. While every effort was made to preserve the artistic quality of the first, the second one contained no visuals that had not been ruthlessly screened to carry the communication message as clearly as possible. The message, of course, was that this building is beautiful, soundly engineered, enduring, economical, and whatever other desirable thing it might be *because* it was built by *our* company.

PURPOSE Figure 10.1 is a diagram of the basic factors underlying the effective use of audio-visual aids. It cannot be overemphasized that the first requirement for

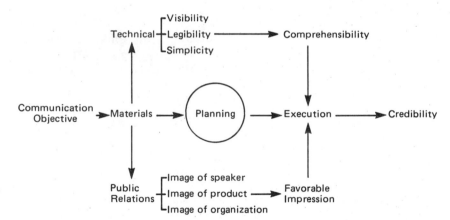

Figure 10.1
Factors in the effective use of audio-visual aids.

effective use of these aids is a clear, specific definition of the purpose they are to serve. Obviously, this purpose will conform to the communication objective of the presentation, but it usually functions in a supportive, reinforcing role. Aids are just what their name implies: aids. They are not normally called on to carry the burden of the message but rather to make a point or an argument clearer or more convincing.

The material must make a relevant contribution to achievement of the communication objective. This is the primary consideration in selecting audio-visual aids, but it is not the only one. A second might be called the public relations factor. Does the material reflect favorably on the objective, the speaker and the sponsoring organization? At the least, can it be said that it does not create negative associations that the viewer will transfer to the speaker? Pictures can be powerfully effective, often in ways the viewer is only dimly aware of. The familiar criticism, "It wasn't *what* was said so much as the *way* it was said," is doubly true of graphic materials. A picture may perfectly illustrate the point you want to make, but in such an offensive way that it arouses hostility instead of agreement.

Or it may make one point at the expense of another. This is a problem the courts face continually in jury trials of gruesome murder cases. It is the court's purpose to ensure that all relevant information is brought clearly and impressively before the jurors. Graphic pictures of the victim may be available that depict the manner of death as nothing else can. This can force a difficult decision on the presiding judge, who must keep in mind that the ultimate objective of the legal process is to render a just decision. How great is the danger that even one juror's objectivity will be so affected by the graphic shock of the pictures as to prevent a fair hearing of the more important questions of whether the accused is in fact guilty, and to what degree?

Antismut campaigners face a classic dilemma in selecting materials to illustrate their subject. Maximum impact calls for display of the most obscene examples of material the speaker believes should not be displayed at all, inviting the accusation that the presentation actually caters to the prurient interests it presumably deplores. This contradiction was neatly illustrated by an organization that crisscrossed Southern California communities with a well-organized and highly profitable antipornography presentation in the 1960s. Its appearance in each locality was preceded by a coordinated campaign of announcements through sympathetic organizations and of advertisements emphasizing the shocking, adults-only nature of the fully illustrated presentation. After one performance, an enterprising interviewer had no difficulty collecting a score of outraged condemnations of pornography from members of the audience, some of whom, it developed, had returned to be shocked by the presentation half a dozen or more times.

TECHNICAL   A second type of criterion for audio-visual aids is technical. In general, these criteria deal with the visibility, legibility and tool-effectiveness of the aids. It is remarkable how often the simplest technical considerations are ignored. It would seem obvious that a message intended to be read or grasped visually needs to be a) visible to all members of the audience, b) decipherable to the most distant member of the audience, and c) simple enough to be understood without detailed study.

Let's take each of these points in order. *Visibility* is usually a question of location of the easel, screen, chalkboard, or stand supporting the material. It seems elementary that it should be a location providing an unobstructed view to all, or to all but an irreducible minimum, of the audience. It should be at a sufficient elevation for those in the rear to see over the heads of those in front, but not so high that front-row viewers have to look up at an uncomfortable angle. About four feet from floor to lower edge of viewing area is usually good. These commonsense conditions are easy to check out when the presentation is to be made in a familiar setting. Problems often arise when a presentation planned with one setting in mind has to be adapted to an entirely different one or when the setting turns out to be different from the one envisioned as the presentation was prepared. In such cases a snap judgment—and not always a satisfactory one—has to be made, bearing in mind the requirements of visibility and comfortable viewing. When any significant fraction of the audience cannot see the exhibits easily and comfortably, it is often better, where feasible, to divide the presentation into two sessions rather than to resort to awkward and distracting maneuvers with the material or the audience.

Figure 10.2
This drawing illustrates poor judgment in the selection of a Visual Aid presentation.

The best location in the world can be defeated, however, if the speaker has the annoying habit of standing between the exhibit and the audience. Granted it is not always possible to avoid blocking somebody's view now and then, it seldom needs to be more than a momentary inconvenience if you are alert to the problem. Before you begin speaking, fix in your mind the sight line to the material from the position of the viewers farthest to the right and left. Then stay out of the area they enclose, or at least don't spend any more time than necessary inside it. When writing or drawing on a board or pad, stand as far forward as possible, and to one side, so that only your hand and arm are in the visual area. Similarly, if you want to indicate a detail, stand to one side and use a pointer or reach into the visual area quickly to point with your finger.

Legibility is a second technical consideration that is too often neglected. How large should the lettering or smallest detail on a visual aid be? Standard eye charts indicate that a person with good vision should be able to distinguish bold plain letters slightly less than one-half inch tall at distances up to about twenty feet. Since visual aids are not ordinarily utilized to test the limits of the audience's vision, it is safe to assume that details much smaller than an inch high or wide are apt to be lost on all but the most intimate, around-the-table audiences. It is important to keep in mind, too, that perhaps half of your audience will have less than average vision and that some legibility is lost for those who have to view at an angle.

Legibility is also affected by type style, color, lighting and background detail. The most practical procedure for determining legibility is to test it under conditions similar to those in which it will be used. Assuming you have good or average vision, you shouldn't subject your audience to graphic materials you can't decipher at a somewhat greater distance than you expect your farthest spectator to be. Adequate letter height in inches will usually work out to half the distance to the farthest listener, in feet, divided by 12.

The third technical problem, *comprehensibility,* is basically psychological in nature. How much can you expect your audience to grasp from a single visual? Experienced speakers know that the ability of audiences to absorb and retain information is far more limited than is generally supposed: a single theme with no more than three to six major points is all that can be covered effectively in a single presentation. Similarly, a single exhibit can make only one point with, if necessary, the most economical of supporting facts or arguments. Thus: "Fuel A is Superior to Fuel B . . . Cleaner . . . Locally Produced . . . Cheaper" is about as much as one card can convey effectively. In fact, many speakers would prefer to divide the message among three cards: "Fuel A is CLEANER than Fuel B," etc.

By the same token, material presented in graph or pictogram form should be kept classically simple. Unless you are making a direct comparison (Performance A versus Performance B), multiple lines plotted on the same graph are almost always counterproductive. Figure 10.3 illustrates this point

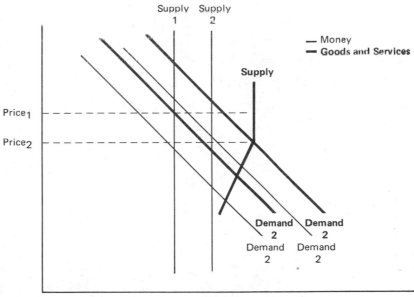

Figure 10.3
A confusing figure.

with considerable clarity. Whether in graphs, line illustrations or slides, elimination of extraneous and distracting elements is essential to effective visual communication.

As important as visibility, legibility and comprehensibility are to clarity, they are equally important to maintaining the vital bond of confidence between audience and speaker. The audience subjected to hard-to-see, hard-to-make-out, confusing graphic materials rapidly loses respect for the speaker. Not only do poorly planned and presented visual aids fail as communication tools, they also erode the speaker's credibility.

There are several other technical and mechanical points that should be noted. Illustrations in books and magazines can seldom be converted directly into good visual aids. If they are properly scaled for comfortable reading at a distance of one to two feet, they are not readable when blown up by means of a slide or overhead projector—at least not within the size limits of most screens or walls. In addition, a graph or illustration intended to be studied on a page is usually too complicated for satisfactory use as a visual aid. It is almost always better to extract the information you need from the printed illustration and use it to construct a new exhibit expressly designed for your purpose.

TIMING Timing is another important consideration. Unless there is a special reason for doing so, no exhibit should be displayed except *in direct connection with the text it supports.* Graphic materials that are exposed prematurely, or that are left in view after they have served their purpose, are often distracting. An exception to the general rule is the exhibit that is deliberately displayed ahead of time in order to arouse interest and curiosity or the one that is left on display so its point will sink in. But these are exceptions that are selected for special purposes.

Photo 10.1
"This picture appeared recently as part of a promotional presentation for a large American Corporation. It was blown up to cover the entire wall behind the speaker and remained visible throughout the presentation. The message? America is in danger of losing the living symbol of its highest standards: Pride, honor, honesty."

A second point of timing has to do with the amount of graphic material an audience can comfortably absorb in a given interval. The generally accepted rule of thumb is that you should *not* plan for *more than about one visual per minute of talk* as a maximum. An exception to this rule is the paced slide show, in which slides, changing every few seconds, almost simulate the continuous flow of a motion film. In such cases, however, the slides are carefully selected and sequenced so that the incremental change from image to image is small enough to prevent the viewer from feeling confused or overwhelmed.

An additional set of considerations arises when the visual aids are to be used repeatedly. *Durability and convenience of storage* then become factors. If they are to be used in a variety of different settings, adaptability and portability are important. Sometimes a flexible approach to presentation media is indicated. A three-dimensional model, for example, may be quite practical for home-base presentations, but a slide of the model might be the only sensible way to present it at distant locations.

REINFORCE-MENT

The role of reinforcement in audio-visual communication is a somewhat different type of technical consideration. Studies[2] have shown consistently that audiences retain a depressingly small percentage of the information presented by lecture alone—ranging from a high of around 50% at the end of the presentation to less than 5% after a few days. Visually presented material fares a little better, ranging from a high of 75% downward to about 15% after a time lapse. A combination of the two types of presentation, however, can produce dramatically improved results—better than 90% immediate retention and a fairly stable level above 60% after a few days—if the two approaches are properly prepared and coordinated.

This last provision is the key point. Both the visual and the audio presentations must be well planned and executed. Moreover, the corresponding sight/sound elements must be presented simultaneously and in as nearly identical terms as possible. Experience, verified by retention data, has shown that material presented visually and immediately described verbally in its own terms, without deviation or digression, is most easily absorbed and retained. For example, when a visual containing words is first exposed, the words should be repeated orally exactly as they appear before going on to discussion or amplification. Similarly, the point of nonverbal visuals should be verbalized as simply and directly as possible. It is true that many people resent the implications of being read to when they can perfectly well see the words themselves. But tests show that, whether resented or not, information is retained best when it is shown visually and immediately repeated orally.[3] Naturally, the resourceful speaker will develop techniques for minimizing the negative implication. Some, for example, make the reading an almost off-hand mannerism, as if it were more for the speaker's benefit than the audience's: "Fuel A is superior to Fuel B because it is cleaner, locally available, and cheaper. Now, how do we arrive at this conclusion? . . ." and into the discussion. There are speakers who can get away with repeating the message twice, thoughtfully, as though using it as a reminder and a filler while formulating the comments to follow.

Although we have dealt primarily with the more familiar types of audio-visual aids—slides, pictures, drawings, graphs, message cards, and the like—it is important to remember that a visual aid can be anything that communicates its message through the eye rather than through the ear. The value of an imaginative approach to presentation aids is illustrated by the experience of a furniture manufacturer.

As had the construction firm described earlier, this company had gone to considerable trouble and expense to develop a professionally produced slide presentation and hired an excellent speaker to take it on a sales tour. Everywhere the presentation was warmly received, but its results were disappointing in terms of sales.

After much discussion the company decided to gamble on a radical approach suggested by a consultant. The slick, beautiful slide show was put in storage and the professional speaker sent home. The company manufactured strong, functionally aesthetic, useful articles upon which people sat, ate and slept. Rugged integrity and solid craftsmanship were to be the keynotes of the new campaign.

A man who had spent twenty years in the factory was selected as spokesman. By conventional standards, he was not a good speaker. He spoke slowly and plainly, not always grammatically, but he was not afraid of audiences and he spoke with an authority that no hearer would dream of challenging. There was literally nothing he did not know about furniture construction, and he projected a pride of craft that went right down to the bone.

Ordinary visual aids would have been inappropriate for such a spokesman. In this case, special exhibits were prepared by selecting a typical chair, table, and other articles of furniture and literally sawing them in half to provide a cross section of the construction. These exhibits were fitted into a crate that was flown from city to city as the new representative retraced the path of the former salesperson. There was always some initial reaction to the man's awkward opening—to his lack of polish and his failure to establish eye contact. But it soon disappeared as his workman's hands began to move over the polished wood and the exposed inner construction of the exhibits. He pointed out the functional logic of the design while he explained in plain, patient detail why this kind of joint was required in this particular location, why this kind of glue and this method of doweling provided the requisite strength at this point, why this upholstery was selected, and why it was necessary to attach and support it in this unique fashion. It was a rare audience that was not absorbed in his presentation by the time he concluded. His credibility was phenomenal. Predictably, his sales record was equally solid and impressive.

As this experience suggests, an imaginative approach to visual aids often pays off. In this case, the exhibits were the key to the effectiveness of the presentation. They were not only revealing in themselves, but they gave an awkward speaker articles with which he was familiar and comfortable and which were capable of evoking his own kind of eloquence. He could not in a lifetime of practice have learned to speak so effectively with conventional slides, charts and graphs.

Obviously, we cannot always count on such a fortunate union of subject, visuals, and speaker. But it is always a good idea at some point in the process of preparing a presentation to let imagination range over the unexplored possibilities for a different approach to visual aids. In some cases, it may prove advantageous to develop different types of aids for different audiences or situations: models and physical exhibits for one type of occasion, charts and cards for another, slides for a third. It will help you develop a flexible, resilient approach that will improve your ability to handle changes and surprises. It is also advisable to give some thought and practice to how you would handle the situation if one—or all—of your visual aids should turn up missing just before you were scheduled to begin your presentation.

In their role of support to the spoken part of a presentation, visual aids are especially valuable in solving specific kinds of communication problems.

We have already mentioned the importance of audio-visual reinforcement of key presentation points with its dramatic effect on audience retention of information. As a part of the same effect, well-planned visual aids help the hearer identify the information the speaker considers important. The appearance of a chart or picture alerts the audience to the significance of its subject matter.

TYPES OF VISUAL AIDS

Visual aids are of greatest service when they are used to objectify, clarify and simplify, show relationships and comparisons, dramatize, add impact, create interest, increase retention, and improve understanding. They can also be effective shortcuts to comprehension. A picture can give an audience a clearer image of an unfamiliar object—its shape, size, color, texture, and comparison with other familiar objects—than many minutes of verbal description. A diagram can make a process comprehensible in seconds. A graph can demonstrate at a glance the meaning of otherwise meaningless statistics, reveal trends, and show unsuspected comparisons and contrasts among related phenomena.

Well-prepared visuals give succinct, memorable answers to the questions that arise continually in the hearers' minds as you speak. What does it look like? How does it work? What does it mean? How does it relate? What are its implications? Over the years speakers have developed an impressive array of visual tools for answering such questions as they arise.

The most natural form of visual aid, so commonplace it is often forgotten when mentioning different types, is *body language*. This includes movement, posture, gesture, and expression. These are dealt with in Chapter 8, but they are mentioned here to remind the reader of their essentially visual role in communication.

Handouts are among the simpler forms of prepared aids. A handout can be anything—a picture, agenda, budget, fact or work sheet, pamphlet, or the like—distributed to the audience for reference during the talk. Handouts serve to involve the listener in an immediate, personal way and can be valuable as a future reference in helping to recall information from the presentation. Their disadvantage is that they can be distracting during the parts of the presentation that do not refer directly to them.

The *demonstration,* once popular in selling, is another form of audio-visual communication that appears to have made a partial comeback in recent years. It is most commonly seen in TV commercials and in department stores where the speaker actually demonstrates the virtues of a tool, appliance, or utensil. This presentation has been expanded to include a handout of a food tidbit in some supermarket demonstrations, creating what might be called an audio-visual-olfactory-gustatory-tactile communication aid!

The *chalkboard* is undoubtedly the most common visual tool, familiar to most of us from our earliest school days. For the speaker who is comfortable with it, the chalkboard is a flexible, effective aid to communication. Using it seems informal, relaxed and spontaneous. Audiences usually relate well to use of the board, becoming involved in the process and anticipating the message as it is being written.

The *chart pad* can be used in very much the same way as the chalkboard, with felt pens or bright soft crayons instead of chalk. The chart pad is a large tablet of newsprint or drawing paper sheets, held together at the top edge, on an easel or stand. The visual message is written or drawn on the top sheet and, as each sheet is completed, it is either torn off or folded back over the top of the pad to expose the next sheet. The messages can be developed as the speaker goes along or prepared in advance and the sheets turned back to expose each message at the appropriate time. When used in this way, it is commonly called a *flip chart*.

Individual *charts, graphs, illustrations, maps,* blown-up *photographs* and similar graphic materials can be mounted on an easel or stand and exposed in much the same way as the individual exhibits of a flip chart.

The *felt board* or *flannel board* is a lightweight board, like a bulletin board, with a flannel surface on one side. Hooktape and magnetic surface boards are used in the same way. The individual exhibits, prepared in advance, are backed with flannel so that they adhere readily to the surface of the board when pressed against it and yet can be easily pulled off. The flannel board is especially convenient for putting together a diagram or other illustration a block at a time and for showing changes and modifications by shifting or changing the components.

All types of projections require more expensive, and sometimes complicated, equipment, considerable preparation, and reduced light for satisfactory results. One of the most popular, the *slide projection*, makes it possible to present all the vividness and detail of good photography in a format large enough to be viewed by a large audience. In the same general class are the *transparency*, for use with overhead projectors, and the *opaque projection*, for any nontransparent picture, illustration, text, or other flat graphic exhibit.

Similar to the slide series is the *slide strip* or *film strip:* a series of exhibits on a strip of movie film for projection a frame at a time. Less dynamic than a motion picture, these projections, when properly sequenced and paced, can nevertheless provide a sense of drama and action in depicting a procedure or process.

The ultimate audio-visual aid is the *motion picture film*, which can capture every nuance of a procedure or dramatic event, can freeze one instant of a high-speed action, or can compress to a few seconds a process that takes hours in real life, such as the unfolding of a flower.

A relative newcomer to the audio-visual field, *videotape*, may assume a position of much greater importance in the future. Basically a movie camera that employs magnetic tape instead of film and a TV monitor rather than a projector, the system has many of the advantages of audio-tape recording. No developing or printing is required, as with film, and the tape can be erased and reused. Scenes just recorded can be reviewed on instant replay, if desired, and erased and re-recorded until the required effect is achieved. For the present, however, its utility is limited by screen size, and, therefore, limit its use with large audiences.

With this brief survey of audio-visual aids, we will focus now on selection, design, and use of the principal types of aids.

The Chalkboard

One of the principal advantages of the chalkboard is its ubiquity—almost every organization, public hall and meeting room has either a fixed or a portable blackboard available. It is also familiar. The audience is not curious about it or distracted by it. In use, it stimulates audience interest and involvement in what is being written or drawn on it. This, in turn, provides the atmosphere of productive tension that often encourages a speaker to do the most effective job of communication.

The board's very familiarity can be a handicap, nonetheless, for speakers who tend to think of it as a prop rather than a tool. Sometimes the chalkboard becomes a barrier and a distraction rather than an aid to communication.

The fact that you are familiar and comfortable with the chalkboard should not keep you from planning your use of it as carefully as you would plan the use of any other visual aid. It should be used only for words, questions, headings, illustrations and similar visuals that clarify, intensify, or reinforce the key concepts of the presentation. Unless there is an overriding reason to do so, it is not generally a good idea to confront the audience at the outset with a board already covered with words, illustrations, or figures. Most audiences react negatively to such a display, possibly because it conjures up painful memories of final examinations. It is distracting because of the tendency to read or try to copy the material during the speaker's opening remarks. A brief agenda, slogan, or statement of theme or objective in one corner of the board can be helpful. But longer material usually should be handled in a different manner. If it cannot be simplified or condensed so that it can be put on the board without excessive disruption during the presentation, perhaps it should be distributed as a handout. If this is impractical and if it must be placed on the board ahead of time, then it might be worthwhile to cover the board with sheets of paper taped to the frame at the top. They can be removed one at a time at the appropriate point, exposing the block of material under discussion.

Writing on the board at great length should always be avoided if at all possible. Usually long material can be condensed by reducing it to key words and phrases. If longer material must be written on the board, it should be broken into short sections, with pauses for oral interjections, comments, and amplification.

As with other visual aids, legibility is a primary consideration in effective use of the chalkboard. Drawings should be large and simple. Words should preferably be printed in uppercase letters in a bold, plain, open style. It is easy for the speaker standing a few inches from the board to forget how small the letters look from the back of the room. With a little practice, most people can learn the art of writing or printing rapidly and legibly on a chalkboard, automatically adjusting the scale to room size. As a rule of thumb, the smallest letters should be no less than 1½ inches high, and the largest twice that size,

Figure 10.4

The relative perceived sizes of a letter as the viewer moves farther away should demonstrate the importance of proper letter sizes in a presentation.

to be read easily at a distance of about 25 feet. Figure E demonstrates the importance of proper letter size. With a little experimentation, one can learn to use this standard as a rough guide to the size required for greater or lesser distances. Legibility is enhanced at all distances by making sure the chalk is blunt enough to yield a good heavy line. Colored chalk adds brightness and variety; it can also be used to distinguish between different points.

Many speakers forget that it is important to be as adept with the eraser as with the chalk. Nothing is quite so distracting as a blackboard covered with material that has been thoroughly discussed and is no longer pertinent or — worse — material left over from a prior speaker's presentation.

Speakers tend to employ one of two general approaches: the building-block, in which one idea or detail is added to what has gone before until a complete outline or model has been developed, and the point-to-point approach, in which each idea is developed independently of what has gone before and what follows. The building-block approach sometimes requires that the key points, at least, be left on the board or recapitulated at one side of it. But the more common and informal point-to-point style is compatible with the relaxed, spontaneous flow of chalkboard communication. Where possible, it is probably best to stay close to the center of the board, erasing each block of material as you finish with it in order to signal the closing of that point and to make room for the next one.

The importance of developing good platform habits and not permitting oneself to become careless in their use is especially evident in chalkboard communication. The speaker needs to be aware constantly of the danger of blocking off the visual material from the view of some persons as well as of the necessity to maintain as much eye contact as possible. These are not easy goals to pursue simultaneously. At first it may seem quite awkward to write or draw without facing the board and keeping one's eyes on the work. However, most people learn rather quickly to stand well to one side of the work, still half-facing the audience, without looking continuously at the work. The countenance is still visible to the audience, and a semblance of contact is maintained. The sense of contact is heightened if the speaker continues to talk while writing or drawing.

The chalkboard is certainly not the answer to all visual-aid problems. There are some, such as those requiring graphic precision, to which it is distinctly unsuited. But it is convenient, flexible, and, with an imaginative and practiced speaker, a powerful communication aid. Its principal psychological advantage is the informal, workmanlike tone it contributes to audio-visual communication.

The Chart

We have already commented briefly on the variety of styles and names applied to the charts used as visual aids — chart pads, flip charts, individual charts and exhibits, illustration charts, and so on. For convenience, we will deal with the various types of graphs in a separate section. Like a chalkboard, a chart provides a surface upon which a message can be either placed during the presentation or prepared ahead of time. The chart has two principal advantages over the chalkboard. It is compatible with printing and with formal art processes, enabling it to project a neater, more precise and more professional image. It is also permanent and can be used repeatedly, if desired.

The familiar flip chart is this type. Frequently used as a key-point outline of a standard presentation, the flip chart in its simplest form may be no more than a series of cards or sheets, each printed with a condensed topic point. As each point is discussed, its chart is flipped over to the back of the pad, exposing the next one. Flip charts can be considerably more elaborate than that, of course, employing photographic blowups, art work, cartoons, graphs, maps, pictograms — in fact, anything that can be drawn or printed.

The informality of the chalkboard can be achieved with the chart by printing or drawing the graphics on a pad of blank sheets. As each is completed it is either folded back or torn off. Some speakers, who wish to maintain overall continuity and who like to refer to earlier points, attach each sheet to the wall or lectern with masking tape as it is torn off. Particularly when different colored felt pens are used to define different ideas, this practice lends color, unity and interest to the presentation.

Flip charts come in a variety of sizes, some of them too large to handle conveniently. At the other end of the scale are eight-by-ten-inch desk-top formats that are too small for anything but one-to-one or small-group presentations. At their largest, charts are seldom satisfactory for audiences of more than seventy-eighty persons.

The Graph

A graph is a special kind of chart that is especially useful in simplifying complex relationships. A graph brings our geometric sense into play to reinforce our ability to visualize quantities, proportions, comparisons and trends. Graphs convey the idea of process, of change, or of interaction as few other communication devices can.

A text author who wishes to present a set of values in an orderly, concise manner may choose to arrange them in a *table*. Tabulated data enable the reader to locate exact figures rapidly, but it requires interpretive study to determine relationships and trends. Except in their most simplified form, however, tables are almost invariably confusing when used as a visual aid before an audience. By referring to a table of reported crimes in the United States year by year, it can be ascertained that the FBI reported exactly 1,026,284 violent crimes in 1975 and 969,823 in 1974. Then, by referring to each year separately, the upward trend over the years can be recognized.

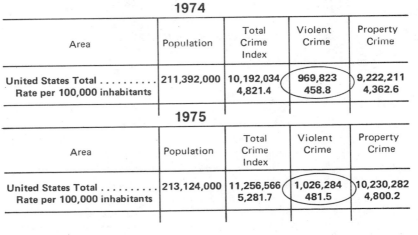

1974

Area	Population	Total Crime Index	Violent Crime	Property Crime
United States Total . . . . Rate per 100,000 inhabitants	211,392,000	10,192,034 4,821.4	969,823 458.8	9,222,211 4,362.6

1975

Area	Population	Total Crime Index	Violent Crime	Property Crime
United States Total . . . . Rate per 100,000 inhabitants	213,124,000	11,256,566 5,281.7	1,026,284 481.5	10,230,282 4,800.2

Figure 10.5
"Excerpts from FBI Crime Index Tables showing an upward trend in violent crime from 1974-1975."

On a conventional *line graph*, the trend would be instantly apparent, although there probably would be some loss of precision in establishing the exact numerical value of each plotted point. One could determine that the crime figure for 1974 was a little more than 950,000, and for 1975 a little more than 1,000,000. Ordinarily this is close enough for the purposes of audio-visual presentation, where the emphasis is more apt to be on trends and general magnitudes than on precise figures. The exact figure can be given orally or printed on the graph adjacent to the point at which it is plotted, if desired.

Typically, a line graph shows how a quantity changes with the passage of time. Each space to the right of the starting point, for example, might represent the passage of one day; each space upward, an appropriate unit of measurement of the changing quantity. Thus, as Figure 10.6 indicates,

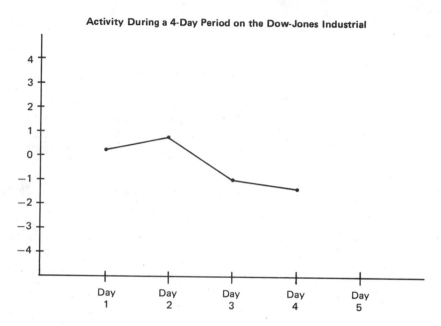

Figure 10.6
Line graph showing Dow Jones averages as a function of time. Note that for each unit of measure on the vertical (Y) axis a mark corresponding to that number is placed above the appropriate unit of measure on the horizontal (X) axis, thus lending the continuity or the appearance of trends.

if you were plotting the daily Dow Jones Industrials averages, each day you would move one space to the right of the day before and then up (or down) to the level corresponding to the Dow Jones average for the period. You would know at a glance whether it exhibited a definable trend.

The same principle applies whether you are graphing the Dow Jones averages, the temperature, or the number of automobiles sold by an agency. The graph relates one phenomenon to another. The second is usually the passage of time, but it need not be. It would be possible, for example, to plot automobile sales against temperature, unemployment, or sunspots, although in each case one of the variables would undoubtedly incorporate a time factor (*e.g.,* sales per hour at a given temperature.)

A second popular type of graph is the *pictorial,* or pictograph. A pictorial graph combines the virtues of illustration with the advantages of the line or bar graph. It conveys magnitude or comparison by utilizing appropriate visual symbols, drawings, or photographs in various sizes or repetitions. Its clarity and eye appeal have made the pictorial graph a favorite among writers of social science textbooks and editors of newsmagazines. Many of us can remember first visualizing the relative military strength of European nations during specific periods through the familiar pictorial map. A larger or smaller drawing of a soldier indicated the comparative size of each nation's army. There were also the agricultural products maps, with the little rows of pigs and sheep, rounds of cheese, and sheaves of wheat. If the army of one state was twice as large as that of another, its representative soldier was twice as large as the other country's. If it produced a third as many pigs as its neighbor, its row of pigs was one-third as long.

In addition to its clarifying role, the pictorial graph can be a powerful rhetorical device. A number in a table or a line on a conventional graph does not convey nearly the emotional impact of a row of coffins, grave markers, or smashed automobiles in dramatizing our national toll in fatal automobile accidents.

Figure 10.7
Line graph, picture graph.

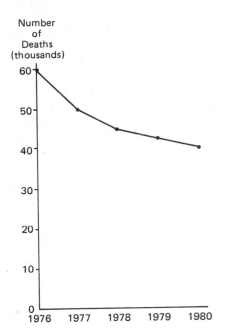

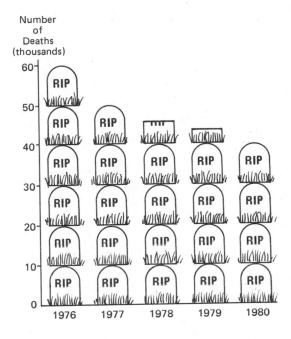

While the pictorial can be more persuasive than other types of statistical or graphic presentation, it is usually a poor vehicle for depicting quantity with any precision. A proportional pictorial graph would show Germany's army to be a great deal larger than Switzerland's in 1939—but how much larger? three times? ten times? fifty times? For most people, it's hard to judge how much larger one illustration is than another. Where quantity is depicted by repeating the symbolic unit, as on the agricultural products map, viewers often have only a hazy idea of the size of the units or the total number represented. A pig population of 931,750 in one country and of 612,200 in another might be represented by pictures of nine and one-third and six and one-eighth animals, respectively. One could tell at a glance that the first figure is larger by half than the second, but the fact that each symbol represented 100,000 animals, and that the totals were between a half-million and a million, would probably not make much of an impression.

For these reasons, the pictorial is often used in combination with other graph styles. A line or bar graph, for example, may be combined with pictures and figures to increase the communication level. Thus, the heroic accomplishment of the first country in the following illustration to double the pig population in three years might be shown on a line graph, rising from about 450,000 at the beginning of 1977 to more than 930,000 at the end of 1979. At the lower (beginning) end of the plot line would be a small pig with the caption "1977—

Figure 10.8
*Pig populations using
picture graph.*

453,100"; at the 1978 intersection, a larger pig captioned "1978—625,900";
and at the upper end of the line, a monstrous pig with the caption "1979—
931,750." The figures, the size of the symbols, and the steepness of the line
convey far more information more memorably than any one of them standing
alone. Still, there is a danger in this approach, too. It is easy to get carried
away with the number of details that might be included and to wind up with
a graph so complicated that it communicates nothing except confusion.

The *circle graph,* so dear to the hearts of economists, is the familiar pie
with different width wedges showing how the budget is divided up. The circle

Figure 10.9
*"Circle graph,
commonly used by
economists, showing
state and local
government expendi-
tures. Note that the
size of each sector is
proportional to the
percentage of the
budget allocated for
the corresponding
uses, thus enabling
the reader to visualize
the various relation-
ships between
sectors."*

graph is not a trend graph; it is a static proportion graph, indicating how a fixed total is allotted and how the various allotments relate to each other and to the whole.

By its nature, the circle graph is restricted to large, general categories. If you try to break it down into details, it becomes unreadable; the wedges become so small that they are no longer useful for comparison. But regardless of the size of the wedges, the circle graph represents a whole, and the total of its parts must add up to 100 percent.

The last general style of graph, the *bar graph,* is another device that does an excellent job of demonstrating comparisons and contrasts, although it is less effective at conveying trends and precise values. The grid and plotting for a bar graph are similar to those for the line graph. However, instead of the plotted points connected with a line, each point is used to mark the height of a bar indicating the amount of the measured quality under the conditions defined by the variable against which it is measured. The bar graph is an excellent device for showing the relative standing of a single variable from day to day or month to month, or of several variables at a single point in time. For example, a bar graph could show a dealer's sale of Cadillacs month by month (Figure K.1.), or a comparison of the sale of Cadillacs, Buicks, Oldsmobiles, Pontiacs and Chevrolets during a particular month (Figure 10.10-2).

Figure 10.10
"Two bar graphs representing car sales. Notice that comparisons may be made between a single variable at different points in time (A), or between several variables at a single point in time."

1.
Number of Cars Sold

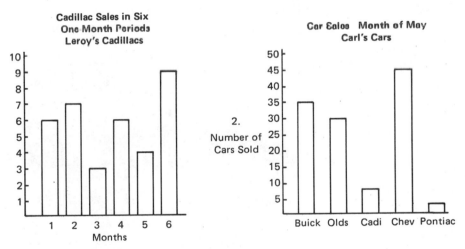

Like the line graph, the bar graph can depict negative results when the bars extend downward from the zero line (or to the left of it on a horizontally oriented graph).

Even at their simplest, graphs require at least a moment of orientation for the viewer to get into the symbolic frame of reference. Which variable is along which axis? What are the units of measurements? What kind of trend is indicated by a rising or falling line? The viewer is ready to deal with the meaning of the graph only after such basic reference points have been grasped. Difficult as it is for some speakers to wait, it is essential that the audience be given time to make this adjustment before plunging ahead. Often the speaker can help by identifying the variables and the axis with which each is associated, thus giving a clue to the overall trend the graph depicts.

Projections

When the audience is too large for a chart or chalkboard presentation, the only practical solution usually is some type of projected image. This makes it possible to blow up a small visual to virtually any size required. It is a main advantage of projections, but they can be used effectively with audiences of any size.

The basic projector principle has not changed significantly since the days of the magic lantern and stereopticon, a century ago. The essential component is a closed compartment containing a bright light. This is projected through a transparent visual or reflected from the surface of an opaque one and then through a lens system. The latter is adjustable so that the resulting image can be focused on a screen at a distance from the projector. In general, the greater the distance, the larger the image, although some projectors with special lenses can create a very large, often somewhat distorted, image over a relatively small distance.

There are several basic types of still projectors, the most popular in recent years being the *slide projector,* the *opaque projector,* and the *overhead projector.* Each has definite advantages and disadvantages with which you should be familiar before deciding whether to use a projector and what type. All of them work best in a darkened room. All of them require equipment that is relatively expensive, take up space in the meeting room, require an adjacent electrical outlet or an extension cord, and creates transportation and storage problems. On the other hand, projectors as a whole are among the most effective visual-aid tools the speaker has.

Photo 10.2
Slide Projector

The *slide projector* is the universal standby. It employs a photo transparency held in a standard two-by-two-inch cardboard or plastic frame. A slide can be made from anything that can be photographed, including charts, graphs, models, drawings, and the like. A slide can be in color or black and white, and the image usually can be projected many times the original size without unacceptable loss of quality.

A well-organized slide presentation can be absorbing and impressive. At the same time, there are drawbacks and problems of which the speaker should be aware before planning to use slides. Not all photographs make good slides. Overexposed, underexposed, or low-contrast pictures usually do not turn out well as slides. A series made up of slides of uneven quality or brightness can become distracting or annoying to the audience. Slides containing details, such as lettering, that cannot be read easily when held at a distance of one foot or more are apt to present legibility problems when projected.

Moreover, the speaker sometimes has difficulty competing with the attention-riveting power of good, interesting, colorful slides in a darkened room, where the visual sense takes precedence over the aural and feedback is hard to assess. Nevertheless, the slide presentation remains among the most effective of communication aids.

Photo 10.3
Opaque Projector

The *opaque projector* eliminates some of the disadvantages of the slide projector—primarily those involved in photographic processing in the preparation of slides. In the opaque projector, the image is created by light reflected from the surface of an opaque visual rather than projected through a transparent one. The size of the material is therefore not so restricted, and it can be much more informally prepared. A drawing, photograph, or a page from a book or magazine can serve.

The disadvantages of the opaque projector are that it is a bulky, noisy machine, hard to set up where it doesn't block somebody's view and requiring a darker room than a slide or overhead projector for satisfactory results.

Photo 10.4
Overhead Projector

The *overhead projector* in many ways represents a compromise among the advantages and disadvantages of the slide and opaque projectors. It can be used satisfactorily in a much lighter room than either of the other projectors, it is quieter than an opaque projector, and the visuals are considerably easier to prepare than slides if you have access to a copying machine.

In the overhead projector, light is directed upward through a lens to focus it on the screen. The standard transparency is a ten-by-ten-inch sheet of clear film upon which the image can be fixed in most copying machines or drawn or written with a grease pencil. The copy is readily accessible during projection. It is easy to cover all or part of it with a sheet of paper and expose the points you want to discuss one at a time.

Unfortunately, the overhead projector is unwieldy to handle or to place where it doesn't block the view for a part of the audience. Because they are designed to project a fairly large image at fairly close range, overhead projectors are usually aimed upward at a relatively large angle, so that the lower edge of the image on a vertical screen is significantly closer to the projector than the top edge, giving the projected image a wedge shape, or keystone effect. This annoying distortion can be counteracted to some extent by tilting the top of the screen toward the audience.

In the long run, the key to effective visual aids is the same as the key to any other part of communication — good visual materials are the product of careful planning and testing ahead of time. Before committing yourself to a type of visual, you should review the advantages and disadvantages of each to determine which is most appropriate to your requirements. Each visual should be analyzed in detail to make sure that it contributes to the presentation objective, does not detract or distract, and has the requisite qualities of clarity and legibility. When the visuals are all assembled they should be reviewed as a group for overall coherence and consistency. And finally, they should be viewed under conditions as nearly like those under which they will be presented.

As a final point, the guideline that applies to all communication, "When in doubt, leave it out," applies with especial force to visual materials.

VISUAL COMMUNICATION: ESSENTIAL CONSIDERATIONS

I. Visual Aids Increase
   A. Perception
   B. Attention
   C. Understanding
   D. And Often Interest

II. Kinds of Visual Aids
   —Nonprojected—
   A. Handout
   B. Demonstration
   C. Chalkboard
   D. Chart
   E. Felt Board

III. —Projected—
   A. Slide Projection
   B. Film
   C. Closed Circuit TV
   D. Opaque
   E. Overheads

IV. Materials for Visual Aids
   A. Maps
   B. Graphs

V. Using Visual Aids
   A. Be sure everyone can see the aid
   B. Make the aid as simple as possible
   C. Check accuracy
   D. Use professional appearing aids
   E. Don't let the aid distract from your message
   F. Use dark heavy lines
   G. Remove aid when you have completed your discussion pertaining to it
   H. Use a pointer
   I. Talk to your audience and not to your visual aid

NOTES

[1] Edgar B. Wycoff, "Why Visuals?" in *Audio-Visual Communications*, Vol. 11, No. 4, April 1977, pp. 39, 59.

[2] For an excellent summary of these studies, see Berelson, B. and G. Steiner, *Human Behavior: An Inventory of Scientific Findings*, 2nd Edition (New York: Harcourt, Brace & World, 1978).

[3] Knower, P., F. Phillips, D. and Keoppel, F., "Studies in Listening to Informative Speaking," *Journal of Abnormal and Social Psychology.* (Jan. 1945), pp. 82-88.

SUGGESTED READINGS

Brown, J. W.; R. B. Lewis; and F. F. Harcleroad. *AV Instruction: Media and Methods.* New York: McGraw-Hill Book Co., 1969.

Wilcox, R. P. *Communication at Work: Writing and Speaking.* Boston: Houghton Mifflin Co., 1977.

U. S. Civil Service Commission. *Visual Materials: Guidelines for Selection and Use in Training Situations.* U. S. Government Printing Office, 1971.

An irritating habit of mine, I've often been told by my closest friends or relatives, is to underline a passionate statement on whatever subject is under discussion with the question, "Do you HEAR me?" What I'm subconsciously asking the person, of course, is not just to listen but to "hear" my undertones, the implications.

On my desk now is a pioneering study which confirms that my question has not been as odd as it has appeared to be. For tests made as part of the study disclose that immediately after listening to a 10-minute oral presentation the average consumer or employee has heard, understood, properly evaluated and retained only half of what was said. Within 48 hours, that sinks by another 50 percent.

The final level of effectiveness—comprehension and retention—is only 25 percent! Even worse, as ideas are communicated from one person to the next, they can become distorted by 80 percent.

With 100 million workers in our nation, a simple $10 listening mistake by each would cost business $1 billion!

The financial toll of poor listening is enormous. Thus, more and more corporations are actively looking for solutions. Chairman and Chief Executive Officer J. Paul Lyet of Sperry Corp. (producer of Sperry Univac computers and other capital equipment products) is a leader in expanding the corporation's commitment to improve the quality of listening among its 87,000 employees.

"Poor listening is one of the most significant problems facing business today," says Lyet. "Business relies on its communication system, and when it breaks down, mistakes can be very costly. Corporations pay for their mistakes in lower profits, while consumers pay in higher prices."

If you're a poor listener, you're much more apt to make mistakes on important business matters. Letters must be retyped, appointments rescheduled and shipments reshipped—all because the proper information wasn't heard, or understood, when first given.

If you're the majority, though, you don't overrate your own listening abilities. For instance, 85 percent of those asked rate

Listening 11

themselves as "average" listeners or less, while fewer than 5 percent rate themselves as "superior" or "excellent."

But your listening ability can be improved. In the few schools which have adopted listening programs, listening comprehension among students has as much as doubled in a few months.
*—Sylvia Porter, "Now Hear This: Americans are Poor Listeners," **Tampa Tribune** (November 15, 1979), p. 15-A.*

The attention given again to listening in recent years is dramatized by Ms. Porter's article and by a series of television commercials currently being run by Sperry Corp. Many people tend to regard listening as a natural, taken-for-granted skill and to assign speakers the responsibility to get and retain listener attention. If the audience goes to sleep, the speaker is assumed to have failed. This assumption has an element of truth. Some degree of audience receptivity is certainly a condition for the kind of listening required for meaningful communication. It is also true that a speaker who wants attentive listeners will make the message as interesting, intriguing, challenging, frightening, or entertaining as possible.

For most purposes, this conventional view is quite serviceable. It fits well with the familiar portrayal of the communication process as a sort of simple telephone system. Words from the speaker's lips enter the process as the input and emerge as an output at the receiver's ear. This model is useful in helping to visualize the mechanics of the process. It also makes it simpler to deal separately with its three basic elements—sender, medium, and receiver.

At the same time, this model's clarity and simplicity reinforces the false assumption that communication is a kind of transmission belt for moving packages of meaning from one bin to another. As effective communicators have known intuitively in all ages, and as modern communication science is making increasingly apparent, that is simply not the way communication works. The real dynamics of the process are quite different, far subtler and more interesting than the telephone analogy suggests.

MEANING AND MESSAGES The telephone analogy implies a conduit system into which meaning pours from one receptacle and, if everything works as it should, out of which the same meaning empties into another. A better analogy, perhaps, is suggested by a coffee-table toy observed on the desk of a colleague. It consisted of a simple open frame with a crossbar from which several steel balls were suspended on strings. At rest, the balls touched each other in a straight line. If you swung the end ball so that it struck the one next in line squarely, the impulse traveled instantly down the line to the ball at the other end. It would swing out in an excursion proportional to the swing of the first ball, which would swing out and back . . . and so on, until the input energy was dissipated. Meanwhile, the intervening balls remained stationary. Apparently what was transmitted through the system was not the motion of the first ball but a quantum of energy that evoked a corresponding motion in the ball at the other end of the system.

Something similar to this, on a vastly more complicated scale, seems to take place in the communication process. The sender begins with the objective of producing a certain response in the receiver. In order to accomplish this, the receiver's perceptions and motivation must be affected in some way. An understanding or meaning appropriate to the sender's purpose must be called up in the receiver's mind. But *meanings* are not what is transmitted in the communication process—any more than swinging motion is transmitted through the stationary steel balls of the kinetic energy model. What the communication process transmits is *messages,* and there is a crucial difference between a meaning and a message.

A message is a symbolic representation of a meaning. It is pictures, gestures, sounds, printed or spoken words, etc. that the communicator selects to represent the meaning to be communicated. The speaker encodes the meaning in a message and transmits the message; the hearer decodes and interprets the meaning. Every step in the process is essential to effective communication, but the critical operation to which all the others must be adjusted is the listener's decoding and interpretation. No matter how brilliantly the message has been encoded and transmitted, it will be a communication failure if the decoder does not interpret the symbols in the same way the encoder does. That's why the receiver is often described as the most important factor in the communication process and why it is so often reiterated that the message that counts is the message that is *received.*

Effective listening, therefore, is a basic communication skill. The object of improving speaking skills is to enhance the quality of the listening process and to compensate for distractions and listening deficiencies in the audience. It is safe to assume that effective listeners are better interviewers than poor listeners. The same assumption, although less obvious, is equally true of conference speaking and public speaking. Since understanding of the listening process is a prerequisite for effective communication, perhaps the best place to start is with an examination of the reasons people listen, and the reasons they don't listen, to a particular message.

BARRIERS TO EFFECTIVE LISTENING

The conscious reasons for listening are many and varied. Frequently we listen out of curiosity or general interest in the topic or the speaker, or we listen out of respect or sympathy for the speaker, even when the topic doesn't interest us. We have all had the experience of lending a sympathetic ear for no other reason than our recognition that the other person needs to talk. On the other hand, we have all also had the experience of falling into a conversation that—because of the occasion, topic, mood, or personalities involved—engaged our full attention and interest. At such times, our perceptions become sharply focused. Outside distractions are tuned out and we lose track of the passage of time. We are extraordinarily alert to meanings and nuances. We seize upon opportunities to encourage the speaker or to make our own responses. This is the kind of concentrated, involved listening that every speaker hopes for. Sometimes it occurs spontaneously. More often it results from a combination of skilled speaker, topic interest, and receptive listener, with speaker and audience making a joint effort to achieve the most effective communication possible.

Ultimately, of course, the key element is the listener's interest in the topic. In the long run, no amount of platform technique and no amount of audience decorum will compel attention if the listener is not interested and sees no benefit to be derived from listening. The listener who is interested in the subject or sees something to be gained from listening, on the other hand, may be able to maintain attention even when the presentation is poor, as generations of bored students can testify.

Usually, however, a part or all of the communication is lost because the listener, for one reason or another, is not listening or, if listening, doesn't "hear" the message or decode it correctly. The reason may be physical—words that, at least to the listener's perception, are slurred or inaudible. The loss of a few words may distort or destroy the meaning of a whole sentence or paragraph. Then, while the listener is puzzling over the missed meaning, additional meaning is lost. The same kind of loss can occur when the speaker uses words the listener is not familiar with or uses them in an unfamiliar connotation.

External Distractions

External distractions also take a toll on effective listening. Background sights and sounds are sometimes tuned out when one's attention is fully engaged, but it doesn't always work that way. Sometimes the distracting element overpowers the automatic tune-out mechanism and even our best conscious efforts to ignore it. Most people have had the experience of trying to concentrate on a performance or speaker while people in adjacent seats carry on an audible conversation. Sometimes it seems as if the very effort to concentrate, combined with annoyance at the rudeness of the disrupters, defeats the effort.

Refutation

Another type of distraction involves a discrepancy that is inherent in the verbal communication process itself. Speakers rarely speak at a rate of more than 200 words per minute. The average is 125-175 words per minute. Most listeners, on the other hand, are capable of comprehending a message delivered four times that fast. The average speaker's words, therefore, command one-fourth or less of the listener's reception capability. What does the active, acquisitive mind do while it is idling at quarter-throttle? If the speaker or listener, or both, are very effective, the extra capacity may be taken up with extracting the fullest possible meaning and connotation from each word and phrase. Generally, however, it is more likely to be occupied with extraneous details, such as the speaker's dress or mannerisms, other people in the room, sensory impressions, past or upcoming events, worries, speculations, daydreams, and the like.

Sometimes the mind's extra energy is engaged in a type of response that can have either a positive or a negative effect on listening effectiveness. In this type of response, the listener is continually analyzing or anticipating the speaker's points. Done properly, this is an invaluable listening technique for the debater or polemical speaker and an asset to any listener. It consists of the habit of critical listening—of simultaneously receiving, decoding and analyzing the speaker's message. Skilled debaters often develop their rebuttal while the opponent's argument is being presented, without missing a word of the presentation.

More often, the listener unconsciously tunes the speaker out while formulating a response or counterargument. A part of the message is lost or imperfectly received, and the listener's understanding and response may well be inappropriate to what the speaker actually says. Even in casual conversation, we often miss a good deal of the other participant's message because we are only waiting for a pause in which to insert our own message. The other person might as well not be speaking, because the communication lines are down. The listener is thinking only about what he or she is going to reply. Speakers need to consider how they can send their messages to avoid refutation. They can build into their speech what the opposition claims and deal with the opposition's arguments. In interpersonal settings the speaker can shorten his or her comments to allow more interaction.

Emotion

Emotional resistance to the message or speaker is another barrier to effective listening. Hearing only what one wants to hear is a common failing, and so is not hearing what one doesn't want to hear. It can be acutely uncomfortable to listen to ideas that attack one's value system or to speakers one finds offensive. It is so disagreeable to some people that they will not listen to speakers they dislike or with whom they disagree. If they cannot remove themselves physically from the sound of the speaker's voice, they listen from behind such forbidding siegeworks that any idea making it over the walls is certain to be hustled off to the torture chamber.

Most people are aware of this listener reaction and make adjustments for it in their communication. It is this instinct that accounts for the well-documented fact that, contrary to the popular assumption, bad news travels very poorly, at least in the upward channels in organizations.[1] Not only are subordinates reluctant to tell the boss bad news, the boss doesn't want to hear it. From the lower echelons to the company president, all members of management have some degree of emotional involvement in the organization's well-being. Any implication that it isn't functioning properly is apt to be heard as a reflection on management competence. It is an automatic defensive reflex for the company president who is informed of low morale and complaints on the assembly line to want to know who was responsible for hiring malcontents. Any threat of a work stoppage is pretty sure to be identified as labor trouble, not management trouble, and attributed to outside agitators.

A related form of emotional resistance results from ingrained bias and stereotyped thinking habits. The delicate decoding process is affected by what the listener believes about an array of subjects ranging from race to cosmology. The listener who believes strongly that crime is basically an ethnic problem or that poverty is the just punishment of the indolent and the immoral will probably receive a far different message from a sociological discourse on crime and poverty than a listener who has no such strong preconceptions. Everyone has biases on some subjects, and it is probably unrealistic to expect to eliminate bias completely from one's thinking. The most we can hope to do—and the best training we could ask for in effective listening and clear thinking—is to cultivate the habit of seeking out and examining calmly ideas that offend, infuriate, and frighten us. Not only does this help to reduce the power that abhorrent ideas exercise over our emotions, but it also helps to identify the astonishing number of biases most of us harbor. An awareness of the areas in which one is apt to react emotionally is an enormous aid to effective listening.

Unsupported Inference

Snap judgments and hasty inferences can be an equally serious threat to effective listening. The listener who "knows exactly what the speaker is going to say" because of the speaker's opening words, appearance, manner or reputation, is not likely to hear anything new in the message, even if it's there. There are times when it is necessary to make a judgment before all the evidence is in, of course. We always have to weigh the urgency of getting on with things against the seriousness of a possible mistake. Unsteadiness and slurred speech are commonly associated with intoxication, but on occasion they are symptoms of a far more serious problem. To ignore an offensive remark at a party because its author appears to be drunk is a different order of judgment than, as a police officer, to lock the individual up on the same evidence.

There is hardly ever enough data to make an absolute judgment to which there are no exceptions. There are extremes on both sides of a reasonable caution. This is neatly illustrated by the story of a scientist, renowned for his skepticism, who was on a train with a rather self-important student and a lad away from home for the first time. The latter remarked naively, "Isn't it interesting that all of the cows in this part of the country are brown?" "You should say," the student corrected him, "that at least the cows you have seen from the train window are brown," to which the scientist appended dryly, "On at least one side."

Under the circumstances, it was no doubt a deserved put-down. Most people would probably agree that it's rash to assume that all cows in the neighborhood look like the few you have seen. On the other hand, it's a reliable observation that most cows are the same color all the way around.

Suspicion

Suspicion of the speaker's motives is another serious hindrance to effective listening. If the message objective is not clear and plausible, the listener's automatic barriers are apt to go up. If you respond to the doorbell to find a smiling stranger offering you a free gift, you have good reason for suspicion, as well as resentment at the insult to your intelligence. But if the stranger explains that the gift is offered by his or her company to anyone who will agree to hear a fifteen-minute sales presentation, you can make a rational judgment whether the gift is worth fifteen minutes of your time and a test of your sales resistance. Never mind that the real motive could be to case your house to see whether it's worth robbing; the explanation offered is reasonable enough to satisfy most ordinary purposes. Ultimately, listening is a voluntary activity; it won't take place if the listener perceives no identifiable self-interest in the message.

This does not mean that an audience will listen only when messages of life-and-death consequence are being transmitted. Attention can be directed, briefly at least, by idle curiosity, a desire to be entertained, or some other less-than-earthshaking motivation. But such listening is usually fickle and transitory. This is why successful entertainers try to keep their material short and varied. It is why an opening that piques the curiosity must lead into something of more substantial interest before the initial attention is lost. In general, the intensity of the listening process is proportional to the perceived self-interest of the listener, with speaking and listening proficiency as valuable secondary factors.

Energy

Effective listening is work. We realize how much energy it requires when we try to concentrate on receiving a message when we are tired and sleepy or when we have been listening for a long period without a break. Gradually, external distractions become harder to ignore; internal distractions, like worries, irritation, reveries and tangential thoughts, take over more easily. This is why experienced conference leaders provide a seventh-inning stretch at appropriate points in a long agenda. Speakers who are alert to audience feedback try to provide the same kind of brief diversion and relaxation when they detect signs of listener fatigue. Sometimes this can be done by changing pace or tone, by injecting an anecdote or humorous interlude, or by getting the listeners to look at something that is not on the platform, to shift positions or to stand up for a moment. If the listeners are genuinely interested, but tired, almost anything that provides a brief respite from the effort of maintaining continuous attention will pay off in renewed alertness.

There are almost as many factors that can contribute to inattention as there are individual listeners, but the ones we have mentioned are among the most common: lack of interest in the topic, imperfect understanding of terms and concepts used by the speaker, external and internal distractions, the discrepancy between speech rate and listening capability, preoccupation with response or rebuttal, emotional resistance or hostility to the speaker or message, bias and prejudgment, suspicion of the speaker's motives, and fatigue. Harold P. Zelko, an internationally known communication consultant, suggests what both speaker and listener should do to improve his or her effectiveness when confronted by these barriers.

Avoiding Barriers to Communication

What speaker should do	Barriers	What listener should do
1. Speak at level of listener's status, interests, experiences, frame of reference	1. Different status, position, self-experiences, frame of reference	1. Think in terms of speaker's status, interests, experiences, frame of reference
2. Adapt to listener's feelings	2. Emotion and prejudices	2. Dispel feelings and prejudices
3. Use common ground and "you" attitude	3. "I" versus "you" attitude	3. Develop "you" attitude
4. Make changes seem attractive	4. Resistance to change	4. Be open-minded
5. Organize clearly for understanding	5. Refuting rather than understanding	5. Listen to understand, not to refute
6. Develop ideas for listener's interest	6. "Extra" time for listening	6. Use listening time constructively
7. Use listener's level of language	7. Language	7. Analyze speaker's language
8. Think logically	8. Crooked thinking	8. Think logically

Zelko, H. P. The Business Conference: Leadership and Participation, ©1969, McGraw-Hill Book Company, Reprinted by Permission.

PUBLIC SPEAKING SETTING One of the speaker's primary responsibilities is to make it as easy as possible for the listener to listen. This apparently simple concept is often difficult for inexperienced speakers to grasp, particularly if their models are taken from the great orations of the past, which are sometimes better examples of literature than of speech.

This means that the speaker's listening skill must have at least two dimensions. It involves the speaker's ability both to listen effectively and to empathize with the listening processes of the audience. In addition to the general factors that affect listening effectiveness — such as acoustics, temperature, physical comfort, and outside distractions — each individual and each audience present special listening problems. A speaker should know as much as possible about the composition of each audience in order to gauge the probable range of attitudes toward the topic, areas of special sensitivity, possible language or vocabulary problems, and so on.

One of the most entertaining young men I have known once asked me to evaluate his public speaking ability because he was dissatisfied with the response he was getting from audiences. "I get good laughs and good feedback," he said, "but in the end it never seems to be enough, and I don't get invited back." His description turned out to be deadly accurate. He kept us chuckling throughout his remarks. Apart from one or two humorous comments about the speech title he had been given, however, we were as much in the dark about his communication purpose at the end of his speech as we had been at the beginning. Consciously or unconsciously, we were all waiting for him to get to the point. The interest level ebbed a little with every minute that he failed to do so, and even our willingness to be entertained would have been exhausted if his sense of timing hadn't prompted him to stop first. When he sat down without having come to the point, his audience was disappointed and left hanging, still not sure what his purpose had been. The audience was being served a meal that included everything from soup to dessert . . . except the main course. This man became an effective speaker when he learned to structure his speech around a solid topic point, using humor to give it life and sparkle.

Inertia

The speaker should also consider the effect of natural psychological inertia on the receptivity of a given audience. We know that generally most people respond better to ideas they perceive as positive than to those they perceive as negative; they would rather hear things that reflect well upon them than things that don't; given two courses, they are more likely to choose the one that requires the least change in their own habits and attitudes. Even people who are dissatisfied with the conditions around them and want to see sweeping changes are usually highly selective in picking their targets. The effective speaker needs as specific an image as possible of the areas the listeners will perceive as positive or negative and what changes they regard as desirable, or at least tolerable. The message that challenges the listener's inertia least has the greatest chance of getting a sympathetic hearing.

Audience Members Responding to Others

We are all familiar with another phenomenon that affects the listening process: the contagion of human response. When one person yawns, others in the group are almost certain to follow suit. People listening to recorded laughter will usually begin to laugh, even when they have no idea what the original laughter is about. Anger and fear provoke corresponding responses. Speakers through the ages have taken advantage of the contagious quality of human reactions by using plants and shills to prompt the kind of response they desire. The recorded laugh track is a modern example of this time-honored practice.

Audience Receptivity

The speaker must never forget that, second only to the message itself, the principal task is to make it as easy and agreeable as possible for the listener to receive the message in the most positive light possible. This is the purpose of audience analysis: getting an accurate picture of the age, sex, educational level, social and economic status, life style, work, interests, outlook and aspirations of the listeners. The message cannot suddenly displace or rip across the fabric of the listener's convictions, values, and habits. It has to be woven into them, displacing as little as possible, clashing as little as possible. Even then, it may be rejected, but it has at least had the advantage of being received and considered—an advantage it would not have had if it had been offered without taking the listener's receptivity into account.

In preparation for addressing a particular audience, the speaker should try to get a fairly definite picture of the listener characteristics in several areas: probable attention span; patterns of reasoning; ability to deal with negative information and ideas; susceptibility to the reactions of others; depth of interest in the topic; analytical and emotional factors in decision-making; preferences in language and vocabulary; amount of repetition required to establish a point.

If the speaker's picture of the listener is fairly close to reality, such a profile becomes invaluable in tailoring the message for maximum effectiveness in reception. No one should expect, of course, that it will be 100 percent on target for any one listener, or on target in any one point for 100 percent of the listeners. The object is to achieve maximum listening for a maximum number of listeners.

Having a specific listener profile in mind can be a decided advantage in constructing the speech. It provides a model against which to test the listening qualities of the speech for the anticipated audience. For example:

(a) General structure: Is there anything about this specific listener that would affect the application of the basic techniques for making a speech easy to follow (showing cause-effect relationships, problem-solution sequences, analogies, comparison/contrast illustrations, etc.)?

(b) Purpose: Is the purpose of the talk not only set forth clearly and specifically, but in a way that shows why this particular listener should be interested?

(c) Introduction and conclusion: Can they be made to relate to the immediate interests of this particular listener?

(d) Illustrations and anecdotes: Can they be made topical for this listener by relating them to a particular profession, locality, event, recreation, characteristic, or similar identification?

(e) Visual aids: What are their positive and negative possibilities in terms of the sensitivities of this particular listener? How can they be most effectively underscored in the commentary? (*i.e.*, "See the little figure on the right in this 'Estimated Impact on Employment' chart? That represents 30 people in this room who will be out of work if Proposition 13 passes.")

(f) Attention-holding devices: How much does the listener really know about the topic? Can interest be held by sprinkling new information through the talk? By building toward the answer to some central question or revelation or some new development?

Audience attitudes and preferences are nowhere more important than in the specifics of platform demeanor and delivery. A rock concert audience is prepared to respond to flamboyant behavior more readily than a conservative board of directors. The same general rule of consistency with audience expectations and preferences applies to all of the elements of platform behavior, from vocabulary and tone to posture and gestures.

A final arbiter of the effectiveness of the preparation and delivery is the audience itself, and many a speech has been saved from disaster at the last minute by a speaker's ability to make on-the-spot adjustments to audience feedback. Listeners always communicate their response to the message received. But since the response is usually unconsciously coded in nonverbal symbols, accurate decoding represents a special listening problem for the speaker. Some inexperienced speakers show a special aptitude for reading the facial expressions, gestures, movements, inarticulate vocalizations, laughter, and coughs—even the silence and lack of expression with which the audience responds to the message. Usually, however, good feedback interpretation is the result of long, careful observation and experience. Then the speaker knows without having to think about it how the tide of response is flowing and can automatically adjust the message and delivery accordingly.

CONFERENCE SETTING

Conference speaking calls for a special blend of listening skill and feedback interpretation. The conference leader is responsible for a whole agenda of delicate operations, any one of which can demand the leader's full attention at a given moment. They include making sure the topic and objectives are fairly and clearly defined and kept constantly before the conference, initiating structure and keeping the proceedings lively and moving along, hearing both the words and the messages, encouraging participation, facilitating and summarizing.

The most crucial task of conference speaking—keeping the interaction process alive and productive—places an extraordinary demand on the leader's communication and listening skills. Even when the leader has strong, definite ideas on the conference topic and objectives, it is necessary to keep the emphasis on the expression and interaction of ideas among the other participants. It is almost equally important to recognize when the contributions become repetitive and nonproductive and to be able to move the discussion along tactfully. Nothing kills listener interest more quickly and thoroughly than empty or irrelevant discourse.

Role Model

In order to facilitate the conference process, the leader usually has to behave as a model participant, exhibiting all of the virtues of effective conference behavior in exaggerated form. It is virtually impossible for a climate of good will, patience, tolerance, receptivity and responsiveness to develop if the leader does not exhibit these qualities to a marked degree. In addition, conference leadership requires a special synthesizing skill that is the product both of a great deal of patient listening and of practice in stating ideas in various ways to bring out their different facets. Often the ideas expressed in the conference format are in a rough, fragmentary form, easily missed by the listeners who are hearing only the words. The highest form of listening goes beyond mere hearing of words and links into the idea-process that the words symbolize. The listener tries to establish contact with the speaker's mind, using the words as clues to the ideas they represent rather than as completed images of the ideas.

The conference speaker has the responsibility of carrying this intuitive or inductive listening process to its next stage, which is a verifying procedure. In this stage, the listener plays back the received idea in different words and perhaps with a slightly different angle of exposure. Whether or not this represents a true reflection of the original idea, the feedback encourages the speaker to restate it in a more precise and developed form. Sometimes this process of statement-and-feedback is highly effective in completing the development of a valuable contribution that would otherwise have gone unrecognized and ignored.

The conference speaker can do a great deal to encourage this kind of inductive listening and idea-drafting. The leader can rephrase and clarify the participant's contributions wherever there is a clue that a valuable concept is being offered in undeveloped form. The contributor may then correct or clarify the rephrasing, and the process can be carried as far as seems productive.

The key process of an effective conference for all participants is listen-respond-listen. The leader's responsibility is to make the process as thorough and productive as possible by (1) insuring that the topic and objectives are clearly understood, (2) encouraging rapport and empathetic listening, (3) providing continuous feedback, (4) keeping the discussion on track and moving, and (5) reducing the number and effect of distracting elements as much as possible. This ensures the most effective listening climate.

INTERVIEW SETTING

Interactions usually take place at a brisk pace in the interview situation. In most cases, the objective is clear, immediate and understood equally by both participants. The interviewer wants to discover as efficiently as possible whether the interviewee has the qualifications to fill a particular position; the interviewee wants to convince the interviewer that he or she does, indeed, have the required qualifications. In a sense, they are in agreement on the direction their communication journey will take, if not upon the point they actually will reach.

Unless there is some communication barrier, the interview normally proceeds at about the pace of an animated social conversation, with remark and response, question and answer following each other. Normally, too, each participant in the interview is trying to analyze the remarks of the other as carefully as possible while the interchange goes on. And each is usually intent on getting a particular fact or a collection of facts or interpretations into the record. Each, therefore, attempts to control the interview, at least to the extent necessary for that purpose.

Since the interviewer is usually in full charge of the interview at the opening, the interviewee must either wait for an invitation to inject the information or seize an opportunity to do so. This is one area in which effective listening often pays off for the interviewee. If the information you want to get into the discussion is relevant and well formulated ahead of time, alert listening will almost always reveal an appropriate place to introduce it. All that is required is a proactive, rather than a reactive, approach to communication.

The difference is crucial. The reactive interviewee only reacts to the suggestions and questions of the interviewer. Questions are answered with as little amplification as possible; little or nothing is volunteered, even when the opportunity presents itself. The reactive individual responds to stimulus but seldom if ever takes the initiative.

Proactive Listening

An interviewee with a proactive approach to communication, on the other hand, answers questions thoroughly, with whatever amplification is justified, and makes opportunities to add information the interviewer may not have thought to ask for. The proactive approach is assertive, without the combativeness sometimes implied by terms like aggressive.

If you are applying for a position in which familiarity with a particular process is desirable, you cannot expect the interviewer to think to ask you if you have any experience with processes requiring similar or comparable skills. As a rule, interviewers do not take kindly to unresponsive or evasive answers to specific questions. It is usually important to answer the question precisely and accurately, and then to expand the exchange to include the material you want to discuss: "No, sir, I've never worked with the Vicco process. However, I am thoroughly familiar with the DeKalb process, which may have some of the same characteristics. I learned it very quickly and never had any problems with it. . . ." or, "If you mean direct, hands-on experience, the answer would be 'no.' But I do have related experience that may be applicable, if you'd like to hear about it."

In every communication mode and process, it is the message that is received by the listener that determines the response, not the message the sender thinks was transmitted. It is therefore crucial to effective communication that we understand the inductive nature of the listening process, whether we are functioning as speaker or audience at any given time.

There are two facets to the understanding of listening: listening as a part of the communication process and listening as a psychological function. As process, listening involves the decoding and interpretation of meanings transmitted in audible symbols, usually words. As a psychological function, listening involves all of the reasons why a particular listener does or does not listen to a particular message. It has been the purpose of this chapter to provide insights into both aspects of listening and the measures that can be taken to improve message "listenability" in both areas.

LISTENING: ESSENTIAL CONSIDERATIONS

I. Listen with a Purpose
   A. As a speaker is your purpose clear?
II. Listen for Main Points
   A. Will the audience locate your main points easily?
III. Listen in Proactive Mode—Accept Responsibility
IV. Listen for the Organizational Scheme
V. Listen for Personal Application
VI. Listen for Information
VII. Listening Problems
   A. Attitude
   B. Attention
   C. Memory
   D. Bias
   E. Setting

NOTES

[1]Huber, George and Jerry Koehler, *Upward Communication in Managerial Decision-Making*, International Communication Association, New Orleans, 1974.

SUGGESTED READINGS

Barker, L. L. *Listening Behavior*. Englewood Cliffs, N. J: Prentice-Hall, 1971.
Brammer, L. M. *The Helping Relationship. Process and Skill*. Englewood Cliffs, N. J: Prentice-Hall, 1973.
Lewis, T. R. and R. G. Nichols. *Speaking and Listening*. Dubuque, Iowa: William C. Brown Co., 1965.
Weaver, C. *Human Listening*. Indianapolis: The Bobbs-Merrill Co., 1972.

The interview is a widely used phenomenon of communication in business and the professions. The skills of communication discussed previously have varied degrees of applicability to the different types of interview situations. Of particular applicability are the earlier chapters dealing with audience analysis and adaptation, delivery, and listening. However, there are a number of unique features of communication to be considered in the development of interview skills. We deal in the next two chapters with the internal, or management interview and with the external, or public relations interview.

FOUR

Jack Marshall manages the upholstery division of a major furniture manufacturing company in the South. Like most managers, he finds the biggest part of his time is taken up with communication. He writes letters and reports; he participates in meetings and conferences; occasionally he is called on to make a speech or presentation.

But 90% of his communication on the job takes place on an informal or only semiformal one-to-one basis. In an important sense, his interpersonal communication style is his management style. It begins the moment he walks in the door in the morning. The way he walks and carries himself, the way he greets his subordinates and superiors, his tone, volume, vocabulary, and facial expression all fit into a complex interpersonal communication system that will continue throughout the day.

In Jack Marshall's day, this communication system will be engaged predominantly in a specific type of interpersonal exchange with special rules and conventions of its own. His agenda for the day may include screening several applicants for office and shop jobs, a cautionary talk with an employee who is habitually late for work, lunch with a representative of a firm that has developed a new fabric-treating process, an effort to discover why a valued employee is leaving the company, and so on.

Such communication interchanges are commonly referred to as interviews. The characteristic that sets them apart from purely social one-to-one communication is that they have a specific purpose that, except for very unusual circumstances, should be perfectly clear to both parties from the outset.

The purpose of this chapter is to describe the communication process in various types of interviews within organizations—employment, appraisal, assignment, review, counseling, persuasive, reprimand, complaint, survey, exit, and other similar situations.

Interviewing Within Organizations 12

NATURE AND SCOPE OF INTERVIEWING WITHIN ORGANIZATIONS

An interview is a structured conversation with a defined purpose. Although it is usually desirable for interviews to be conducted in a friendly, relaxed, conversational atmosphere, this should not be permitted to obscure the fact that the interview differs in fundamental ways from a typical conversation. The two most important differences are structure and purpose. The interview may adopt some of the amenities and style of the informal conversation. It may turn out to be a pleasant experience for the interviewer and interviewee. But it would not have taken place unless there were an organizational purpose to be served, and it is a failure unless that purpose is served.

The interview is structured to achieve its purpose as directly and simply as possible. The typical interview consists of four steps: 1) identifying the occasion and purpose of the interview, 2) exploring the relevant information and opinions, 3) conclusion, resolution or action, and 4) follow-up, report or record.

Usually step 4 — and often part or all of step 3 — takes place after the conversational exchange. Frequently step 1 is self-evident and is therefore passed over or given only the briefest recognition as an introduction to step 2: "I see you're applying for a position as a designer, Ms. Jones. Can you tell me a little about your background in this field?" Step 3 may be deferred: "Will it be all right if I call you tomorrow morning to give you our decision on this?" Step 4 may be a full report verifying that the action was carried out and what the results were, or it may be no more than a check mark against a name, indicating that the interview did take place.

Later in this chapter we will discuss the steps in the interview process in detail, with particular attention to the content of each step. Here, we will review the various types of interview situations within the general interview format.

For managers like Jack Marshall, a large class of interview situations involves employees and employment, beginning with the hiring interview and ending with the termination or separation interview.

In the hiring or screening interview, the interviewer ordinarily begins with two pieces of information: a job description for the position to be filled, and an application and/or resumé from the applicant. Some interviewers like to review the resumé before bringing the applicant in for the interview. Others — particularly when the applications have been prescreened for relevance — find it more efficient to go over the resumé for the first time with the applicant during the interview. In any case, the body of the interview will be devoted to exploring the applicant's qualifications in sufficient detail to determine whether, in view of the job requirements and the available alternate candidates, an employment offer is justified. If the offer is made, another interview, or a continuation of the same one, may be required to negotiate or clarify the terms. The record and follow-up may consist of the opening of a personnel file for the new employee or — in the case of unsuccessful candidates — the disposition of the resumé (return to applicant, file for future reference, discard, etc.).

Modern department management involves continual communication in the interview format. The periodic performance review entails a joint examination of the employee's progress to determine his or her qualification for continuation or advancement. A decision to terminate an employee is usually communicated in a personal interview. The objective here is to provide a clear explanation of the conditions of the termination and the reasons for it. It is customarily preceded by one or more warning interviews. In these the employee is formally put on notice of unacceptable performance or conduct and the improvements required for satisfactory rating. It is especially important that a meticulous record be made of warning interviews, since they are often the basis for a termination decision. Some organizations require the employee to sign a copy of a warning notice or summary of a warning interview.

An exit interview is often conducted when an employee voluntarily transfers from the department or leaves the firm. The purpose of this interview is to determine whether some organizational failure or oversight prompted or contributed to the employee's decision to leave. The results may improve the organization's ability to hold onto trained and experienced personnel in the future.

In addition to its suitability as a vehicle of employment and personnel communication, the interview format is also effective in dealing with non-personnel operations. Production schedules, orders, and changes are usually most efficiently communicated by means of written memos and standard production forms. But where the order involves a heavy commitment of time or materials or a possible conflict of priorities, it may turn out to be more efficient in the long run to take up the problem in an interview format with the production supervisor. In the face-to-face meeting all of the ramifications, potential conflicts, and possible problems can be brought up and dealt with on the spot. Left to routine channels, the difficulties may go by without comment, or they may become the subject of memos and countermemos for weeks.

The interview is also useful to organizational managers in monitoring the overall health and activity of the organization. Periodic operations conferences are traditionally employed to keep on top of plans and potential problems. But some participants are reluctant to speak up in a conference, particularly if what they have to say is critical or controversial. They may be equally unwilling to initiate a private discussion but would be willing to open up if provided an opportunity to do so in a setting in which they felt comfortable. Every manager is aware of the explosive potential of problems that are not brought up or grievances and resentments that are not aired. They all seem to surface sooner or later, usually when least expected and when they can do the most damage.

For these reasons, some managers try to maintain a deliberate program of brief, informal interviews with all of their coworkers and subordinates. Regularly once a week or once a month they try to spend a few minutes with each of the people they supervise or interact with on the job. "Taking pulses," is the way one manager refers to these monitoring interviews, likening them to the routine monitoring of patients by a doctor. They are simply conversational fishing expeditions, designed to develop information about the current activities of the organization and to draw out suggestions, complaints and problems that might not surface otherwise. They also serve a morale-building purpose by demonstrating the manager's continuing interest in the work and opinions of each individual in the organization. They require special interviewing tact and skillful use of the open-ended question—a skill that will be discussed in detail later in this chapter.

In general, interview skills are the basic communication tools adapted to a special intimate format and sharply defined objectives. Because it is normally conducted on a one-to-one, face-to-face basis (ignoring telephone interviews for the moment), it can take on the informal tone of a conversation.

For the same reason, it requires special flexibility and control by the interviewer to maintain the relaxed atmosphere without lapsing into the aimlessness of informal conversation. In addition to the responsibility for carrying the initiative in establishing rapport, obtaining or giving information, and furnishing motivation, the interviewer has to remain constantly alert to feedback clues. Interviews demand agility in adjusting to the attitude of the other participant, particularly if the interview involves emotion-charged matter, or if its outcome is personally important to one or both participants.

Interview objectives are usually simple and limited: getting or giving answers to specific questions, giving instructions or directions, or effecting a change in the performance, attitude or motivation of an individual.

KEY FEATURES IN THE INTERVIEWING PROCESS

Although the interview shares the general characteristics of the communication process, it has a unique form designed to achieve its specific communication objectives. It also has certain features and conventions that must be recognized and understood in order to use it effectively. Some of the most significant of these will be discussed in this section.

Dyadic Communication

The interview is intrinsically dyadic—that is, in its basic form it usually involves two individuals in a communication interchange. There are, of course, interview situations involving three or more individuals, but the essential structure of the true interview is bipolar. Communication flows between two points even though others may be present as witnesses or intermittent participants. Even when one or both poles are occupied by a number of participants—as when a board interviews a group of applicants—the active roles are usually passed around to different pairs of participants while the others remain passive observers. At any given moment, the communication is a dyadic exchange between one board member and one applicant.

In order to gain the fullest benefit of the interview format, it is important to keep this dyadic element in mind. It can give the exchange a personal directness and immediacy that can be intensely productive without losing the quality of friendly informality. This quality can be lost in an instance if either the interviewer or the interviewee has a feeling of being ganged-up on.

Agreement of Objectives

Usually both the interviewer and the interviewee know from the outset exactly what the interview is intended to accomplish. In fact, one of the criteria for an effective interview is its orderly progress and efficiency, evidence that the participants understand and agree on their objective.

There are exceptions to this rule as to any other. When exploratory interviews are being conducted among several possible candidates for a promotion, it is not always possible to make a full disclosure of the objective. A plausible alternative purpose is sometimes substituted, or the interviewee is simply informed that the reason for the interview cannot be disclosed. However, the comedy scene in which the employee goes through an interview believing he or she is going to be fired only to discover that a promotion is in the works, or vice versa—plays much better on the TV screen than in real life. The same is true of the cat-and-mouse game of questioning an interviewee without revealing where the questions are leading. This is universally resented as a prosecuting tactic that has no place in a business organization. In addition, it is usually far less effective than a straightforward pursuit of a clearly defined objective.

Cycle of Communication

An interview is an exchange, with communication responsibilities shared by the participants. Communication typically passes back and forth in a statement-response or question-answer cycle. The interviewee is the focus of the process and should arrive prepared to deal with the questions and opinions that can be anticipated. It is not the job of the interviewer to monopolize the interview with lectures but rather to provide opportunity and encouragement for the fullest participation by the interviewee.

Reciprocal Influence

It is inherent in the idea of an interview that each participant has something to contribute to the achievement of its objective. If either could do it alone, the interview would represent a waste of time. Even in cases where the input is unequal—for example, where the purpose is merely to inform one of the participants—the interview is pointless unless some present or future action, cooperation, consent, or acquiescence on the part of the passive participant is a part of the objective.

Even though one person may contribute more than the other, the product of an effective interview should represent a true synthesis or blend of inputs from both participants. The information and ideas of each modify and influence the thinking of the other as well as the final outcome. In an employment interview, for example, the interviewer probably begins with a fairly definite idea of the minimum qualifications for the job to be filled. Jack Marshall may tell an applicant for a job in the upholstery department: "We're really looking for somebody who understands cutting and fitting. I don't believe you list any experience in these operations." The applicant responds, "That's true. But I do understand the operations. They were covered very thoroughly in my training at Upholsterer's International. And I used the same basic calculations and operations in my two years as a pattern-maker at Industrial Fabrics."

Originally, Jack's inclination was to eliminate any applicant lacking direct cutting and fitting experience. Now he has the input to consider the qualification in a new light: is training plus experience in a related operation sufficient to meet the requirements of the job? Perhaps he will decide it is and accept an applicant that he would otherwise have rejected summarily. The new employee enters the department with an awareness of the skills that will require special attention and improvement. The interview objective has been achieved for both participants by finding an area of compromise between two elements that, so long as they remained separated, would have prevented a satisfactory conclusion.

It is the reciprocal nature of the communication cycle that enables the interview to serve as a problem-solving tool.

Mutual Involvement

The interview format permits the participants to influence each other and the outcome by providing for a direct exchange of information and ideas. It does not, however, guarantee that a productive interaction will take place. That requires an ingredient that the format cannot supply—the willingness of the participants to become involved: to engage the issue and each other; to share their information, speculations and questions in a mutual exploration of the interview objective and of possible ways of attaining it.

Questions

The interviewer's basic tool is the question. In fact, the interview can be thought of as a complex question-and-answer process. Asking the right question is the key to starting the interview off in the right direction, carrying it from step to step, eliciting the required information at each step, and arriving at the desired conclusion.

At the same time, it is a serious mistake to think of the interview as merely a series of questions and answers. Nothing is more deadly nor more destructive of the real potential of the process than an interview that proceeds like a verbal true/false test. The real strength of the interview is the interaction of information and ideas that occurs in the process of interchange and adjustment as the dialogue proceeds. The questions give it structure and direction and act as levers to move it from stage to stage.

The degree of freedom the interviewer has in selecting and arranging the questions may determine the degree of formal structure in the interview. Generally speaking, a highly structured interview is organized around a set agenda of questions from which there is little or no deviation. A nonstructured interview follows no preconceived pattern, or one that is set by the interviewee.

The structured interview has certain advantages. For one thing, it helps in meeting the requirements of the civil rights and labor relations statutes for equal treatment of all interviewees within such jurisdictions. It can be timesaving by helping the interviewer to avoid either redundance or failure to obtain necessary information. On the other hand, it makes it easy to fall into the trap of turning interviews into impersonal, unengaging, repetitious question-answer routines.

The unstructured interview has no set agenda or guide to follow. It acquires its direction from the interchange itself or from the impulse or inspiration of one or the other of the participants. It encourages follow-up of possibly pertinent side issues that are often ignored in a structured format. It is more creative, involving and personal, and it can be more productive, than an interview with a rigid pattern. Its weakness is that it can be time-consuming and inefficient. Where there is little rapport between the participants, it can be unproductive; when rapport is good, it sometimes faces the danger of degenerating into a directionless social conversation.

Some employment interviewers are able to combine the best features of structure and nonstructure by dividing the interview into two parts. The first part consists of the employment application and a brief formal review of the applicant's responses to the application questions. The second part of the interview is nonstructured, introduced with an open-ended question, such as "Now can you tell me something about yourself?"

This illustration points up an important distinction between the two types of questions that normally figure in information-seeking communication. It is important for the interviewer to understand the difference between open and closed questions because they serve different purposes and produce different results.

Closed questions tend to dictate both the form and the content of the answer. They are specific, concrete, and ask for a fact or judgment: "Where were you born?" "Do you think you can handle this job?" Open-ended questions are more concerned with feelings, philosophies and general reactions. They give the interviewee much more latitude in shaping the response and in volunteering information. Often they provide insights into the interviewee's personality and thought processes that could not be obtained by specific probing. However, like the nonstructured interview with which they are associated, they are timeconsuming and sometimes produce far more irrelevant than relevant material.

Primary and Secondary Questions

A helpful division in the preparation and implementation of interview questions is to classify them into two categories, primary and secondary. Primary questions are employed to introduce a new line of thought. They indicate an inquiry into a new area. Examples of primary questions include: How will your experience as a salesperson make you a better manager? Do you type? How would you describe your management style? Who has had the most profound effect on your life?

A secondary question is designed to stimulate further information on the topic introduced by the primary question. The aim of a secondary question is to uncover relevant information that explains or embellishes the information received from the primary question. When asking a secondary question you are attempting to "follow-up" the first question. Examples of secondary questions include: Would you explain further? Why do you suggest that? Would you please continue? Can you describe your reaction in detail?

The use of primary and secondary questions helps the interviewer in developing a specific theme, and provides the interviewer with an opportunity to elicit information in an organized pattern. Primary and secondary questions can be open or closed. For the most part, primary questions are planned in advance of the interview, and if more than one person is being interviewed, each can be asked the same questions. On the other hand, secondary questions emerge from the particular responses given by each interviewee. Thus, the primary questions provide a basis for comparing and contrasting individuals; secondary questions provide for manifesting individuality.

PLANNING THE INTERVIEW

Whether structured or unstructured, the interview is a specific process designed to produce a specific kind of result by means of specific communication operations and effects. The fact that it may not follow a predetermined pattern does not mean that an effective interview can be unplanned, undirected and spur of the moment. The planning is apparent in the pattern of the structured interview; it is less visible, but no less necessary, in the unstructured interview. The planning begins from exactly the same point in both cases. Whether the interview is to be structured or unstructured, the planner begins by visualizing the interview's intended outcome and the kinds of responses that must be evoked from the interviewee in order to achieve it. The personal interviewer may intend to locate and hire at a reasonable figure a new employee with certain skills, experience, and personal qualities. The structured interview would be organized around a series of direct, closed questions about the applicant's training, work history and record: "Do you have training or experience in skills A, B and C?" "Why did you leave your prior jobs?" and so on. The unstructured interviewer intends to acquire the same information, volunteered by the interviewee in a more involving, informal interchange. This interview might begin with general exploratory questions: "What kind of organization and job would be most satisfying to you?" "Did you find that to be the case when you were working at X Company?" "What do you regard as your most important professional qualities?" and so on, each question depending partly on the response to the last one and partly on the information that remains undeveloped. Competently handled, either style of interview should provide what the interviewer is seeking — the information necessary to make an informed decision about the applicant's suitability for employment.

As this example suggests, the structured interview is more effective in mass interviewing to fill jobs requiring essentially mechanical skills, while the unstructured interview may be more productive in assessing the qualifications of candidates for a job involving personal initiative and the ability to handle people and concepts skillfully. But in either case, the difference is in the structure, not in the planning or foresight by the person responsible for its organization and success, the interviewer.

The seriousness of this responsibility and the disastrous consequences of poor planning were indelibly impressed on this writer following his first assignment to interview a number of candidates for a fairly responsible position. A great deal of time and effort went into preparation for the interviews, but it was expended on only half of the problem — a close examination of the position to be filled — with virtually no forethought to the interviews themselves. The result was not unstructured; it was simply chaotic! There was no coordination among the questions and responses from interview to interview, so that the end product was sixteen different impressions without enough in common to compare one to the other. The final selection was a product of desperate intuition. The fact that the new employee did not turn out bad on the job had nothing to do with the selection process!

A short time later, an opportunity to work with an exceptionally skillful interviewing team provided a contrasting education in the key role that planning plays in conducting an efficient, effective interview cycle. Each employment interview was designed to answer three questions in the mind of the interviewer: Can the applicant do the job? How well can the applicant do the job? Will the applicant fit into the organization? Each of these questions was broken down into subquestions designed to elicit the information necessary to form a conclusion. The style of the interview was up to the interviewer, but no interview was to be considered completed unless there was sufficient information to make a judgment in each of the three question areas.

The same general process applies to all types of interviews. The first and most important step is planning, beginning with a clear definition of the objective and isolation of the two or three questions that must be resolved in order to achieve it. These then become the major topics around which the interview is organized and into which all the detail questions are fitted.

A number of other technical questions need to be settled in the planning stage. Among the earliest of these decisions should be selection of an interview style. As we have noted before, the degree of structure and formality to be employed is affected by a number of factors, including the type of interview and its objective, the personality of the interviewer, the number of interviews to be conducted and the time available. It is important to establish the interview style early because it will affect the way most of the details are planned and handled.

Once the style is established, it is wise to consider how a mutual understanding of purpose will be verified. Even in so obvious a situation as an employment interview, it helps to eliminate misunderstandings and focus the interchange if some acknowledgment is made that the purpose is to find the best applicant for a specific job. If there is any possible ambiguity—in a disciplinary, termination, or exit interview, for example—it is even more important to make sure at the outset that the participants are in agreement on the topic and objective. Nothing is more disconcerting than to discover in midstream that the interviewer is talking about one subject and the interviewee another. Sometimes it is necessary to make clear what the interview does not involve as well as what it does. An exit-evaluation interview may find it necessary to allay any suspicion that the organization is trying to change a departing employee's mind: "The company respects your decision and wishes you the best possible luck in your new position. But when a valued employee decides to leave, it is important to us to understand the things that went into the decision to find out if there are any improvements we should make in our approach." The purpose of such clarification is to remove any unwarranted implication of pressure and to alleviate any reticence the interviewee may feel about discussing past resentments or organizational shortcomings.

It must be recognized that there are certain interviews—such as the sales presentation—in which a blunt announcement of purpose ("Ms. White, I intend to sell you that automobile"), however refreshing, is not considered psychologically advisable in most cases. Fortunately, the sales situation is usually sufficiently unambiguous, and most prospects sufficiently familiar with sales routines, to permit the selling objective to be stated in terms of selfless devotion to serving the buyer's needs. What is resented, however, is a direct misstatement of the objective—the sales pitch that begins, "I'm not here to sell you anything," or disguises itself as a disinterested opinion poll or a benevolent enterprise.

Interview Climate

A basic responsibility of the interviewer, and one that is too often neglected, is the establishment of the *communication climate*. Climate refers to the collection of physical and psychological factors involved in the interview setting. Unless there is a specific reason to the contrary, we want the interviewee to be physically comfortable in terms of temperature, ventilation, lighting, seating arrangements, space, decor, noise, and distractions. Some thought should also be given to putting the interviewee at ease psychologically. This can help remove the anxiety that many people experience in the interview situation and establish a friendly, nonthreatening sense of rapport and frankness.

The psychological atmosphere is usually set in the first few minutes. The interviewer identifies the purpose of the interview; makes any appropriate comments on the manner in which it will be conducted, the type of questions that will be asked and the reason for them; and explains any unusual conditions or problems. Usually the interviewee will be encouraged to comment and ask questions in order to clear up possible misunderstandings and to set up a true interchange rather than a question-and-response process.

These marks of respect and consideration, along with the conventional amenities—a cordial greeting, offer of coffee, and so on—all contribute to the relaxed, comfortable climate that produces the best results in most interview situations. There are certain circumstances in which interviewers make a deliberate effort to establish an uncomfortable or intimidating atmosphere, but these are not among the typical situations dealt with in this discussion.

Once established, the climate should be maintained throughout the interview. One of the easiest ways for the interviewer to ensure its continuation is by listening attentively to what the interviewee has to say. It is also important to make sure that the interviewee's questions are answered, that he or she thoroughly understands the questions that are asked, and that ample time is allowed for considering and making answers. If there are going to be points of disagreement, it is usually better to hold off raising them until late in the interview.

In Chapter 11, Listening, several types of listening processes are described that are particularly applicable to the interview, among them behaviors such as a nod, a smile, or an interjected phrase ("I see," "Yes," "Go on," etc.) that tells the speaker you are listening with interest and approval. This kind of feedback is as important to the interviewee, even though it may be absorbed unconsciously, as it is to the interviewer. Often the encouraging effect can be enhanced by the interviewer's echoing or repeating the last few words of the interviewee's comment and using them as the trigger for the next comment or question.

Achieving Interview Objectives

After the introduction and any preliminaries, the main development of the problem or objective occurs in the body of the interview. Here the key questions are asked and the key information developed or supplied. The interview has been planned and set up, the climate established, and the objectives defined in order for this working session to proceed as effortlessly and productively as possible.

Here, if at all, is where the hard information will be developed to determine whether or not the applicant is qualified for the job; where the interviewer learns what influenced the departing employee's decision to resign; where the full reasons for a warning, reprimand or discharge are laid out and discussed.

The body of the interview calls for the interviewer's best performance and most effective skills to proceed with tact and courtesy into what may prove to be sensitive areas, to keep the interview moving, and to motivate full participation on the part of the interviewee. Early in the interchange, the interviewer usually does most of the talking and asks most of the questions. In the body, the contribution of the interviewee should become much more pronounced.

Whether formal or informal in structure, the body of the interview tends to fall naturally into one of two or three simple communication or problem-solving patterns. One of these is the linear sequence, a series of questions and topics that build, one on the other, toward the objective. Another is to place the problem or objective at the center of the discussion, considering it from all angles. A third is historical, an examination that concentrates on the process by which the problem or objective arrived at its present state.

The body of the interview culminates in the *action* phase. This phase, following naturally from the consideration process, represents a clear commitment of the participants to some response to the interview objective. In an employment interview the action stage may consist of an offer and acceptance of the terms already discussed, an agreement that it would be unproductive to explore the topic further, or an agreement to consider the terms and discuss the matter again. A sales presentation has roughly the same action phase with respect to the product offered for sale. In the warning or disciplining interview, the interviewer spells out the consequences of the objectionable conduct, and the interviewee agrees or refuses to correct it, and so on. The action phase, obviously, is the climax of the interview process, toward which the entire interchange is directed.

The summary is the tidying-up phase of the interview in which its relevant inputs, action and conclusions are restated and, if warranted, recorded. It is important to summarize the interview before ending it in order to avoid misunderstandings on what was said or agreed on or, if no agreement was reached, what the points of difference are. The summary and record are the link to any postinterview follow-up.

Problems of the Interview Process

As with all interpersonal exchanges, the interview is affected by the variables of human personality and attitude. This is especially true with respect to the ingrained attitudes and prejudgments that go under the general heading of bias. A bias is like a filter that distorts an individual's perceptions of the outside world. Everybody exhibits bias in some areas. Most people, for example, will respond positively to a fluffy, cuddly kitten and negatively to a hairy tarantula, despite the fact that a cat's bite is far more apt to be dangerous than a tarantula's.

We tend to think of bias in relationship to groups of people who are in some way different from what others conceive of as representative, or powerful, or worthwhile people—the poor, the handicapped, the elderly, the young, women, minority groups. Bias attaches some negative prejudgment to its targets—they are assumed to be less competent, intelligent, honest, reliable or fastidious than others. But biases are not necessarily attached only to groups; most of us harbor unconscious assumptions about or reactions to individual characteristics or mannerisms. People may be penalized in our minds for being ugly according to our particular standard of beauty or for having "beady" eyes, a "shifty" gaze, a "limp" handshake, a "weak" chin, a "sloping" forehead, or a face or head of the wrong size or shape for our preconceptions.

Not all biases are negative, of course. Sometimes people reap an advantage from conforming to an accepted standard of beauty or from belonging to the "right" ethnic, religious, professional, or age group.

Biases in either direction reduce the objectivity and effectiveness of the interview process in which they play a part. Eliminating bias from one's outlook is difficult and, in the ultimate sense, probably impossible. But specific biases can be reduced or eliminated and their effect on one's professional performance neutralized by a rigorous, honest examination of personal assumptions and attitudes about individuals and groups. Recognition of one's biases may not effect any immediate change, but it does make it possible to make allowances for them. Often the mere awareness of bias encourages one to take note of the evidence that it offers a distorted picture of reality. In the long run, bias can be negated effectively only by submitting it persistently and thoughtfully to the test of reality.

A special form of bias arising from the hierarchical structure of organizations can have an insidious effect on the objectivity of the opinions and information presented in the interview process. One of the most interesting cases of this type of bias took place several years ago in a large company. A job satisfaction poll taken in one department indicated a phenomenal, practically universal, sense of satisfaction among the department members. A second poll produced almost the opposite results. The principal difference between the two was that while the first one was conducted by the department manager, the second was conducted by an outside professional and the identity of the participants was protected.

Even in less blatant cases, it is a cardinal tenet of organizational communication that upward-flowing messages, from subordinate to superior, tend to emphasize the positive and suppress negative information and opinions. Since the interviewer who is responsible for setting up and conducting the interview is usually higher in the chain of command than the interviewee, there is a special responsibility to recognize and neutralize as far as possible the built-in bias of the hierarchy.

These are only samples of the kinds of pitfalls that can be encountered in the interview situation. Most of them can be anticipated and counteracted by thoughtful preparation and a liberal application of empathy, the most important single quality an interviewer can possess. Empathy is not the same as sympathy, or feeling sorry, for the other person. It is, rather, a practical, social application of the golden rule: the ability to put yourself in the other person's shoes and to imagine how he or she feels in the situation you have arranged. You may be one of those fortunate people who possess natural empathy. If you are not, it is worth the time and effort to develop a sense of the feelings of others. It is the one quality that can make all your communication skills easier to acquire and apply and your interviews more effective and facile to plan and conduct.

INTERVIEW- ING WITHIN ORGANIZA- TIONS: ESSENTIAL CONSIDERA- TIONS

I. Types of Organization Interviews
   A. Employment
   B. Exit
   C. Evaluation
   D. Persuasive
   E. Informational
   F. Counseling

II. Steps of Interview Process
   A. Identifying occasion and purpose
   B. Exploring relevant information
   C. Conclusion—resolution or action
   D. Report or record

III. Preparation
   A. Audience analysis
   B. Data collection
   C. Setting

IV. Types of Questions
   A. Open and closed
   B. Primary and secondary

V. Establishing Communication Climate
   A. Comfort
   B. Space
   C. Lighting
   D. Noise
   E. Atmosphere

SUGGESTED READINGS

Benjamin, A. *The Helping Interview.* Boston: Houghton Mifflin Co., 1969.

Bolles, R. N. *What Color is Your Parachute?* Berkeley, Cal: Ten Speed Press, 1978.

Downs, C. W.; G. P. Smeyak; and E. Martin. *Professional Interviewing.* New York: Harper & Row, 1980.

Stewart, C. J. and W. B. Cash, Jr. *Interviewing: Principles and Practices,* 2nd Edition. Dubuque, Iowa: William C. Brown Co., 1978.

Bernard Macnaughton, vice president for a large aerospace company, must meet with newspaper and TV reporters to explain why his company should be exempt from noise pollution laws at a local airport. He is extremely nervous and fears this situation. We refer to it as a public interview. Generally, in a public interview, a representative of the organization supplies information about the organization to one or more representatives of the media — the press, radio, or television. Over the years the media interview has become one of the most important organizational vehicles, apart from advertising, for communicating with the public. Its importance can hardly be exaggerated. Most large organizations have a special officer or department whose sole responsibility is public relations. Even in these cases, however, too little attention is usually given to preparing managers at all levels to handle external communications effectively. Many medium and small organizations make no provisions at all.

As a result, their story is apt to be told badly when it is told. During the late 1960s and early 1970s consumerism, environmental concerns, and a revival of muckraking journalism, combined with a growing public cynicism, began to raise questions about ethics and practices that many organizations were not prepared to handle. Their representatives, like Bernard Macnaughton, were unprepared and consequently extremely apprehensive about communicating with the public. After years of being treated with special deference, business and professional leaders no longer enjoyed automatic credibility on corruption, pollution, pricing, safety, and a host of other questions, either in the public forum or in the stockholders' meeting. Instead, they found themselves subjected to persistent, probing, and sometimes embarrassing questioning.

Typical business responses were anger, suspicion and withdrawal. The most innocuous question was apt to be met with a defensive "No comment." The dark suspicion that the media were engaged in an antibusiness conspiracy grew to the status of an article of faith. What was actually taking place was more complex and less sinister.

What the business community experienced as hostility was in reality a loss of the privileged status it had once enjoyed as the principal support of the media through advertising. In the days when the business community was fairly compact and monolithic, a single advertiser or a small number of advertisers might hold the power of life or death over a newspaper. However, as the press matured as an industry in its own right, its sources of advertising revenue became (at least for the survivors) broader and more diversified. No single advertiser or bloc any longer had the power to dictate

Public Interviews 13

consistently what the policy and content of any major segment of the press should be. Moreover, the day of the press empire dominated by the personality of a single individual was past. The effect of the managerial revolution was to stiffen resistance to all influences that might detract from the objective of maximizing profit. The road to this objective was circulation, and the press found itself able to concentrate its attention as never before on the task of creating an attractive product for a mass audience.

The requirements of the news-consuming public likewise underwent significant changes during the third quarter of the twentieth century. Institutions, such as the federal government, the military, and General Motors Corp., that had once been regarded with almost automatic respect, by the public and the media, suffered a precipitous loss of credibility. Paradoxically, at the same time the news of the day enjoyed an unprecedented rise in popularity.

These were some of the significant conditions of the market to which the media organizations addressed themselves. The press is no longer subservient to the control of narrow outside influences and is thus freer to move as any other independent industry might to develop a product that responds to the requirements of its market.

NEWS AS A COMMODITY

Most people do not have any great difficulty in conceiving of a commercial newspaper as a commodity. It is a package designed to make a profit for the publisher, principally by charging the business community for the service of exposing commercial messages to potential customers. Advertising rates, however, are based largely on readership. Since few people would buy newspapers only to read the advertisements, a potpourri of informational, inspirational and entertaining items is packaged with the advertising to attract the attention of as large a segment of the target public as possible and keep it turning the pages.

All of this is fairly elementary. What many people find more difficult to grasp, however, is that the individual news item is often a commodity — a product carefully designed to appeal to a specific market. The traditional description of a news story — an objective account that tells who-what-when-where-why in the opening sentence and supplies accurate details in descending order of significance in the sentences that follow — is descriptive enough, but it doesn't really answer the most important questions.

What do we mean, for example, by "objective"? by "accurate"? by "news"? In the day to day operation of the press, somebody has to decide what is and what isn't news, what is the most important, what is of lesser importance, and what isn't important enough to print. Somebody has to decide which are the more significant and which the less significant details and also what the angle or main point should be. Somebody has to decide what the boundaries of the story should be. What should be selected out of the continuum of related events and reactions to make a complete story?

For example, the public relations department of a company might issue a press release beginning:

XYZ SPENDS $50,000 TO KEEP METATE RIVER WATER CLEAN. A new $50,000 filtration system removes more than 95 percent of the industrial chemical content of water discharged by XYZ Company into the Metate River, Company President George Smoothly told at a stockholders' meeting today. . . .

The release might then go on to give additional details from the president's report, describing the XYZ Company's contributions to the health of the local environment, to the economy, and to employment, as well as its new products and future plans.

Once the release might have been accepted and printed pretty much as received, thus limiting the story to an accurate account of the company president's speech. Today, there is a much greater chance that the story would be seen in a much broader perspective. The company's release might be combined with additional information from other sources:

NEW FILTER REDUCES XYZ RIVER POLLUTION
— But Not Enough, Government Board Says
Even with a new $50,000 filtering unit that removes 95 percent of its toxic chemical content, the waste water the XYZ Company dumps into the Metate River has a pollution level still higher than federal regulations permit, the Herald Dispatch has learned. . . .

This story might then go on to recount both the company's contributions to the community and the burden it imposes on the ecology, the public health, and the recreational potential of the river. This story would almost certainly be considered antibusiness by the XYZ Company while the original release would be considered probusiness by ecologists. Either version meets the abstract conventional criteria for a news story. The first accurately reports on a speech. The second focuses on a situation and reports with equal accuracy on two of the many related factors that play a role in the situation. Instead of following the XYZ Company through to the end of the story, for example, the second paragraph might point out that XYZ is only one of 187 companies struggling to clean up their effluent and the difficulty they are encountering in meeting the federal standard. Or it might focus on the effect of various chemical loads on the river's ecosystem and how this effect relates to the regulations.

The point is that any of these or many other possible approaches can produce a legitimate news story. The approach actually adopted may be influenced by outside pressure or individual bias, but the chances are strong that what it will reflect to the greatest degree will be the reporter's and editor's judgments of what it takes to sell the most papers to the largest number of people in a given market. The larger and more diverse the market, and the greater its choice of media, the more the pressures tend to cancel each other out and the greater the chance for balanced reporting.

The reporters and editors are the mechanics and technicians of the editorial side of the industry, just as the typographers and pressmen are of the printing side. Whatever their personal biases or shortcomings, their professional objective is to produce a commodity that will sell on a given market. They go about it in much the same way the working staffs of other businesses go about turning out marketable underwear, automobiles and packaged foods. It is this, and not some dark antibusiness conspiracy, that accounts for the "hostility" of the media toward the once-privileged business community.

Chester Burger, management consultant and former CBS national news manager, sums up the situation succinctly by quoting NBC commentator David Brinkley: "When a reporter asks questions, he is not working for the person being questioned, whether businessman, politician, or bureaucrat, but he is working for the readers and listeners,"[1] and comments:

If indeed the working press, reporters, and correspondents bear an anti-business animosity, opinion polls tell us that such attitudes are quite representative of public opinion generally in the United States today. Rather than dismissing newsmen and news media as hostile, they may be the very ones to whom business ought to increase its communication, because they typify the attitudes of millions of Americans.[2]

This is not to say that the mechanism functions ideally, or even terribly well, at all times and in all places. News organizations—especially smaller and less affluent ones—still can be and are vulnerable to advertiser pressure. An individual publisher's, editor's, or reporter's bias may still color a story or a publication's policy. Vendettas are not completely unknown even today in the publishing world. Fads and sensations tend to displace hard news when the media cater too slavishly to the popular mood of the day. Television news personalities often regard themselves as entertainers rather than reporters, performing accordingly. On the scene reports and footage from Vietnam were being heavily cut, rewritten or killed at the editors' desks for months before the ghastly realities of that war finally broke the dam against exposure. The list of obstacles in the way of objective, factual news reportage can be extended indefinitely. There probably is no such thing in the real world as a fully told, completely objective, completely accurate news story.

All of this makes it even more remarkable that the system functions as well as it does. The overall quality and scope of reportage available to the average consumer is far better today than it was only a few decades ago. An organization's story can be told effectively through the media. All that's required is a story worth telling and a working knowledge of how the system operates.

UNDER-STANDING TODAY'S MEDIA
One of the most interesting phenomena of modern politics was the rapid, steady rise of Jimmy Carter from the relative obscurity of the Georgia governor's mansion to national prominence and then to the White House. There is little indication that Carter was especially adept at getting his message across through the media in the early years of his career. And, like all public figures, he did not always find it smooth sailing. Even after he became President some important White House announcements received inadequate exposure because their release was not timed to take advantage of press deadlines.

Nevertheless, more than one observer has credited the attention he devoted to studying the working press with his ability to get his story across to the public in his own campaign. As one observer remarked astutely,[3] "In his march to the presidency, Carter perhaps came to understand the media better than any understood him."

One of the media principles Carter put to good use was the attention-getting power of the unexpected.[4] He recognized that a candidate who performs just about as expected in the primaries gets far less media attention than one who provides a surprise. A winning candidate who squeaks through when expected to win by a landslide gets extra coverage of an unwelcome flavor. The story is not that he won but how close his opponent came to upsetting him. On the other hand, a candidate who comes in second when expected to come in fifth has a good chance of getting a better press than the actual winner, plus getting an image of vitality and momentum. Accordingly, the Carter organization's extremely modest predictions helped to promote the newsworthy image of an interesting challenger coming up fast from the field.

Even with preparation, it's difficult to anticipate all of the questions that can come up in public communication situations, as both successful and unsuccessful political candidates have learned to their sorrow. During the 1976 pre-election debates, nearly a hundred million television viewers virtually watched the tide of the campaign turn in a few seconds when President Ford entangled himself in an ill-considered comment on foreign policy.

Fortunately, the consequences are not often that serious. But they can be troublesome enough for the organizational spokesperson who has failed to prepare for the unexpected, at least to the extent of having a pleasant "No comment" or "I can't go into that now" or simply, "I don't know" ready for an emergency and sticking to it. Inexperienced speakers often think such a confession will be interpreted as a sign of incompetence. It can be far more incompetent to try to give an answer that has not been thought through adequately, as one telephone company executive discovered a few years ago.

In charge of an informal press conference on company appointments and facilities, he was confronted with a casual, unexpected question about future sales of telephone instruments. In an attempt to answer it off the top of his head, he made an inadvertent reference to "the competition." To his dismay he had triggered a flurry of questions the telephone company preferred not to have raised but that the reporter knew instinctively would interest far more readers than anything else they had discussed. Most people, he realized, were only vaguely aware that one could buy telephone instruments from an independent manufacturer, or that it was legal to do so.

Once the subject was opened, the company executive felt he had no alternative to continuing to try to answer questions he was not prepared for. Reluctantly, he admitted that a number of local firms had installed not only telephones but extensive auxiliary equipment as well, purchased from independent manufacturers, and that there was some doubt that the telephone company would be willing to service equipment not purchased from it.

The story, as published, turned out to be far better publicity for the previously little-known competitor than it was for the telephone company. The reporter had nothing against the company but he recognized the difference between a story that would interest a lot of readers and one that would interest only a few. The telephone company executive had let himself be trapped, losing control of the interview, because he was unwilling to cut off a line of questions he had not prepared for and because he did not have a clear picture of how and why news stories are angled the way they are. The interviewee should never forget that the reporter is there to develop his or her own product, not to promote the product of the interviewee. That happens only if their interests coincide.

THE RESIDUAL MESSAGE

There is a subtle difference between the basic communication aims of the interviewee and the interviewer in most media interview situations. The primary objective of the interviewer is to create a product that will attract the interest and attention of an audience. The specific content or how long it will be retained is of secondary importance.

The objective of the interviewee, on the other hand, is to create a lasting impression—an image or statement that the audience will carry away as the ultimate effect of the communication. It is not necessarily identical to the message the sender has transmitted or even to the one received at the time of communication. It is the message that remains in the receiver's mind to color future thought and action. It may consist of no more than a vague, associated mood, or a positive or negative attitude, or a fact or two, or a general idea. Whatever its content, it is the end product of the communication.

The residual message is shaped by a variety of influences: the initial information and attitude of the reporter, the accuracy of the sender's assessment of the reporter, the skill with which the message is developed and delivered, the receiver's perception of the sender and the sponsoring organization.

For the interviewee, particularly the press interviewee, implanting the desired residual message is a two-stage process, only one of which is under any degree of direct control of the interviewee. In the first stage, the interview, the message has to be transmitted to the interviewer with sufficient impact to carry through into the second stage—the story that is printed or broadcast. This can happen only when the interviewee starts out with a clear idea of what the residual message should be, plus a working understanding of the interviewer's job and the interests of the audience.

The Interviewer

If you are going to anticipate journalistic behavior, you need to have some realistic picture of the pressures and constraints under which the journalist works.

To begin with, it is important to keep in mind that there is nothing the interviewer would like more than to get a great story from the interview with you—the lead story on the network six-o'clock news or the upper right two columns on the front page of the newspaper, with a banner headline and a by-line. The more the editor learns to rely on the reporter and the more the public learns to recognize and respect the by-line, the more successful the reporter. For you this factor, like the familiar comedy routine, is both good news and bad news.

It's good news because it means an alert reporter will do everything possible to get a good, attention-getting story out of the raw materials you provide and to get it into print. The bad news is that the story that winds up in print may not be the one you wanted told if the reporter sees another angle that will provide a better story.

You must also be aware of the pressures of time and media space on the reporter. Everybody has heard of the journalistic deadline but not everybody understands how it works. Whether it is intended for broadcast or printing, the writing of the story is only the first step in a complex process that is keyed to the final product. A newspaper is scheduled to be off the press at a specific time. All of its complicated distribution system depends on meeting the schedule regularly. The printing time for a press run of a given size can be predicted within minutes. Before the presses can roll, however, press plates must be prepared and checked. The plates can be prepared only after each page has been composed and set up, complete in every detail—body type, headlines and subheads, photographs, dates and pagination—with everything in place and adjusted to fill the available space.

Before that, however, the paper has to be made up, page by page and column by column. Space has to be apportioned, type set, pictures sized and screened, and the whole assemblage checked and proofed. Before that, headlines and subheads have to be written, typographical details settled, and all editing, rewriting, and checking completed on the stories that have been selected from among those available for inclusion in that issue.

Each stage of this complex chain of events requires a well-defined period of time for its completion. Add them all together, and turn the clock backward from the time the issue is due off the press by the number of hours required for all of them, and you have the copy deadline. If your story is to be ready for a particular issue, the interview must be scheduled to give the reporter time before the deadline to write your story and any others he or she may have been assigned.

Not everything in the press is subject to a particular deadline, of course. Some stories, like features, human interest, and investigative reports, are not necessarily tied to any particular day's events. Often edited and set in type ahead of time, they can be inserted at the editor's convenience. A large part of the paper, such as ads, features, columns, comics, editorials, and even early news items, may already be in type by the copy deadline, with holes left for late-breaking news and deadline copy.

Most routine organizational news is not time-critical. At the most it may become outdated after a certain length of time. Consequently, announcements of personnel changes, new products, acquisitions, ground-breakings, and general institutional features are often released well ahead of the anticipated publication date with a notation, "Release Before (date)," or, if the story is a prerelease, "Release After (date)."

Television has a slightly different time and deadline problem. The typical television news item may be anywhere from one-tenth to one-third as long as the published version. If it is an important late-breaking or continuing story carried on a local station, it may be put in front of the newscaster after the broadcast is under way, during a commercial or while the camera is on another speaker. It may be carried without any graphic support at all or with a still picture or drawing occupying all or part of the screen. If the story warrants, a crew may be sent out for live on the scene coverage and filming or taping material that will be edited and used on later broadcasts. An interview that is filmed is subject to the same editing and amplification that a published item might undergo.

The prime news event for many television stations is the early evening broadcast, sometimes referred to generically as the six-o'clock news. For local network affiliates, these broadcasts usually consist of a half-hour or hour of local news leading into the network's national/international roundup. The typical network roundup has three components: the network's home-city and in-studio segment, the international segment transmitted by network correspondents and stringers in various overseas locations, and the national affiliate segment consisting of local stories of national interest as reported by the affiliates' newscasters. Every day there is fierce competition among reporters and among affiliates across the nation for that thirty-, forty-five-, or sixty-second moment of glory that comes with getting a local story before the millions of viewers of the network news. If your story has a legitimate national-interest angle, you can bet that your reporter will do everything possible to get national exposure for it.

A similar situation applies to the press. To have a story picked up by the wire service is a feather in the cap of a local reporter.

So far, we have discussed the effect on the interview and the resulting story of the training and professionalism of the reporter. The experienced journalist understands the value of novelty, conflict, controversy, and scandal in arousing and holding reader interest. He or she is usually persistent and inventive in the pursuit of controversial comments, inadvertent admissions and surprising developments, all of which can be unnerving enough. But not all reporters are experienced and well-trained, which can create equally difficult problems for the interviewee.

Although the situation is far better than it was only a few years ago, journalism is not among the highest-paid professions. Particularly at the general reporting level, you may encounter young, poorly trained reporters who compensate for their lack of experience by exaggerated aggressiveness. This is especially true of those surviving anachronisms of an earlier generation of the press, the newspaper whose reporting reflects the personal biases of a controlling family or individual.

One of the authors still recalls with embarrassment the fiasco that developed when, as head of a program on a California campus, he was interviewed by an obnoxious young reporter from a local paper published by a crusty octogenerian with a long list of public phobias that included colleges and professors. There was good reason to anticipate a hostile interview and a biased story.

The apprehension was thoroughly justified. The reporter, with liberal cooperation from the interviewee, turned the interview into a model of everything modern objective journalism tries to avoid. He opened with several gratuitous slurs aimed at the university and the faculty, and then fired his opening question: "If you know as much as you claim to, why do you have to work for a university?" It triggered an automatic response: "If you're such a hot reporter, why can't you get an honest job with a decent newspaper?" The rest of the interview was in a similar key, and the resulting story was written in the same tone of juvenile hostility displayed by both sides in the interview.

Although it is not often that one encounters such flagrant animosity among today's journalists, the interviewee should be aware that it can happen and should have a strategy ready in case open hostility, or any other factor, causes the interview to degenerate to such a point. Unless you are very sure of your ability to control yourself and your material and to keep the interview moving in the direction you desire, it is probably best simply to terminate it. In the example related above, termination would certainly have been preferable to engaging in a pointless exchange of insults.

But regardless of the attitude of the reporter, there are two things that are absolutely necessary to the interviewee: you must know with complete clarity and precision what residual message you want to leave, and you must make advance preparations for the interview. That means making mental notes of what you want to say or writing your points out in detail and rehearsing them. The surest path to disaster is the belief that you can bluff or ad lib your way through an interview.

It is also helpful to take whatever measures are necessary to give you an attitude of confidence and optimism about the interview (Liquor, however, is not advised). For example, you should not be in the least embarrassed to rehearse, in front of a mirror, if necessary, or to memorize at least a few key phrases. If possible, and if it makes you feel more comfortable, arrange for the interview to take place on familiar ground, in your own office or building. If you have any reason to fear you may be misquoted, or just on general principles, do not hesitate to tape record the interview for your own reference.

You should never be afraid to lay down reasonable ground rules. An interview is not a fishing expedition; usually it has a specific, well-designed subject. You have a right to expect that if you are prepared to discuss that subject openly and thoroughly, you should not have to range all over, fielding extraneous and distracting questions. *Parade Magazine* (April 2, 1978), quoted an admirably succinct and good-humored set of ground rules laid down by one interviewee:

> I will submit to an interview, providing you ask no questions about my past, especially my first three marriages; you ask nothing about my finances—I don't know anything about them anyway; and you submit your story and photographs to me and my press agent for final approval.

Even though this particular list was designed to protect a celebrity from being picked over in areas that were not germane to the purpose of the interview, the general approach is sound for any interview. The restrictions must be fair and appropriate, of course. It is unlikely that a newspaper reporter will agree to submit a story and photographs for approval; on the other hand, a reporter for a trade journal or even a general circulation magazine may very well be willing to do so. If you are the chief executive of a processed-food company that has just been charged with responsibility for seventy cases of botulism, you cannot expect to restrict an interview to a discussion of your new company logo. If you are the file clerk who won the company contest for a new logo design, you have every right to exclude questions having to do with corporate policy and legal problems.

PREPARING FOR A PUBLIC INTERVIEW

As suggested earlier, the first and basic step in preparing for an interview is to determine precisely what *residual message* you want to leave with the ultimate audience. This has two important effects on your overall preparation. It helps you to focus on the single point that you want to make and therefore to relate the relevant information to it, while eliminating material that does not contribute to it.

It also helps you to state each item of information in a way that relates it to the basic message. If your subject is a new company facility and your message is that your company will provide even better service in the future, then each major feature of the new facility is described in terms of the contribution it will make to improved service. Organizing your material for the interview around the residual message helps to structure it and to implant the residual message in the interviewer's consciousness.

The second step is to review the media possibilities. To the extent that you have a choice, what medium would be most effective for telling this particular story? Is an interview really necessary? Could it be handled just as well with a press release, possibly accompanied by one or more pictures and followed up with a call to the reporter? Do you need fact sheets, backgrounders, photographs, or other prepared materials for the interview? Is it to be a one-to-one interview or a press conference? If a press conference, should you open with a prepared statement? Should you take up as much time as possible with the statement, leaving a minimum of time for questions? Should you distribute printed copies of your statement?

The third step requires you to consider what you know about the *interviewer* or interviewers and the media you will be dealing with. Do you have any clues to their philosophy or audience? Are there any peculiarities or unique interests present that might affect your approach one way or the other?

The fourth step is to *anticipate* the interview. Try to put yourself in the interviewer's head, formulating the questions you would ask if your roles were reversed. Then consider the most effective way to answer them. Keep in mind the reporter's guidelines: the who-what-when-where-why-how formula with the climactic information or conclusions stated first and the supporting material following in descending order of importance. This is sometimes a difficult and awkward pattern to learn to handle, particularly if you are a person who habitually thinks in an orderly, linear fashion, from cause to effect, from hypothesis to conclusion, from earlier event to later event. You have to learn the technique of selecting the crucial elements. For example, the summary statement you would normally place at the end of the development, you would now move up to serve as an introduction.

Chronologically you might have the following experiences:

1. You return home after a weekend trip.
2. You notice an open window you thought you had closed.
3. You enter the house.
4. You discover many items are missing.
5. You note the window has been jimmied.
6. You conclude your home has been burgled in your absence.

The journalist's order for these events would move #6 to the top of the list, followed by #4, #5, #3, #1, and #2. Toward the end of the list, the order might vary, depending on the writer's style, angle and available space.

The final step is *filling in details* and alternatives. If the subject is simple or you are extremely familiar with it, all the preparation may occupy no more than a few minutes of thought. But it is practically impossible to overprepare. Since you can never anticipate exactly what the reporters' questions or angles may be, it is important to have as many alternate angles and back-up facts of your own as possible. Nothing is more disconcerting than to have an answer fixed in your mind and then to discover that it doesn't fit the question.

It is usually a mistake to try to handle even the most casual interviewer off the top of your head, as a participant in a recent industrial conference learned at the cost of a negative reference to his organization in a roundup story on the conference. He had not anticipated being interviewed and submitted to it on the spur of the moment. His information was accurate, but he adopted an ill-considered breezy approach that grated on the interviewers. In a few impromptu remarks, he made three crucial errors: he called the conference a show, he called the background material propaganda, and he employed the word I to the point that he appeared to be taking credit for both his company's and the meeting's accomplishments. The interview came back to haunt him, not only in the published account, but with his colleagues as well.

INTERVIEW STRATEGIES

There is something intrinsically intimidating about being interviewed. There is a tendency to feel helpless, at the mercy of the interviewer. Experienced reporters know this very well, and they utilize it when it is to their advantage. Confidence in your own material, purpose and preparation can go a long way toward dispelling the qualms with which most people approach an interview.

Half the battle is won if you go into the interview with secure knowledge that your objective is a worthy one, that you have considered all the questions that are likely to come up, and you have a clear picture of the message you want to deliver, along with the facts to support it. It will add to your sense of confidence if you also have worked out in advance a method of approach, or strategy, for the interview as a whole or for the individual questions.

There are a number of standard approaches to consider, depending on the nature of the material and of the interview situation. Where the subject is controversial, you need to decide ahead of time whether you are going to adopt a balanced or an aggressive approach. Are you going to try to handle both sides of the issue? Or are you going to include only material supporting your own point of view? Sometimes the latter is the best attack, although the general opinion is that it is usually sounder to give some recognition to both sides of a controversial issue without being forced to do so by questions. Again, the nature of the material and strength of your case should provide a clue to whether you should deal with the negative material before, or after, the material supporting your point of view. The one approach that is almost universally condemned is sandwiching your point between slabs of negative material. This is considered a weak approach because of the well-documented tendency of readers and listeners to remember the first and last part of a presentation or point better than the middle.[5]

You also need to consider how explicit you are going to be. Some subjects lend themselves to a cold facts approach much better than others; sometimes the nature of the material or the situation dictates that a point can be developed only by implication. Like most people, reporters have a decided preference for the explicit and will try to pin you down to specifics, often even after you have indicated that you have gone as far as you are willing to go. In such cases, it is usually better to state that you cannot be more specific than you have already and to stick to your guns.

One of the clearest and most effective techniques for developing a point is the problem-solution approach. It consists of isolating and defining the problem around which each of your points is built. Then you give the solution you have achieved or that you propose. This approach gives the interviewee a great deal of leverage if the interviewer accepts the original definition of the problem, because any subsequent question or objection can be referred to the problem and the possible alternative methods of solving it.

Cause and effect is often a useful technique for clarifying why a particular problem was not solved or a recommended approach not employed. It begins with the recognition that nothing is free in the universe, that nothing is acquired without giving up something else. With an engine of given capacity, for example, you can increase the speed of the motion you take from it at the sacrifice of power, or vice versa, but you cannot increase both the speed and the power simultaneously, other things remaining equal.

When your message is that a particular action is unwise, the most effective argument is often one that shows that the consequences of the action would be more damaging than anything that might be gained by it. Since it often deals with hypothetical effects, this is an argument that is easily abused. There was once a Southern senator who argued passionately against a federal school-lunch program for undernourished children because, he said, their parents couldn't afford to provide them with a lunch, and it would be detrimental to the family if they got the idea the government cared more about them than their parents did.

Cause-effect is also effective in other kinds of situations, such as describing a complicated process or explaining how some highly confusing situation came about.

The "Yes," or consensus strategy, is often used by speakers or interviewees who want to de-emphasize the areas of disagreement on a particular topic. It has been referred to as the "Yes, but . . ." or the "Yes, and also . . ." approach. The speaker makes a point of agreeing with the position implied in a question or statement and then proceeds to define the degree to which he or she differs or goes beyond the position: "I certainly agree that busing school children is undesirable; but it is far preferable, and less detrimental to the children, to permitting racism to fester in the classrooms for another generation. . . ." "Yes, I do believe that something should be done to preserve the family farm. And I also believe the same measures should be extended to improve the plight of the migrant farm worker. . . ."

When used adroitly, the consensus strategy has the effect of focusing on the problem as something external upon which both parties, despite minor differences in approach, are working together.

A great deal depends on the kind of point you are developing and the kind of interview situation you face. It is a good idea to consider various approaches in context to see if one does not appear to fit the circumstances better than the alternatives. Even when that does not turn out to be the case, it is far better to have thought through the possible approaches before you are actually confronted with the question.

Interview Behavior

In addition to the general preparation, attitude, and approach to facing a media interview, there are specific behavioral choices which may improve the chances of communicating your message effectively.

Proposition 1: *Begin with the news, then explain.*

We have already discussed the way facts are normally ordered in a news story. Try to form the habit of presenting your material in the same order: (a) This is what we have done; (b) This is why we did it.

Proposition 2. *Answer direct questions directly.*

This doesn't mean that you have to allow the interviewer to force you to answer questions. It does mean that you should avoid hedging and evasiveness at all costs. If you feel a question is out of line or unfair, you are entitled either to say so or to answer directly that it is not a question you can deal with at this time. If you don't know the answer, it's all right to say so—with an offer to get the answer as soon as possible if the question is legitimate. Remember that you're not on the witness stand; you have a right to make qualified answers or to expand on your answer if you feel doing so will get your point across better.

Proposition 3. *Don't lie or exaggerate.*

This is a pragmatic, not an ethical, imperative. It is almost impossible to make a lie of any significance stick. It's painful to admit that you or your organization made a mistake, and you don't have to dwell on it, but the media and the public have always shown themselves far readier to forgive a mistake than a coverup.

Proposition 4. *Don't argue with the reporter.*

This is a game that you lose, even if you win. If you argue with the reporter or lose your temper, the reporter is going to have the last word where it counts — with the public you are trying to reach.

Proposition 5. *Don't let the reporter put words in your mouth.*

Be careful of "denial" questions. One's impulse is to reply to such a question as, "Did you fire your former assistant because she was black, or because she was a woman?" with "I did not fire my former assistant because she was black or because she was a woman." Once the words are in your mouth, they are subject to quotation in a way that makes you, not the reporter, responsible for associating the firing with race or sex. It's far better to state the case objectively and without rancor in your own words, or to deal frankly with the difficulty of answering insinuating or loaded questions.

Proposition 6: *Don't talk off-the-record.*

Don't believe the myth that you can prevent a reporter from using something you say just because you claim off-the-record status for it. The reporter may go along with you to the extent of not quoting you directly, but any information you give a reporter belongs to the reporter from then on and will be used if it is deemed newsworthy.

Proposition 7. *Put everything you can in the public context.*

You're naturally concerned with your organization and its accomplishments and problems. But you're talking to a public audience that is really interested in the public effect of your company's ideas and actions. To you, the new facility is a sign of the company's growth and success. To your audience, the important thing is that it will mean new jobs and better service.

Proposition 8. *Follow up*

If there is any excuse to do so, give the reporter a call after the interview to provide the additional information you promised or to clarify a point that may have been slighted in the interview. So long as it doesn't sound as if you're pushing or trying to interfere, it's a welcome gesture that often prevents publication of an inaccurate story.

Even with the best of preparation and strategy, there will no doubt be interviews that go sour. But overall, your ability to take charge of the interview and control it will be in proportion to the thought and effort you put into it. In those cases when you cannot fully control the course of the interview, you can at least hold your own well enough to make sure that your story gets a fair hearing.

PUBLIC INTERVIEWS: ESSENTIAL CONSIDERATIONS

I. Determine Question at Issue
   A. Get accurate information
   B. Rehearse potentially difficult questions
   C. Have a colleague evaluate your rehearsal responses
   D. Memorize a few key phrases
   E. Determine interview ground rules
II. Interviewee Behavior
   A. State the pertinent facts
   B. Answer questions directly
   C. Avoid exaggeration
   D. Avoid argument
   E. Insist on accurate statement of your views
   F. Do not allow others to inaccurately state your position
   G. Never talk off-the-record
   H. Maintain calm, unemotional manner
III. Understanding Media
   A. Recognize reporter's objectives
   B. Realize interview reported will be only segment
   C. Consider time and space restrictions

NOTES

[1] Burger, Chester, "How to meet the Press," in *Harvard Business Review,* July-August, 1975, pp. 62-70.

[2] Burger, "How to Meet the Press," p. 62.

[3] Brown, C. J. et al., *Media and the People* (New York: Krieger, 1978). p. 341.

[4] Ibid, pp. 341, 342.

[5] Gulley, H. and D. K. Berlo, "Effects of Intercellular and Intracellular Speech Structure and Attitude Change and Learning," *Speech Monographs,* Vol. 3 (1956), pp. 288-297.

SUGGESTED READINGS

Downs, C. W.; G. P. Smeyak; and E. Martin. *Professional Interviewing.* New York: Harper & Row, 1980.

Gordon, R. L. *Interviewing: Strategy, Techniques and Tactics.* Homewood, Ill: The Dorsey Press, 1969.

Metzler, K. *Creative Interviewing.* Englewood Cliffs, N. J: Prentice-Hall, 1977.

Sherwood, H. C. *The Journalistic Interview.* New York: Harper & Row, 1972.

In this final section your attention is directed to evaluation interests of public communicators and to their evaluation by individuals responsible for scheduling them. These evaluations can be important to the speakers, who, we hope, have an interest in objective evaluation of their presentations. This kind of feedback is of significant value in refining one's delivery and content. To individuals responsible for conferences, information about the most effective program portions and/or presentations is of major importance for future programs, projects and personnel.

The examples which we provide can, of course, be modified to be made most useful to specific purposes. We hope they are also helpful to persons seeking models to adapt to their own communication behavior.

FIVE

Roger Watkins has just finished making an important speech before the local Rotary Club. Now he is anxious to find out how effective he was.

In his speech, he sought to gain support for a rezoning application that is vitally important to his company. Five years earlier, the company failed to predict its future growth accurately, and now it desperately needs more room to expand. But first it has to secure approval of a zoning change to permit commercial use of land originally designated residential. He knows that city councils and planning commissions often tend to resist such changes on general principles, and he also expects opposition from local environmentalists. The Rotary membership, on the other hand, has usually shown itself to be sympathetic to the needs of the business community. By showing the advantages of the rezoning, not only to his own company but to the economic health of the community, he hopes to gain sufficient support to offset the anticipated opposition to his company's proposal.

Roger's general impression is that his talk went over well. The Rotarians listened with friendly, and apparently approving, attention. Afterwards, several members complimented him and expressed opinions that were in agreement with his conclusions. One listener challenged him on a minor point but appeared to be satisfied with his defense of it.

But this is only an impression, based on random surface indications. It was a predictably sympathetic audience; moreover, it was one accustomed to giving speakers a courteous hearing. A hiss or a boo under the circumstances would have been a much more reliable sign of disapproval than attentiveness, or even applause, of active approval. Nor should Roger read too much into the ritual of complimenting the guest speaker. It may mean no more than that he didn't seriously offend anyone and didn't talk too long. As for the expressions of agreement, it is usually difficult to determine from a casual exchange how deep they go and whether they represent anything new in the listener's attitude. The listener who raised an objection indicated, at least, that he or she was following and weighing the points Roger made and presumably was, to some unspecified extent, affected by them.

In most cases, this equivocal kind of evidence is all the speaker will have to evaluate a performance. Unless the response has been lively and partisan, it is usually difficult to get anything more than a limited, subjective impres-

Evaluating Public Communication in Business and the Professions

14

sion of the impact, if any, of one's communication effort. Even when there is vigorous feedback, it is often confined to a vocal minority. Unless the majority becomes sufficiently involved to engage in some form of polling activity, such as competitive applause, feedback may not be an accurate barometer of the overall audience response. In addition, feedback doesn't normally give much indication of changes in attitude made as a result of the speaker's presentation.

It would be helpful—if it were practical—to follow each speech immediately with a carefully designed audience survey to determine a) what the individual listener's information and attitudes on the subject were before the presentation; b) whether the attitudes had been affected by the presentation and, if so, whether they were reinforced, weakened, or reversed; and c) what effect, if any, the presentation is expected to have on the listener's future behavior.

Such specific information is not usually available for any significant segment of the audience. It may be provided informally by a few listeners who are sufficiently motivated to describe their reactions to the speaker. By and large, however, the speaker who wants an on the spot evaluation will be forced to rely on close observation of indirect indicators of audience attitudes and changes.

To this point, we have proceeded on the reasonable assumption that effective communication has something to do with the impact the speaker's message has on the listener's attitudes. We cannot expect to measure such subjective effects with any high degree of precision. But in order to achieve a reasonable degree of accuracy, we need to identify not only the results we can expect from successful communication but also what criteria to follow in identifying them.

CRITERIA FOR EFFECTIVE COMMUNICATION

In Chapter 4 we discussed the necessity of establishing a clear and realistic communication objective as the first step in developing a presentation. Effectiveness criteria are the general tests you apply to audience response to determine whether and how effectively you have attained the objective you aimed for.

The primary requirement of any communication effort is that your message be heard and understood. This minimal criterion is so obvious that it often goes unmentioned or, worse, is ignored. But if it is not met, it is not possible to meet any of the other criteria of effective communication. Satisfying it involves all of the fundamentals of communication—the clarity with which you express ideas, your organization of materials, your platform skills and demeanor, audience receptivity, and the physical surroundings. The most brilliant speech imaginable can be wasted if it is presented to a large audience by a speaker with a weak voice and no amplification. Even if the prepared text or format has to be drastically altered to meet unexpected conditions, the first law of communication is to be heard and understood at all cost.

Even the most carefully planned clarity of communication can be torpedoed by undetected ambiguities, as a story related by Louis L'Amour proves.[1] After his first literary success, he was asked to address an amateur writers' club. He decided to impress upon them the importance of building every short story around a single unifying theme. In order to emphasize the point, he repeated several times during his talk that you are not ready to start writing a story until you can state it in a single sentence. When he asked for questions, one lady stood up timidly and said, "Mr. L'Amour, you said we should be able to reduce a short story to a single sentence—but you forgot to tell us what the sentence is!"

Most experienced speakers have been confronted with similar communication failures, often when they thought they were being extraordinarily lucid. That's why some speakers invite feedback on the most apparently obvious points. It gives them a chance to state "what the sentence is" in case communication is being blocked by a misunderstanding they had failed to anticipate.

The basic criterion, then, is this: Was the message understood? Assuming that it was, the second criterion involves the listener's perception of the message. Was the response positive or negative and does it conform to the intended response? This response, operating at several levels, is affected both by the judgment and personality of the listener and by the persuasiveness of the speaker.

Roger Watkins may base a part of his appeal for support for a change in the zoning ordinance on ideological grounds. He would assume that a Rotarian audience would be favorably predisposed toward business enterprise and hostile to regulations that appear to hamper it. He may also expect a sympathetic response to suggestions that the change he proposes will contribute to the financial activity and prosperity of the community in which they all have a stake. In addition, he may devote special attention to projecting the kind of personal and company image—enterprising and public-spirited—that is consistent with his message. This would offset a possible suspicion that his proposal is merely self-serving. The more levels at which a positive response can be evoked, the stronger the response is likely to be and the greater the chance that it will produce the kind of action the speaker desires.

Two basic criteria, therefore, are involved in evaluating the effectiveness of communication:

Was the message understood?
Was the desired response evoked?

Through careful attention to verbal and nonverbal feedback during and after the presentation, the speaker may be able to evaluate the audience response fairly accurately. It may remain unclear, however, how much of the response can be attributed to the presentation and how much predated it. A third important criterion follows: How strong was the response? It is difficult to assess and is linked to the evaluation of overall effectiveness discussed in the next section.

COMMUNICATION EFFECTIVENESS AND OVERALL EFFECTIVENESS

Up to this point, we have ignored one obvious criterion of effectiveness, the only one recognized by some evaluators: Was the overall objective achieved? Was Roger Watkins' rezoning application approved? Was the candidate elected to office? Did the applicant get the job? If the answer is "yes," the communication was effective. If not, it failed.

The logical weakness of this rigid standard is obvious. It is perfectly possible for an event to take place or not take place for reasons that have nothing to do with a particular communication effort of which it is the subject. Roger's speech before the Rotarians could be totally effective, and the rezoning application might still be turned down because the opposition had a stronger organization. His Rotarian address could be a waste of time because everybody in the organization was already committed to his point of view. In that case, it would have been a far more effective tactic to try to talk to an environmental group or, better, an uncommitted group, where effective communication would work to change the alignment of forces in his favor.

Making achievement of the ultimate objective the only criterion for evaluating communication effectiveness can be especially demoralizing in ego-involving situations, such as job interviews. Companies often have a highly detailed picture of the qualifications they require for a particular position. Therefore, whether an applicant has the required qualifications is ultimately a question of fact, not of rhetoric. It is possible to communicate poorly and still land a job for which the interviewer believes you are qualified, or to communicate very well and not get a job for which you are believed not to be suited. The infuriating term overqualified has become a personnel department cliché recently with unsettled employment conditions.

When one speaks purely to entertain or instruct, the objective is very closely related to the communication process and its evaluation criteria: Was the message understood? Did the audience perceive it as entertaining? This is not the case where the ultimate objective—securing a job or getting approval of a zoning change—involves processes and decisions that take place outside the communication interaction.

The real world sets limits on all processes. In the job interview, the interviewer's overall objective is to recruit a qualified applicant. The interviewer's communication objective is to present the organization's needs in the best possible light and, within the limits of reality, to persuade the best-qualified candidate to accept the job. These are linked, but distinct, objectives—one tactical and the other communicative. You may fail to secure a particular applicant for any number of reasons—poor communication, lack of rapport with the interviewee, bias, or even incompetent interviewing. If you persistently strike out in securing the best applicant, it may be a result of poor tactics, rather than poor communication.

Even in relatively simple situations the confusion between communication objectives and overall objectives can create an evaluation problem. If I run out of gas on the freeway and call my spouse for assistance, which she renders, I have achieved both my communication and my overall objectives. If she doesn't comply, the failure can be communicative, tactical or personal. It is a communication failure if, in my impatience, I convey an incomplete or counterproductive message. Her response may be, "You didn't say you wanted me to bring you some gasoline. I thought the point of your call was that you'd be late for dinner," or "You hung up before you told me where you were," or "If you want cooperation, you'll use a different tone of voice." On the other hand, if I habitually run out of gas and call her for help, she may have understood my message perfectly and simply decided that enough was enough.

We have dwelt on this point because the importance of clearly defined criteria is the essential point of this chapter. You cannot evaluate communication effectiveness accurately by using standards that apply to or include noncommunication processes. In most goal-oriented efforts, you are dealing with at least two different kinds of objectives, only one of which is strictly communicative. The other is an ultimate or overall objective, which includes both communicative and other processes. The two kinds of objectives are evaluated by two different kinds of criteria.

EVALUATION OF PUBLIC SPEECHES

To aid in the evaluation of your own communication efforts, we present three sample speeches which may be evaluated in terms of the criteria which we have discussed throughout the book. Of course, you are reading the speeches rather than experiencing the oral communication in the context where it was delivered. Nevertheless, you have the opportunity to observe the application of many of the principles under discussion.

We have also included some forms which will be useful in gathering information and evaluating the success or failure of yourself and other communicators in a variety of settings. The forms may be used first for evaluating the illustrative speeches from business and the other professions and then for application to one's own oral presentations.

Sample Speech #1—the Ceremonial Demand

In Chapter 4 we discussed the demand of the audience and occasion as a first consideration for the speaker. We said that even before the purpose of the speaker can be completely developed, this audience demand must be classified and analyzed. We identified major demand categories of ceremonial, reportorial and propositional. The following examples are from actual communication situations where speakers found it necessary to adapt to this first consideration. Each of these speakers had a specific purpose which was then pursued through a particular organizational pattern and appropriate supportive material.

The first of these examples is a speech by Dr. John Lott Brown on the occasion of his formal inauguration as president of the University of South Florida. The audience and occasion clearly demand a ceremonial speech. The speaker must speak to the importance of higher education, the greatness of the particular institution, and the nobility of the mission of the university community. Note how the speaker recognizes all disciplines of the university, the importance of the community participation, and the issues facing the world at this moment. The ceremonial speech does not break much new ground, but it is required to assert shared values of the speaker and audience. The members of this audience would find little in this speech with which to disagree; they would probably be appreciative of the speaker for stating the ceremonial necessities.

The speech was delivered on April 15, 1978 on the university campus. It was a warm spring afternoon. The speakers' platform and seating for the audience were constructed in an outside area especially for this occasion. The audience of faculty, students and representatives from the metropolitan area witnessed the formal installation of the president and introductory speeches. Of course, band music and flags were a part of the scene as well as academic robes and regalia.

> Today, in 1978, more than twenty years after it was conceived, the University of South Florida is still a very new university. Perhaps the newest in the nation when compared to other institutions of similar size and scope. The period in which this university has developed has been exciting. Generations of students in colleges across the country have progressed through the activist years of the sixties and early seventies into what appears to be a curious mixture of idealism and materialism represented in varying strengths on

university campuses today. Technological developments which have occurred during the lifetime of this university have been awesome in their complexity while at the same time so frequent and so accessible that they have been accepted by many as commonplace. The miracle of the transistor, put to work so effectively in the early sixties, has been superseded by the advent of a technology which permits the creation of an entire computer on a tiny chip less than one-fourth inch square. Scientific revelations about the nature of the life code in the structure of genes has progressed to the point where scientists can seriously entertain the frightening though exciting possibility of experimental creation of new life forms. The United States, spurred to achievement by the accomplishments of the Russians in the late fifties, succeeded in putting a man on the moon by 1969 and then bringing him back home again safely. These things have happened since the birth of the majority of students in this university today.

Unfortunately, humankind can count no comparable major achievement in the realm of human relations or international relations. Changes have occurred; there is significantly less tension among the great powers than existed in the early 1960s, the time of the Berlin Wall and the Cuban missile crisis. We now enjoy a kind of détente with Russia, and a dialog has at least begun with China, the largest of all nations. The turbulence in the Middle East has increased, decreased, and increased again through several cycles. The good intentions for improved inter-American relations of the early 1960s have not really been translated into effective action.

These are the times in which we live. They pose a challenge to all of education, particularly higher education, to equip our citizens with the knowledge essential to cope with an ever more complicated society. Our technological advances have been accompanied by and have contributed to an explosion in the rate at which information is created. The almost exponential increase in the number of articles appearing in technical, scientific and scholarly journals has posed severe problems for which there are not now apparent practical solutions. Our libraries and other information storing and processing centers are hard pressed to cope with the situation.

In the first half of this decade, the sudden and unexpected exploitation of their political advantage by the oil-producing nations has profoundly influenced the economic balance of the Western world. The American dollar, once the standard on the international monetary market, has been severely weakened by the massive outflow of our currency which accompanies the excess of our imports over exports. Our response to the energy crisis has been to increase the percentage of our imported oil from 30 percent of the total used in 1974 to 50 percent of the total used now. We continue to travel twice as far in cars that are less efficient in comparison to those used by many of our neighbors in the Western world.

In the face of all these circumstances, the process of higher education in many of our nation's finest universities remains remarkably unchanged as compared with the conditions that have prevailed for many, many years. Although some changes have occurred, the organization of departments and colleges is little different than it was ten, twenty, or thirty years ago. Most of those who are responsible for the process of higher education have received little or no specific training in the nature of that process and its implementation. Classic methods of teaching, with many of the broader introductory subjects being presented in large classrooms, continue to prevail. Response to economic difficulties has in many instances been to decrease the number of class sections and increase their size, still further increasing the burdens on faculty. Little effort has gone into the exploration of newer techniques for teaching that might be more economical. The rewards in higher education continue to be based on research and scholarship to a greater extent than on the ability to teach. Many universities continue to be seen by the general public as aloof from, if not disdainful of, broader aspects of human affairs. Educators continue to see universities as dominated by graduate programs which command the major portion of the financial resources available. The perceived aloofness of university communities, real or imagined, continues to contribute to antipathies between universities and their host communities.

In spite of the fact that much of higher education can be seen as a continuation of the traditional mode, there are important discernible trends that have been accompanied by significant change in the nature of higher education. Social forces have created new opportunities for women, for minorities and for financially less advantaged students. Formerly exclusively male dominated professions, medicine and the law, are gradually opening to women in ever-larger numbers. Many more women are undertaking education in engineering and scientific fields. Barriers to equitable higher education opportunities for black students are breaking down, but much remains to be done.

The average age of students is steadily increasing. In our own university, the average age has reached approximately 27 and in many community colleges is closer to 30. More people are seeking more education throughout more of their lives! The reasons for this can be found in the fact that there is more to know as well as in a greater appreciation of the importance of knowing. The educational process is never-ending. Continuous study is essential just to keep up with major technological developments. There are social pressures of various forms on an increasingly larger percentage of our population to seek a college or university education. Partly in consequence of this, the population of college students has increased much more dramatically in the past dozen years than has the general population. In 1965, there were approximately five million college and university students in the United States. By the fall of 1977, this number had increased to over eleven million. In most recent years, the increases have all been the result of an increasing proportion of women students.

A large proportion of the undergraduate student body appears to be motivated by a kind of "vocationalism." They are concerned with the acquisition of skills that can be immediately translated into remunerative careers, into earning power. There continues to be a demand for the traditional humanist education, although that demand is perhaps diminishing under the onslaught of economic pressures in the case of the younger students. In the case of older students, there may be an increasing awareness of the many values afforded by higher education in the humanistic tradition. Recent studies suggest that a broad liberal arts education is associated with greater success both in one's professional and one's personal life. A significant majority of top business executives have been found to have a strong liberal arts background. Better educated people are less likely to have been divorced, are more likely to express satisfaction with their role in life and are found to have superior earnings when compared to those with lesser higher education.

Many in higher education believe that standards have deteriorated. It has been stated that those responsible for the institutions of higher education have relaxed their standards and relinquished their responsibility for the maintenance of quality. As a result, institutions of higher education have begun a new cycle, perhaps overdue, of debating the optimum nature of higher education. The faculty of Harvard, Berkeley and our own institution, along with many others, are re-examining the question of a required core curriculum and various techniques for ensuring a certain minimum level of understanding of the language, of history and society, of philosophy and ethics, of social and natural science and mathematics, and of foreign languages and cultures in addition to the techniques of oral and written expression on the part of students awarded a Bachelor of Arts degree. The students, at least those at Harvard, have suggested that a re-examination of teaching skills on the part of faculty may be more important than more specific core curriculum requirements. Students have pressed for "relevance" and many faculty have faced a severe dilemma in justifying to themselves their pursuit of esoteric subject matter areas in the face of a world confronted with myriad sociological and political problems of the gravest sort. Nonetheless, faculty must remain free to pursue scholarship in many areas that may seem to have little practical relevance.

Trends in higher education, along with those in our society at large, provide considerable assurance that we can expect more and more students to be drawn from an ever-widening range of ages and that many more students in the future will be required to combine their educational experience with gainful employment, both at the undergraduate level and at the graduate level. Increased appreciation of the importance of higher education for the fullest enjoyment of life, quite independent of effects upon earning power, will continue to bring many more students into higher education programs serving students of all ages.

What is seen as anti-intellectualism by those in the universities continues to stand in the way of improved relations between the community and the university, between town and gown. This problem is not as severe as it has been, however. It is still further reduced in those institutions which have taken the initiative in devising programs to meet the requirements of their own communities.

I have come to the University of South Florida because I see it as an institution which can achieve a leadership role in higher education. If we are to achieve this we must cast our lot with our community. We must serve students in a wide range of ages and we must provide special programs for business and industry in our area. At the same time, we must remain a university with an appropriate balance among the social and natural sciences, humanities and fine arts on the one hand, and professional programs on the other. We must accept our responsibility as a university for the preservation of our intellectual and cultural heritage.

To fulfill our mission successfully, we must examine the process of higher education very carefully. There are undoubtedly ways in which the efficiency of that process can be increased. Increasing costs and the relative reduction in the level of funding available for public higher education render it essential that we seek to improve efficiency. We must examine the techniques of higher education in relation to the goals we seek to achieve. In areas such as engineering, science, business, education, nursing and medicine, we must contrive to equip our students with self-confident competence so that they will go forth with the assurance that they can master in their roles in society. Such a goal requires a process in which there are many opportunities for experience in the contexts to be encountered after graduation. Such opportunities can best be afforded by preceptorships with appropriate businesses, industries or community agencies. Many of our colleges have already begun to develop cooperative programs with businesses, industries and public agencies. We are fortunate to be a part of one of the largest and most rapidly growing areas in our state and in the nation where such opportunities abound.

In the arts, sciences and humanities we must somehow strive to inculcate understanding and appreciation. If the educational process is successful, understanding and appreciation will be accompanied by an appetite for the continuing pursuit of these subjects. We are fortunate in receiving strong support for our fine arts programs from the community. We must strive to deserve and encourage even greater support.

It would be difficult for us to have chosen a better setting for our institution. The past seventeen-year history of this institution is one of remarkable growth and achievement: it presages even more remarkable advances in the future. Our task is to adapt to contemporary needs: the genuine integration of the university with the community, the creation of opportunities for students of all ages to find the education they seek in our programs, the acknowledgement of our obligations to the business and industrial-technological interests in our community, and at the same time constructive guardianship of the intellectual and cultural heritage of our society.

In all of these endeavors, we must seek to improve the process of education, to evaluate our students on the basis of their competency and their appreciation, not on the basis of criteria that may be only remotely related to the true purposes of higher education.

Our task is large and demanding. It requires the concerted energies of many people and the full cooperation of the university and our friends in the community. I look forward to my role in the continuing development of this remarkable university, working in support of our faculty toward the fulfillment of the most optimistic visions of my predecessors.

Sample Speech #2—the Reportorial Demand

In another instance an audience makes a reportorial demand. Certainly the speaker has a specific purpose in mind, but it must be adapted to the demand of the audience and occasion for expertise on an identified topic. The audience seeks information and has assembled for the purpose of receiving it from someone who knows—an expert.

In this speech Arno Knapper, president of the American Business Communication Association, is making a report to his membership as they assembled in convention on December 29, 1977. Mr. Knapper titled his address "Business Communication, ABCA, and Me." Speeches such as this one and others delivered at meetings of professional associations are most often in this reportorial mode. The speakers report on their findings to a group of colleagues with similar professional interests.

> When I was named first vice president of ABCA, I immediately went to Lilian Feinberg and asked her to chair this session because I thought she would be short and to the point in making my introduction. Well, I don't know the point of what she said; but she is short! And my speech may be even shorter. Thank you, Lilian.
>
> Any president of a professional association will tell you that addressing one's colleagues as their president is indeed a humbling experience. For all of you who believe that I need humbling experiences, I am pleased to tell you that your wishes have come true. Frankly, I do feel humble; and, you know, the feeling is pretty good.
>
> Two years ago I thought I had my presidential address written. I may have had one written then, but I have written several different versions since. This one is the most recent, not necessarily the best. It just happens to be the one I settled with. After several versions, I decided I would be presumptuous to think that I could tell my colleagues something they didn't already know. I decided that it would be folly to think I could deliver a speech that would compare to the delivery of Jessamon Dawe or Norman Sigband, or that I could put on a performance that would compare to one by Phil Wolf. So, after several attempts to do those things, I finally decided that I must do my own thing. So, what is my own thing? Glenn Griffin would probably say, "Lead a community sing!" (Incidentally, Glenn may have stayed away from this convention for fear I might do just that.) But fear not, I decided upon something else. I decided to do a *pas de bourrée* through my life in business communication and ABCA. As with most dances, I think mine too has a message.
>
> I want to share with you some of the things I have learned and how I came to learn them. I want to share with you some of my thinking about business communication. And I want to share with you some of my thinking about ABCA. Toward that end, I want to look at what I think ABCA is, who I think we are; where I think we are, and where I think we are going.
>
> I became acquainted with business communication in a step-by-step exposure and learned something in each step.
>
> My first exposure to business communication came in a typewriting class where I learned that a good communication was a well-typed one. And this is all I thought it was at that point in my life!

This is what I call my form and style stage, and how little I really knew!

Then I learned that a good business communication not only was well typed but that the grammar and English mechanics were also supposed to be in conformance with some standard of acceptance. I had never dreamed that the English and grammar I had studied was for any purpose other than for writing poems, short stories, and English themes. This was my grammarian and composition stage; and how little I knew!

Then I found out that a business communication must have certain good qualities, and those qualities were stated in most of the early business communication textbooks. Each book seemed to have a variation on the same theme: a gimmick, a plan, a quality, a principle. This stage of my learning occurred in college, and I thought at the time I knew all there was to know about business communication. This was my writing-technician stage. And again, how little I really knew!

Up to that point I had learned a lot of techniques, but I had little real understanding of what business communication was all about. About that time I got acquainted with ABCA. I started reading (and thinking) on my own and came to realize that a good business communication was really supposed to convey something meaningful. I found that the semanticists and logicians offered me a great deal of helpful insight into business communication. They seemed to open up a whole new perspective. This was my semantic and logic stage; again, I realized how very little I really knew!

By this time in my life I was teaching business communication, and this is when I really began to learn. I learned that communication takes place within some context; that the purpose of a communication is to get something into the mind of a receiver, not just out of the mind of a sender. I learned that I must understand something about the behavior of people if I am to get something into a receiver's mind. I learned that, if I am to understand human behavior, I must also understand the setting or context within which that behavior takes place. This is my organizational behavior stage; and this is about where I stand today. And, again, how little I really know!

I have learned some things along the way, though. Each of these stages in my *pas de bourrée* had a meaningful place in my life with business communication. I am convinced that the things I have learned in my various stages must be given some attention when I teach or perform in the process of effectively communicating with others.

As I look back over these stages of my learning, I tend to think about the people who seemed to be identified with the various stages, and I have come to realize that ABCA embraces them all; the form and the stylist, the grammarian-composer, the writing technician, the semanticist, the logician, and the organizational behavioralist.

By embracing all of these specialists, ABCA has been something for almost everyone. For many years, ABWA seemed interested primarily in business-letter and report-writing matters, but the board of directors correctly observed that the association had grown to include many more things than letters and reports. Consequently, a change of name seemed appropriate and change it we did, from American Business Writing Association to American Business Communication Association. I was on the board at the time and well remember the discussions we had. One of the discussions was whether to include an "s" on "Communication." As you know, the "s" was omitted because the scope of the Association was well beyond just communications.

With the new name, we chose not to define *writing* and *communication* synonymously. We were into business or purposeful writing of all kinds; we were studying the theory of communication; we were concerned with something called process of communication, and we were drawing models showing what actually happens when communication occurs or should occur. We were dealing with media of communication; oral communication was gaining a place in many of our courses; and we were talking about something called organizational communication.

Today we are talking about other new things, nonverbal communication and body language, for instance. Some members are concerned that "business" in our title is too restrictive since the word may imply profit and exclude not-for-profit communication. "American" is also a bit restrictive for what we are. Perhaps another change in name is just around the corner, but let's not speculate on that now.

Our literature has become closely related to the literature of behavioral science. We have broken away from flying by feel and by the seats of our pants. We are now using some rather scientific and sophisticated tools. We talk about symbolic logic, regression analysis, exponentials, standard errors, levels of confidence, need-hierarchy, Theory X and Theory Y, Transactional Analysis, and something called management.

Our textbooks have turned away from types of transactions and from tricks to outwit the unsuspecting reader. Our texts are now geared more to situational analysis and problem resolution through good thinking.

We have come to realize that communication is not something in and of itself. Instead, we have fully recognized that communication is a multidimensional subject in an interdisciplinary world. Communication is about something that occurs in some context for a meaningful purpose. Communication does not simply exist until it breaks down; nor is there necessarily a lack of it when there is an absence of it. A complete communication does not exist until something is not only out of one mind but also into another mind and received in the same perspective.

No longer are we qualified to teach business communication simply because we can type a pretty letter, spell some words correctly, regurgitate some rules of grammar, discuss what something really means, and exchange jargon from the behavioral sciences. The business communication teachers of today must know something about form and structure, the language, semantics, logical inference, value judgment, descriptive statistics, social psychology, and organizational behavior, to name a few! Business communication is not just a literary skill; it is also a behavioral science. Furthermore, it sure helps to know something about marketing, finance, accounting, computers, banking, economics, labor relations, literature, politics, history, and the physical and biological sciences!

ABCA is a unique organization. ABCA has a warm congeniality unknown to many professional associations. Historically, we have been a group of friendly participators, delighted to exchange our ideas and to learn from one another. We have utilized our individual strengths, and we have successfully resisted the temptation to cast everyone into the same mold. Consequently, I am not much interested in trying to define who we are, what we are, where we are, or where we are going. Making precise definitions would enter us into a zero-sum game of I win and you lose, or you win and I lose. Precise definitions will limit our horizons, narrow our thinking, and limit our interaction, including some while excluding others. And that would be the antithesis of what we really are.

In my quarter of a century in ABCA and particularly in my travels this year to the various regional meetings, I have talked to many people and I have come to four conclusions about ABCA:

1. We are who we are;
2. We are what we are;
3. We are where we are; and
4. We are going where we're going

In the vernacular of Transactional Analysis, we are in our Adults — I'm okay, and you're okay. Let's keep it that way!

Sample Speech #3—the Propositional Demand

At other moments the audience and the occasion produce expectations that the speaker will take a position on an issue of controversy. The nature of the topic and the identity of the speaker with the topic in question create a demand that the speech be other than ceremonial or reportorial.

The following speech was delivered by C. C. Garvin, Jr. on January 24, 1977. As chairman of the board of Exxon Corporation, the speaker was expected to meet a propositional demand as he spoke to the Columbia Business School Club of New York on a topic entitled "Toward a New Beginning in Energy Policy." The energy crisis, the new administrative postures, and the actions of the oil industry were well known to the audience. The expectation was that the speaker must take a position in support of his industry and defend its policies.

Let me begin by expressing my appreciation for the opportunity to speak before the Columbia Business School Club. Your organization has established a distinguished forum for the business discussion of public issues. Never has there been more need for businessmen to participate in such discussion and do their part to contribute to the formation of public policy.

Most people would agree that with the inauguration of Jimmy Carter as the thirty-ninth President of the United States, we can expect major new initiatives in public policy. Our new President must respond to the great challenges facing the nation in many areas. Few can really envy him the awesome responsibilities of his office. In this connection you may recall what Adlai Stevenson is supposed to have said in a lighter moment: "As a boy I thought I might grow up to be President, but I soon dismissed it as the risk every American child has to take."

During the campaign, the President repeatedly emphasized that after the political and economic shocks of recent years, the time has come for us all to make a new beginning. Indeed it has. If we are to meet our pressing problems adequately, we must rebuild confidence in our major institutions. We must restore a spirit of cooperation. And we must work hard together to achieve solutions.

But good resolutions are easy. Sound policies, based on the most realistic appraisal of the possibilities, are not. If President Carter is to lead us toward solutions, he will need to exercise tireless patience, as well as the utmost skill in negotiation, compromise and conciliation.

Nowhere is this more true than in energy policy. Energy is the lifeblood of our economy. Without assured and at least moderately increasing energy supplies, we cannot achieve the economic growth which we must have to provide new jobs, raise living standards, clean up the environment, fund new social programs or reach many of our other national goals.

Progress will be hard, for at least two important reasons. Our major energy suppliers, the oil companies, have themselves become a significant part of the problem in the eyes of many people. And even with everyone pulling together, our energy choices are in fact sharply limited, especially in the short run. I would like to consider both these issues with you today, and then share a few thoughts I have about energy policy under the new Administration.

Just why are the oil companies so suspect? The obvious reason is of course that consumers have had a bitter taste of fuel shortages, followed by a steady diet of energy price increases—both unpleasantly seasoned by a short-lived spurt of oil company profits.

In trying to deal with this issue I am reminded of a story which the late General Anthony McAuliffe used to tell. General McAuliffe was the commander during the Battle of the Bulge, who sent the famous reply, "nuts," to a German surrender ultimatum. The incident made him famous. But he came to hate talking about it at every lunch, dinner and cocktail party, where he was always introduced in the same way. "One evening a dear old Southern lady invited me to dinner," he said. "I had a delightful time talking to her and her charming guests, because during the entire evening no one even mentioned the nuts incident. As I prepared to leave and thanked my hostess for such an enjoyable evening, she replied 'Thank *you* and good night, *General McNuts.'*"

With apologies to General McAuliffe, my point is that we in the oil industry have not yet been able to shake the effects of one dominant impression that has been left in the public mind by the events of the past few years. People feel that *they* are having to make sacrifices while the companies are benefitting, probably at their expense.

There are also other familiar reasons for the public's distrust, reasons associated with the drastic loss of confidence in all our major institutions—Vietnam, Watergate, the vicious combination of recession, unemployment and inflation. Yet still other reasons are more fundamental, having to do with all business, not just big oil. The corporation *seems* impersonal by nature, and this invites distrust. As the saying goes, companies seem to have "no heart to touch, no rear end to kick." Let me note here that I find this allegation highly disputable, especially the second half. In our industry we can show any number of bruises administered at the hands, or feet, of sundry governments that would effectively disprove it.

Another cause of public skepticism about business is the fact that people have long had ambiguous feelings about the profit system, especially lately. On the one hand, Americans generally do believe in the economic importance of profit-oriented activity. On the other hand, they distrust the profit motive. They may not consider it inherently contrary to the public interest, but they do consider it very much distinct from the public interest. Many people undoubtedly felt their worst suspicions about the profit motive were confirmed by the recent revelations about unethical business practices.

Finally, society has been coming more and more to judge business in the light of new values and broader aspirations. These have in part found voice in a multitude of special interest groups concerned about the environment, consumer protection, job safety, equal opportunity and other aspects of the quality of life. There is no doubt that business has sometimes been slow to respond—partly out of inertia and partly because of the serious practical difficulties of satisfying the sometimes conflicting aims of these groups.

All these reasons for the public's distrust are not justified, but clearly some are. In any case, it is appropriate at this time of national rededication to affirm that we at Exxon fully recognize our obligation to take positive action to merit renewed public confidence. As business managers, you may be interested in a few of our current policies which in our view are bringing our activities more squarely in line with today's public expectation.

In the effort to increase energy supplies, our prime responsibility, we have in the last few years been stepping up our investments to the level of about twice our earnings. In the next four years we plan to spend about $22 billion on capital investment and exploration, about half of that in this country. We are strenuously working to develop all types of conventional and unconventional energy resources—oil and gas, coal, synthetic fuels, nuclear, solar and others.

In our financial reporting we have taken the initiative in making major changes. We hope these will go a long way to help make our operations more understandable to our shareholders and the public. In the last few years we have been breaking our earnings out by geographicical region. In our upcoming annual report we will go still further, breaking them out for major segments of our business. Readers will know more about the results we have achieved in such areas as: petroleum exploration and production; petroleum refining, transportation and marketing; chemicals; and so on.

Just recently we passed a watershed in corporate governance. Only 12 years ago, the company's board of directors was staffed entirely by employees. Now, nonemployee directors represent a majority on the board. We are convinced that this is another important step toward more completely assuring our shareholders and the public that our top managers are responsive to outside concerns and that their managerial performance is being judged objectively.

We have a very forthright position on business ethics, set out in a written statement which we circulate annually and which we insist all managers observe and enforce. Of course we believe that we have shown time and again that our integrity is not merely a set of statements on a piece of paper, but a body of principles firmly embedded in the tradition of our company. We believe that we have developed a reputation as a company worthy of public trust. But, as many companies, including our own, have been forcefully reminded in recent years, only constant vigilance will enable us to sustain that trust.

Cutting even closer to the bone, we have taken public positions which we think are in the public interest, but which could be considered directly contrary to our economic interests, narrowly construed. Strange as it may be to hear, we think that in light of the energy realities no oil company should rejoice if the consumption of petroleum products increases too rapidly.

We believe that a new energy conservation ethic *must* be established in this country. To support it, we have changed the emphasis of our advertising and public communications to encourage our customers to use our products wisely, yes, even sparingly! We have offered our customers literature and advice, some of it extensive and technical, on ways to increase efficiency in their energy use. We recommended as long ago as 1972 that monies from the Highway Trust Fund might be used to support feasible mass transit projects, not just highway construction. And we have suggested the government consider the possible need for higher taxes on energy consumption, new controls on the end-use of some energy supplies and special incentives to spur more energy conservation. Of course, such steps should be taken only after evaluating their effect on all sectors of our economy and society.

In a number of other major areas — environmental conservation, job safety, charitable contributions — I think our record shows a sense of responsibility to today's public concerns.

Exxon is not unique in the oil industry. Taken in its entirety, I believe, the record of the oil industry shows that it can live up to the task entrusted to it. Concerns about the industry's character have taken the nation on a detour. It has done some good to be sure: All the parties involved have gotten a better idea of the lay of the land, reexamined their own positions and learned to know each other better. But now it is time for us all to get back on the main highway and get on with the job of finding solutions to our *real* energy problems.

Most of you are doubtless familiar with the main outlines of these problems. Oil and natural gas are this country's major energy sources and we can reduce our dependence only gradually in the balance of the century. Yet the United States, not too long ago self-sufficient in oil, is now using ten times as much oil and more than twice as much natural gas as it is finding each year. We believe and fear that within three years this country will be importing more than half its oil. And we will be coming to depend increasingly on just a few countries in the Middle East to meet the growth in our oil demands.

We have been left with relatively few things we can do. Our country must expend every reasonable effort to conserve energy. But, while essential, conservation will take us only so far before it leads to a dangerous abstinence and a withering of economic muscle. This country must hasten the exploration for and development of the full range of domestic energy resources—not only oil and gas but also coal, nuclear and such new resources as solar and fusion. Neglect of any of these, but especially those available in the near future, could throw intolerable burdens on the others. The outcome would in all probability be a potentially unsustainable demand for oil imports.

Even with the most aggressive development of domestic supplies, however, progress will be slow, demanding long-lead times, heavy capital investments and in the case of unconventional energy resources, extensive research and development. In a task of this magnitude and duration, perhaps the greatest strain of all will be on our perseverance and strength of character.

It seems to me that industry, with its vast and varied array of technological and managerial skills, is equal to the challenge ahead. But the role of government will be essential. Only government, backed by a consensus of the people, can set the priorities, and make available the resource lands, of which it owns the great bulk. Only government can strike the proper balance between all the economic, environmental, regional and social needs involved.

So it is natural to ask: What has President Carter been saying about energy? He has said much that we at Exxon can applaud. He clearly knows that with no quick answers in sight, strong leadership is a must, both to awaken people to the urgency of the energy problem and to rally sustained, widespread commitment to long-term solutions. He has advocated several strong, practical conservation measures. Just a few days ago he urged us all to lower our thermostats. He has also suggested stiff mileage standards for autos, improved mass transit facilities, and higher insulation requirements for buildings. Most significantly, I think, he has made clear his conviction recently on nationwide television that whether we like it or not, the price of energy must inevitably go up—and that in the long run this is likely to exert a highly effective pressure on all of us to hold down energy waste.

To us this position seems very powerfully to suggest the advantages to the country of moving more swiftly to lift price controls from domestic oil and gas production. The President has been reluctant to draw this conclusion, except perhaps for natural gas. But to us this seems to be ultimately the only effective way that energy consumers and producers can adjust their economic decisions to the realities of the situation. Under the present arbitrary system of controls, we are all buying and selling energy in this country at prices which are lower than the cost of replacing it.

For example, with domestic oil and gas production declining, every extra gallon of gasoline we demand must be supplied from imported oil at a higher price than the consumer pays. The situation is even worse with natural gas, which has been regulated at prices below competing fuels since 1954. As a nation, we should face up to the fact that artificially low prices for energy can only encourage consumption, discourage exploration and production and almost guarantee shortages eventually.

We realize only too well that decontrol would inevitably raise the fear that oil companies will benefit from so-called *windfall* profits while consumers must sacrifice. If this is the obstacle to decontrol, we think this matter should be addressed on its own merits and alternative solutions considered. Surely there are simpler and better ways to handle problems like this than to suppress prices artificially.

The new Administration also is likely to show a strong interest in plans to streamline and harmonize government energy responsibilities. Right now a crazyquilt of some sixty government agencies is involved, with fragmented, overlapping and inconsistent purposes. Government should be a system of checks and balances, but under the present government energy system it sometimes seems that all we have is checks. The nation would avoid much delay in energy development if the policy groups in the different agencies could get together and enunciate consistent, long-range energy policies which would be touchstones for all government leasing and regulatory activities. Relations between these agencies and the states need to be better coordinated. And certainly we could greatly step up the efficiency of our entire energy effort if we could eliminate red tape and the very costly duplications in government data gathering.

In considering future energy policies, we at Exxon are deeply concerned about proposals to force oil companies to halt their efforts to develop other kinds of energy. Exxon has undertaken such efforts because we have seen an energy future with the same shape as the President has himself described on several occasions. Declining oil resources will necessitate a shifting of the energy burden to other resources, primarily coal, nuclear and solar. As an energy company, it is *logical* for us to make the shift along with everyone else. Such work represents a *logical* extension of our technological and managerial skills. Won't existing laws and regulations deter any abuses which might arise during such efforts? If the oil companies are shut out, it will almost certainly *reduce* competition in these areas rather than *enhancing* it as proponents of these measures maintain. In the process, it will reduce production, stymie energy research and raise prices to consumers.

The President has not supported other proposals to break up oil companies into separate oil production companies, refining companies, transportation companies and so on. He has not supported them on the grounds that the resulting loss of efficiency would force consumers to pay more. He has said that he wants to be assured that there is competition in the energy industry, and that where it is proved inadequate the existing antitrust laws could provide the remedy. We could not agree more heartily with these ideas, which we think apply equally to the proposals to block energy diversification. So we hope that when the new Administration and the Congress have given the proposals further study, they will reach the same conclusion. The real challenge is to galvanize the support of all companies qualified to get on with the mammoth energy job ahead, not to frustrate their efforts.

As for us, we pledge ourselves to work constructively with the new Administration to find and implement an energy policy consistent with this country's great needs. We recognize that perceptions may differ, that a flexible give and take, tolerance and imagination must be the rule among those who contribute. In no other way can we dispel the atmosphere of mistrust that has prevailed. In no other way can we rebuild the spirit of cooperation that we must have to make a *new beginning,* a new beginning toward finding common solutions to our common problems.

Forms

When invited to deliver a speech the speaker will need to gather information about the audience and occasion. We have earlier discussed the kind of data needed. The speaker should not be hesitant in any way to ask for pertinent information from the person who extends the invitation. A check sheet similar to the following might be reproduced and completed as soon as possible after accepting the assignment. Parts A and B might be submitted to the contact person for the information called for. However, the speaker can obtain more specific information by simply asking the questions by phone or in person.

Part C includes the analysis the speaker does based on the information collected in the first two sections. No specific plans can be made by the speaker until he or she has assembled the information about the occasion and the audience.

Speech Assignment Data Sheet

Part A: Occasion
1. Contact person _____ _____
      name   phone #
2. Date of speech: _____ 3. Time: _____
4. Place: _____ _____
      name   address
5. Name of audience group: _____
6. Other program items: _____
7. Proposed speech length: _____
8. Type and size of room: _____
9. Seating arrangement: _____

Part B: Audience
1. Size of audience: 20 or fewer _____; 20 to 50 _____;
      50-100 _____; more than 100 _____;
      more than 200 _____.
2. Sex: mostly males _____; mostly females _____; mixed _____.
3. Age: teenage _____; young adults _____; middle age _____;
      elderly _____; mixed _____.
4. Predominant common characteristics: _____;
                                                   educational
   _____; _____.
      employment   objectives
5. Reason for attending: _____
6. Identify previous speakers _____
   for this event: name
                      _____
                                topic

Part C: Speaker Analysis
1. Major audience demand is:
      Ceremonial _____; Reportorial _____; Propositional _____.
2. Purpose statements:
   _____
   _____
   _____
   _____.

3. My thesis is: _____
   _____.

4. Some special sources I should consult:
      a. _____
      b. _____
      c. _____
5. Audio-visual materials needed (if any):
      a. _____
      b. _____
6. Additional questions for contact person:
      a. _____
      b. _____
      c. _____
7. Proposed title: _____

Sometimes the program chairperson and/or the speaker can request an audience reaction to the presentation. The value of such information to the speaker is obvious as a useful way of improving his effectiveness. For the program leader, the information is valuable for planning future programs and in assessing audience interests. The following form can be adopted for collecting audience reaction.

Audience Reaction Sheet

Your reactions to the speaker(s) in today's program are solicited as an aid to future planning. Please take a couple of minutes to complete this sheet and return it to

_____ at _____.
      program chairperson   location

Speaker: _____ Topic: _____

Date: _____ Location: _____

Encircle the number which best characterizes your reaction.

1. Did you find the topic appropriate for the audience?   no 1 2 3 4 5 yes

2. Did the speaker seem qualified to speak on the topic?   no 1 2 3 4 5 yes

3. Was the speaker well prepared for the presentation?   no 1 2 3 4 5 yes

4. Was the speech organized in a way which aided the audience?   no 1 2 3 4 5 yes

5. Was the speaker's delivery effective?   no 1 2 3 4 5 yes

6. Did the audience seem attentive?   no 1 2 3 4 5 yes

7. Was the seating arrangement appropriate?   no 1 2 3 4 5 yes

8. Could you hear adequately?   no 1 2 3 4 5 yes

9. Was the introduction appropriate?   no 1 2 3 4 5 yes

10. Would you like to hear this on another occasion?   no 1 2 3 4 5 yes

The person who will serve as a contact person or as a program leader will need to collect information for future reference and for use in introducing the guest speakers. The use of a form such as the one which follows can minimize the number of calls necessary after the initial contact is made:

Scheduled Speaker Data

Speaker: _____ Date Contacted: _____

Address: _____ phone _____

Event: _____ Date & Time: _____

Location: _____ Length of
Presentation: _____

Proposed Topic: _____ Fee (if any): _____

1. Speaker's title or position:
    _____

2. Expertise on proposed topic:
    _____
    _____

3. Relationship of topic to audience:
    _____
    _____

4. Speaker's educational background:
    _____
    _____
    _____

5. Speaker's major activities:
    _____
    _____
    _____

6. Speaker's family (if appropriate):
    _____
    _____
    _____

7. Anecdotal speaker item:
    _____
    _____
    _____

Evaluation of Conferences

Of course much of the preceding material and some forms can be used in the evaluation of conferences. Conferences regularly consist of many speeches and public presentations. They may most closely apply to ends sought or required of the reportorial speech and can be similarly evaluated.

Conference chairpersons and planners have need to gather special kinds of feedback from their participating audiences. Persons in business and other professions find the conference so much a part of their regular activity that they become quite sophisticated in their ability to evaluate such sessions. Furthermore, these audiences are frequently eager for the opportunity to express their enthusiasms and disappointments in a constructive way. The following form adapted from a book by Harold Zelko illustrates a useful evaluational device:

Conference Program Evaluation Form*

Name of Conference: _____

Place: _____ Date: _____

A. Arrangements:
    1. Meeting Rooms:
    2. Housing:
    3. Meals:
    4. Other:

B. Program:
    1. General plan of conference:
    2. Subjects covered:
    3. Sectional meetings and programs:
    4. Speakers:
        contributed most (why)
        contributed least (why)
    5. Case or work groups:
    6. Group participation:

C. Other matters or suggestions:

Use below for further comment

_____

*Adapted by permission: Zelko, Harold P., *The Business Conference: Leadership and Participation.* McGraw-Hill, 1969, p. 201.

Evaluating the Interview

The interviewer has a somewhat different task in evaluation than do the evaluators of speakers and conferences. Little is gained from interrogation of the interviewees about the process unless there are large numbers from which generalizations could be compiled. In most instances the numbers are small and the different objectives of employment, evaluation and informational interviews call for specific evaluations.

The steps in preparation for interviews have been described earlier and guidelines or plans for any session could be developed from these. However, there are available lists of questions used in the employment interview from which you might select questions to incorporate into sessions which you conduct. The following list of thirty-eight questions are among those asked by employers during interviews with college students. Of course, we should not attempt to ask all these questions but select those which seem best designed to gain useful information. Some questions are more significant to some types of positions and organizations than are others. Thus, evaluation of the interview should include evaluation of the questions selected by the interviewer.

Questions Often Asked During an Employment Interview

1.   What courses did you enjoy the most in college?
2.   What type of work interests you?
3.   What are your strengths?
4.   What are your hobbies?
5.   Why did you select your college major?
6.   What are your long-range objectives?
7.   In the jobs you have had, which one did you enjoy the most?
8.   How would you evaluate your ability to speak in front of an audience?
9.   What were your college grades?
10.   What information have you heard or read about our company?
11.   Tell me about your extracurricular activities. Which ones did you enjoy the most?
12.   What three adjectives best describe you?
13.   What are your weaknesses?
14.   How do you plan to achieve your career goals?
15.   What do you expect to be doing ten years from now?
16.   Does it make a difference in what part of the country you are located?
17.   What do you expect in salary?
18.   Tell me about yourself. What kind of person are you?
19.   Are you willing to travel?
20.   Have you had an injury or a serious illness?
21.   Do you plan to study for an advanced degree?
22.   What are the most important requirements for you to accept a position?
23.   How effective are your written skills? Would you consider yourself to be an excellent, average, or below-average writer?
24.   Are you willing to work long hours?
25.   Which do you prefer, working with others or by yourself?
26.   Are the grades you received in college a good indication of your ability?
27.   Why did you select the college you attended?
28.   What was your homelife like when you were growing up?

29. Why did you decide to interview for a position in our company?
30. Did you pay your own college expenses?
31. What kind of working climate do you prefer?
32. Is the size of the organization important to you when considering a job opportunity?
33. How would you anticipate making a contribution to our organization?
34. What major accomplishment gave you the most satisfaction?
35. What motivates you to produce your greatest effort?
36. How do others describe you?
37. What type of job are you seeking?
38. Why do you think you might like to work for our organization?

Evaluation of the participants in the interview process may be difficult, but simple forms designed to measure the performance of the interviewer, the interviewee, or both can be devised. Different interview objectives will suggest variation in the material requested by the form. In other words, the evaluation of a performance interview may vary significantly from the sales interview or employment interview.

The following form was designed to evaluate interviewees during an employment interview. It serves as the basic model for constructing evaluation forms.

INTERVIEW CRITIQUE FORM*

Interviewee's Name _____ Date _____

I. Please rate the *interviewee* on a scale from 1 (worst) to 10 (best) on each item.

    A. OPENING
Introduce Self _____
Shake Hands (if appropriate) _____
Get Interviewer's Name _____
Give Resume to Interviewer _____
Smiling and Eye Contact _____
Understandable Speech _____
Positive Attitude _____
OPENING TOTAL _____

    B. ANSWERS TO QUESTIONS

	Clarity	Completeness	Enthusiasm
Education	___	___	___
Work Experience	___	___	___
Activities	___	___	___
Goals	___	___	___
ANSWERS TOTALS	___	___	___

    C. CLOSING
Questions for Interviewer _____
Learned Procedure for
  Filling Position _____
Shaking hands (if appropriate) _____
Thank Interviewer _____
Positive Closing _____
CLOSING TOTAL _____

II. What was the best part of the interviewee's performance?

III. What could the interviewee do to improve?

*D. Carter, K. Cissna & K. McDonald, "Interview Seminars", U of South Florida, 1980. (reproduced with permission).

SUMMARY In this final chapter we have provided models, forms and guidelines for the evaluation of public communication for business persons and other professionals. These materials may be used in the form presented or amended to fit specific uses. In any case, one of the most serious errors which any communicator can make is to fail to assess his/her effectiveness in every communicative situation. As we have said repeatedly, judgments about us as persons and as professionals are made regularly on the basis of our effectiveness as communicators. Therefore, we should continue to monitor our communication production to guarantee the most positive evaluation by our associates.

NOTES [1]Edwin, J., *Louis L'Amour,* Interview in Los Angeles Times, March 12, 1971.

SUGGESTED READINGS Hopper, R. and J. L. Whitehead, Jr. *Communication Concepts and Skills.* New York: Harper & Row, 1979.

Koehler, J. W.; K. W. E. Anatol, and R. L. Applbaum. *Public Communication: Behavioral Perspectives.* New York: Macmillan Publishing Co., 1978.

Ritchie, J. B. and P. Thompson. *Organizations and People,* 2nd Edition. St. Paul, Minn: West Publishing Co., 1980.

Tortoriello, T. R.; S. J. Blatt; and S. De Wine. *Communication in the Organization: An Applied Approach.* New York: McGraw-Hill Book Co., 1978.

Index

†